KEEPING FINANCIAL RECORDS FOR BUSINESS

Working Papers 1-9

Robert A. Schultheis, Ph.D.
Southern Illinois University
Edwardsville, Illinois

Burton S. Kaliski, Ed.D.
New Hampshire College
Manchester, New Hampshire

Dan Passalacqua, M.A.
Oak Grove High School
San Jose, California

VISIT US ON THE INTERNET
www.swep.com
www.thomsonlearning.com

South-Western
EDUCATIONAL PUBLISHING
Thomson Learning™

Production Services: Litten Editing and Production

Mason, Ohio

South-Western Educational Publishing is a division of Thomson Learning.
Thomson Learning is a trademark used herein under license.

ISBN: 0-538-69175-1

3 4 5 6 7 8 Gl 05 04 03

Printed in the United States of America

CONTENTS

Name ______________________________

Score ____________

Record Keeping and the Computer

CHAPTER 1
Job 1

Problem 1–1, page 6

1. ____________ 6. ____________
2. ____________ 7. ____________
3. ____________ 8. ____________
4. ____________ 9. ____________
5. ____________ 10. ____________

Problem 1–2, page 7

1. ______________________________
2. ______________________________
3. ______________________________
4. ______________________________
____

Problem 1–3, page 7

1. ______________________________
2. ______________________________
3. ______________________________
4. ______________________________
5. ______________________________
____

(This page is without text copy.)

Name ______________________

Score ____________

Sample Problem, page 8

NAME	AMOUNT DUE

Problem 2–1, page 14

DESCRIPTION	AMOUNT SPENT

Problem 2–2, page 15

COMPANY NAME	AMOUNT OWED

Problem 2–3, page 16

Credit Cards	Lost or Stolen	OK
1.		
2.		
3.		
4.		
5.		
6.		
7.		
8.		
9.		
10.		

Problem 2–4

You are a general office clerk in a discount department store. The store provides customers with charge account cards embossed with the customer name and account number printed in OCR style. Your supervisor wants you to check a list of charge accounts to see if they are canceled.

Directions

Below is a list of charge account numbers printed in OCR as they appear on the credit cards. Following that is a printout of canceled account numbers. Compare each credit card number on the list to the printout. If you find the card number on the printout, place a check mark under the Canceled heading. If you don't, place a check mark under the OK heading.

List of Charge Account Numbers	Canceled	OK
281082	________	________
283278	________	________
287238	________	________
288082	________	________
294334	________	________
294343	________	________
298716	________	________
300902	________	________
317879	________	________
319765	________	________
353207	________	________
373299	________	________
379878	________	________
379929	________	________

Canceled Accounts

28 088 2
28 723 8
29 433 4
29 781 6
30 090 2
30 976 5
31 320 7
35 987 8
37 329 9

Problem 2–5

You are an office assistant for the Edmonton National Bank. The bank teller wants you to check a list of bank accounts to see if any are overdrawn.

Directions

Below is a list of bank account numbers printed in MICR. Following that is a printout of overdrawn bank account numbers. Compare each account number on the list to the printout. If you find the account number on the printout, place a check mark under the Overdrawn heading. If you don't, place a check mark under the OK heading.

List of Bank Account Numbers	Overdrawn	OK
2407 549		
2078 145		
2477 956		
2484 598		
2385 107		
2499 007		
2189 311		
2098 338		
2271 850		
2210 879		
2414 561		
2438 198		
2308 176		

Overdrawn Accounts

2098 383
2120 879
2189 113
2407 549
2414 561
2484 589
2744 956
2803 176

Name ______________________

Score __________

Sample Problem, page 19

Student No.	Correct	Error	Not in Class
1			
2			
3			
4			

Problem 3–1, page 20

Student No.	Correct	Error	Not in Class
1			
2			
3			
4			
5			
6			
7			
8			
9			
10			
11			
12			
13			
14			
15			

Problem 3–2, page 22

Vendor No.	Correct	Error	Not on List
105			
106			
107			
108			
109			
110			
111			
112			
113			
114			

Name ______________________________

Problem 3–3

You are an accounting clerk at Duval Carpets, Inc. One of your duties is to maintain the accuracy of customer accounts.

Directions

Compare a customer balance list prepared by a computer and a list made by the accounting department. If the names and balances are on both lists and are exactly the same, put a check mark in the Correct column of the checklist below. If the names and balances are on both lists but are not exactly the same, put a check mark in the Error column. If a name on the computer list is not on the accounting department list, put a check mark in the Not on List column.

Customer No.	Customer Name and Balance
301	Sobus Merchandising Co. Balance: $100.56
302	Spar Valley Products Balance: $0.00
303	Square Deal, Inc. Balance: $1,278.49
304	Station House, Ltd. Balance: $673.10
305	Staubeck Linens, Inc. Balance: $1,809.23
306	Stavoroff Bros., Inc. Balance: $239.88
307	Stawvill Publishers, Inc. Balance: $1,906.33
308	Stayson Mills Balance: $480.29
309	Steale Sail Company Balance: $89.34
310	Steben Pottery, Inc. Balance: $285.37

Accounting Department
Customer Balance List

Sobus Merchandising Co.
Balance: $100.56

Square Deal, Inc.
Balance: $1,287.49

Station House, Ltd.
Balance: $673.10

Stuabeck Linens, Inc.
Balance: $1,809.23

Stawvill Publishers, Inc.
Balance: $1,096.33

Stayson Mills, Inc.
Balance: $480.29

Steale Sail Company
Balance: $89.34

Stebin Pottery, Inc.
Balance: $285.37

Customer No.	Correct	Error	Not on List
301			
302			
303			
304			
305			
306			
307			
308			
309			
310			

Problem 3–4

You are an office assistant for the Northwestern Music Club. It is your job to keep membership lists up-to-date and accurate.

Directions

Compare the membership list prepared by a computer and a dues paid list made by your department. If the names are on both lists and are exactly the same, put a check mark in the Correct column of the checklist below. If the names are on both lists but are not exactly the same, put a check mark in the Error column. If a name on the membership list is not on the dues paid list, put a check mark in the Not on List column.

MEMBERSHIP LIST

Member No.	Member Name
1001	Waldo Eleander
1002	Ernesta Johnson
1003	Manfred Pollack
1004	Carl Swartz
1005	Debra Klein
1006	Constance Ades
1007	Trent Williams
1008	Julio Gonzalez
1009	Freida Holtz
1010	Theodore Palmer

Dues Paid List

Waldo Elender
Ernest Johnson
Carl Swartz
Debra Kline
Constance Ades
Trent Williams
Julio Gonzalez
Freda Holtz
Theodore Palmer

Check List

Number	Correct	Error	Not on List
1001			
1002			
1003			
1004			
1005			
1006			
1007			
1008			
1009			
1010			

Name ____________________________

Problem 3–5

You are an office assistant in a sales department. One of your jobs is to enter into the computer the names of possible new customers from the handwritten notes of salespeople. After entering a name and address, you verify it by comparing what is shown on your computer with the handwritten note.

Directions

Compare the handwritten notes to the computer screen that appears on the next page. If the names and addresses on both the screen and the note are the same, put a check mark in the Correct column. If they are not exactly the same, put a check mark in the Error column. If you find a name on the notes that is not on the screen, put a check mark in the Not Entered column.

Handwritten Notes

1. Sam Masconi
   38 Woodline Drive

2. Julia Valencia
   746 Argonne Blvd.

3. Levy & Sons, Inc.
   9802 Marine Road

4. Lawson Construction Co.
   412 Riverside Avenue

5. Elan Mortgage Corp.
   8080 First Street

6. St. Louis Dredging Co.
   12 Levee Road

Problem 3–5, Concluded

Computer Screen

```
Sam Masconi
38 Woodline Drive

Julio Valencia
746 Argonne Blvd.

Levy & Sons, Inc.
8902 Marine Road

Lawson Construction Co.
412 Riverside Avenue

St. Louis Dredging Co.
12 Levee Road
```

Customer No.	Correct	Error	Not Entered
1			
2			
3			
4			
5			
6			

Name ______________________________

Score ____________

Sample Problem 1, page 25

Step 1

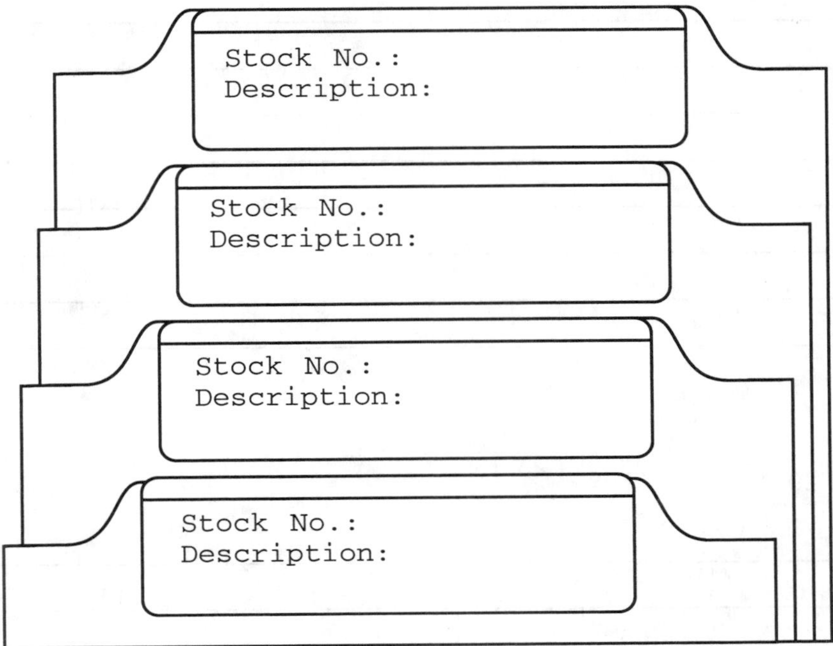

Step 3

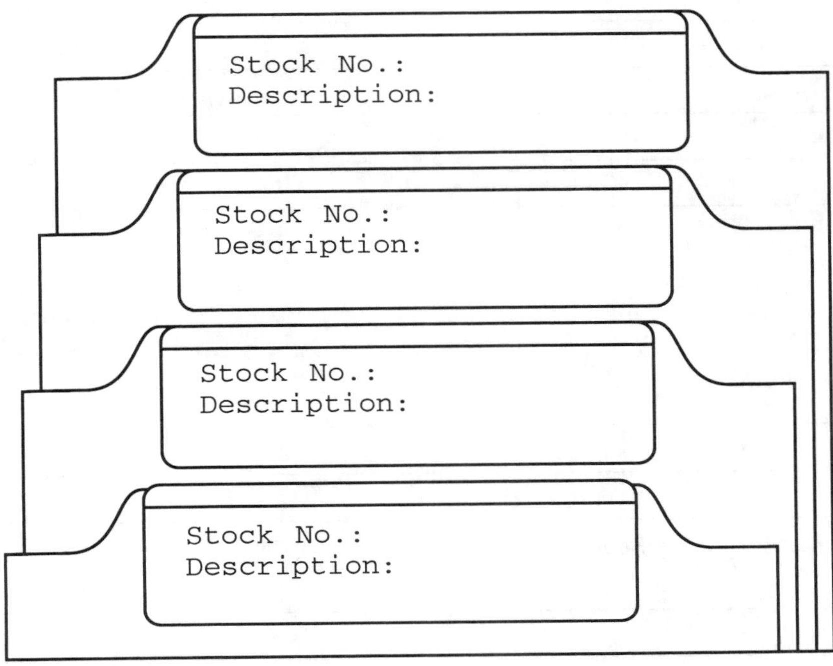

Sample Problem 2, page 27

Problem 4–1, page 29

Employee Number	Employee Name	Employee Number	Employee Name

Problem 4–2, page 29

North	South	East	West

Problem 4–3

You are an office assistant at a consulting firm. You are to make a schedule of the consulting visits of the firm's executives by date. Sort the schedule of visits below so that the earliest visit is listed first.

Date of Visit	Location
June 12	Lancaster, PA
July 22	Philadelphia, PA
September 3	Washington, D.C.
August 13	Baltimore, MD
July 11	Dover, DE
August 31	New York City, NY
October 3	Norfolk, VA
June 21	Tampa, FL

Directions

a. On the first three lines provided, write the heading:

Markham and Patterson, Inc.
Consulting Visits
May 10, 20--

b. Under the heading, write the column headings "Date of Visit" and "Location."

c. Sort the list of visits above *chronologically* by placing the visit with the earliest date first.

d. Verify your work by comparing the names and dates in the original list to your list and counting the names in both lists.

____

____

____

Date of Visit **Location**

____

____

____

____

____

____

____

____

Problem 4–4

You are an office assistant at Wilder College and must sort chronologically the list of seminars below, which are scheduled for next year.

Date	Seminar
March 14	National Ornithology Society
January 27	Word Processing Association
April 21	National Secretaries Association
February 17	Corvette Owners Association
February 6	American Society of Railroaders
March 31	St. Louis Gardeners Club
April 1	Trout Fishing Club of Trenton
February 16	Denton Swim Club

Directions

a. On the first three lines provided, write the heading:

Wilder College
Seminar Schedule
20--

b. Sort the list of seminars chronologically. Record the seminar with the earliest date first.

c. Verify your work by comparing the seminar names and dates in the original list to your list and counting the number of seminars in both lists.

____

____

____

Date	**Seminar**

Problem 4–5

You are a cashier at the Fantasy Clothing Store. One of your duties is to prepare a list of the total cash received each week. You are given the list of weekly cash receipts below, which is sorted numerically. Sort the list so that it is in chronological order.

Cash Receipts	Week
$19,235	January 24
18,807	February 21
18,545	February 7
18,538	March 14
18,422	February 28
18,276	January 31
18,102	March 7
18,078	March 28
18,067	February 14
18,030	March 21

Directions

a. On the top three lines provided, write the heading:

Fantasy Clothing Store
Weekly Cash Receipts
January 24–April 4, 20--

b. Sort the list of cash receipts chronologically. Put the week with the earliest date first.

c. Verify your work by comparing the amounts and dates in the original list to your list and counting the number of items in both lists.

____

____

____

Week	Cash Receipts
________	________
________	________
________	________
________	________
________	________
________	________
________	________
________	________
________	________
________	________

(This page is without text copy.)

Name ____________________________

Score ____________

Sample Problem, page 32

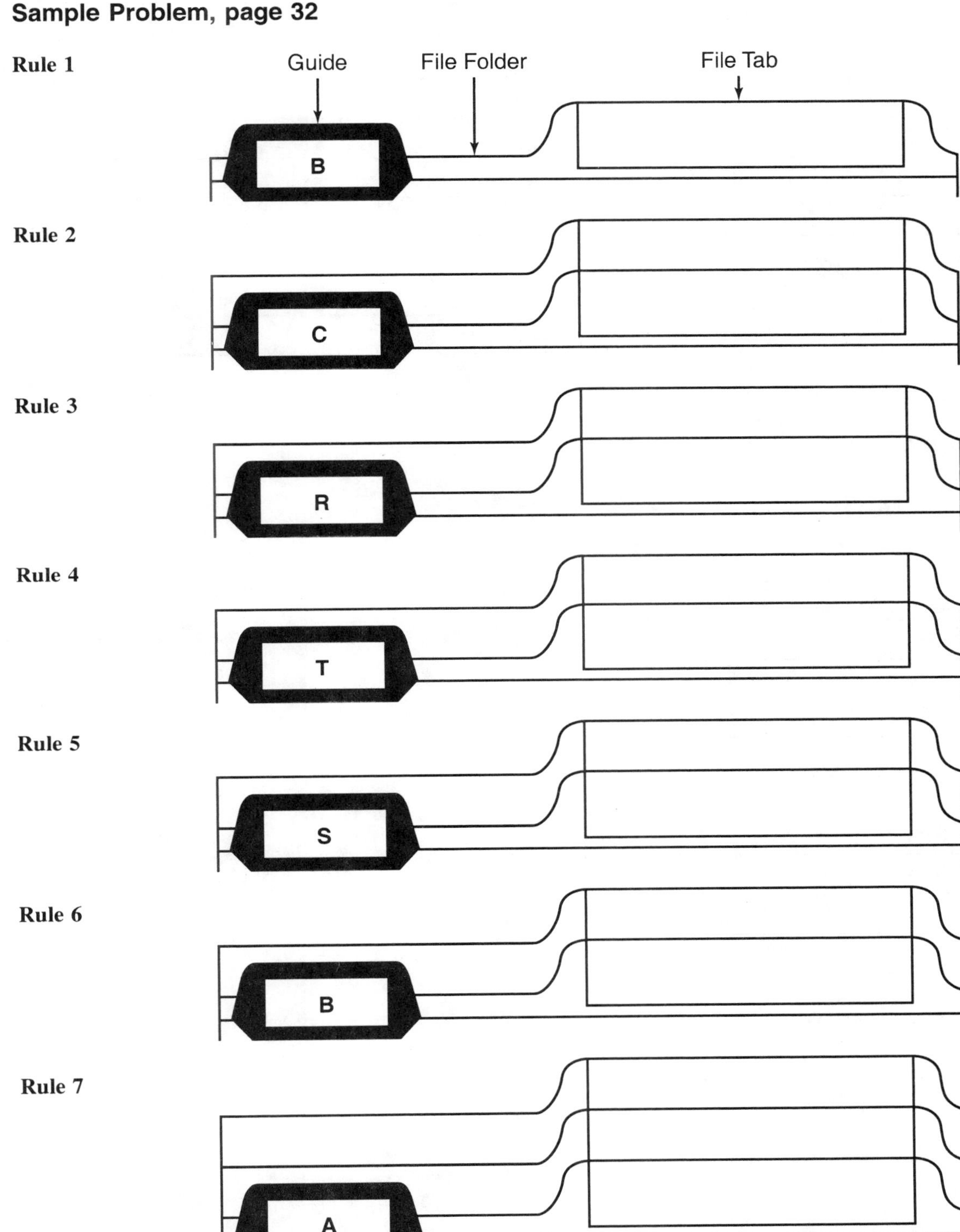

Problem 5–1, page 36

1. ______
2. ______
3. ______
4. ______
5. ______
6. ______
7. ______
8. ______
9. ______
10. ______
11. ______
12. ______

Problem 5–2, page 37

1. ______
2. ______
3. ______
4. ______
5. ______
6. ______
7. ______
8. ______
9. ______
10. ______
11. ______
12. ______

Problem 5–3, page 37

1. ______
2. ______
3. ______
4. ______
5. ______
6. ______
7. ______
8. ______
9. ______
10. ______
11. ______
12. ______

Problem 5–4

You are a sales clerk for Garfield Theater Company, a distributor of movie films. You are asked to make a card file for the sales force in your office.

Directions

a. Write the names below in indexing order (surname first, followed by a comma and the first name or initial). Use the Indexing Order column for this task.

Arthur Bliss	Alvin Robbins
Richard Kavanaugh	Chris Bliss
Timothy Robbins	Lena Madison
Kristen Adamson	Anthony Bliss
Lester Madison	K. Adamson
Helen Goro	Sara Goro

b. Using Rules 1 through 4, file the names in alphabetical order in the Alphabetical Order column.

Indexing Order	Alphabetical Order
1. ____________	1. ____________
2. ____________	2. ____________
3. ____________	3. ____________
4. ____________	4. ____________
5. ____________	5. ____________
6. ____________	6. ____________
7. ____________	7. ____________
8. ____________	8. ____________
9. ____________	9. ____________
10. ____________	10. ____________
11. ____________	11. ____________
12. ____________	12. ____________

Problem 5–5

You work as an office assistant for the Edwardsville Chamber of Commerce. One of your tasks is to make a card file of members who have just joined the Chamber of Commerce.

Directions

a. Write the names below in indexing order (surname first, followed by a comma and the first and middle name or initial). Use the Indexing Order column for this task.

Michael Kuhn	Brian T. Knecht
Eleanor Kleister	Oliver Kuhn
Knecht Shipping Company	Lancer Supply Company
Eleanor R. Kleister	Brian R. Knecht
Kleister Furniture Company	Byron Knecht
Lancer Society	Brian Wholesale Company

b. Using Rules 1 through 7, file the names in alphabetical order in the Alphabetical Order column.

Indexing Order	Alphabetical Order
1. ______	1. ______
2. ______	2. ______
3. ______	3. ______
4. ______	4. ______
5. ______	5. ______
6. ______	6. ______
7. ______	7. ______
8. ______	8. ______
9. ______	9. ______
10. ______	10. ______
11. ______	11. ______
12. ______	12. ______

Problem 5–6

You are a records clerk for the Enloe Photo Studio. You are to make a card file for the new customers listed below.

Directions

a. Write the names below in indexing order (surname first, followed by a comma and the first and middle name or initial). Use the Indexing Order column for this task.

Danice R. Eads	Danice Eads
Nora Alice Earl	Earl Herbert Ross
Earl Ross Company	Early Computer Company
Earl Lumber Company	Nora Earl, Incorporated
Nora A. Earl	Edward Eads
Nora Alice Early	Eads Trucking Company

b. Using Rules 1 through 7, file the names in alphabetical order in the Alphabetical Order column.

Indexing Order	Alphabetical Order
1. ______________	**1.** ______________
2. ______________	**2.** ______________
3. ______________	**3.** ______________
4. ______________	**4.** ______________
5. ______________	**5.** ______________
6. ______________	**6.** ______________
7. ______________	**7.** ______________
8. ______________	**8.** ______________
9. ______________	**9.** ______________
10. ______________	**10.** ______________
11. ______________	**11.** ______________
12. ______________	**12.** ______________

(This page is without text copy.)

Name ____________________

Score __________

Sample Problem, page 40

Step 1

EQUIPMENT MENU

1. ADD EQUIPMENT RECORD
2. UPDATE EQUIPMENT RECORD
3. DISPLAY EQUIPMENT RECORD
4. PRINT EQUIPMENT RECORDS

ENTER CHOICE ☐

Steps 2 and 3

EQUIPMENT RECORD

EQUIPMENT NUMBER ☐☐☐

EQUIPMENT TYPE ☐☐☐☐☐☐☐☐☐☐☐☐☐☐☐☐☐☐☐☐

DESCRIPTION ☐☐☐☐☐☐☐☐☐☐☐☐☐☐☐

AMOUNT ☐☐☐☐

DATE PURCHASED ☐☐/☐☐/☐☐☐☐

VENDOR ☐☐☐☐☐☐☐☐☐☐☐☐☐☐☐☐☐☐☐☐

Problem 6–1, page 43

a.

EQUIPMENT RECORD

EQUIPMENT NUMBER ☐☐☐

EQUIPMENT TYPE ☐☐☐☐☐☐☐☐☐☐☐☐☐☐☐☐☐☐☐☐

DESCRIPTION ☐☐☐☐☐☐☐☐☐☐☐☐☐☐☐

AMOUNT ☐☐☐☐

DATE PURCHASED ☐☐/☐☐/☐☐☐☐

VENDOR ☐☐☐☐☐☐☐☐☐☐☐☐☐☐☐☐☐☐☐☐

b.

EQUIPMENT RECORD

EQUIPMENT NUMBER ☐☐☐

EQUIPMENT TYPE ☐☐☐☐☐☐☐☐☐☐☐☐☐☐☐☐☐☐☐☐

DESCRIPTION ☐☐☐☐☐☐☐☐☐☐☐☐☐☐☐

AMOUNT ☐☐☐☐

DATE PURCHASED ☐☐/☐☐/☐☐☐☐

VENDOR ☐☐☐☐☐☐☐☐☐☐☐☐☐☐☐☐☐☐☐☐

Problem 6–2, page 44

a.

STUDENT ENROLLMENT RECORD

STUDENT NUMBER	☐☐☐-☐☐-☐☐☐☐
LAST NAME	☐☐☐☐☐☐☐☐☐☐☐☐☐☐☐
FIRST NAME	☐☐☐☐☐☐☐☐☐☐☐☐☐☐☐
MIDDLE INITIAL	☐
HOME STREET ADDRESS	☐☐☐☐☐☐☐☐☐☐☐☐☐☐☐
HOME CITY	☐☐☐☐☐☐☐☐☐☐☐☐☐☐☐
HOME STATE	☐☐
HOME ZIP CODE	☐☐☐☐☐-☐☐☐☐
DATE ADMITTED	☐☐/☐☐/☐☐☐☐
DORMITORY ASSIGNMENT	☐☐☐☐☐☐☐☐☐☐☐☐☐☐☐

b.

STUDENT ENROLLMENT RECORD

STUDENT NUMBER	☐☐☐-☐☐-☐☐☐☐
LAST NAME	☐☐☐☐☐☐☐☐☐☐☐☐☐☐☐
FIRST NAME	☐☐☐☐☐☐☐☐☐☐☐☐☐☐☐
MIDDLE INITIAL	☐
HOME STREET ADDRESS	☐☐☐☐☐☐☐☐☐☐☐☐☐☐☐
HOME CITY	☐☐☐☐☐☐☐☐☐☐☐☐☐☐☐
HOME STATE	☐☐
HOME ZIP CODE	☐☐☐☐☐-☐☐☐☐
DATE ADMITTED	☐☐/☐☐/☐☐☐☐
DORMITORY ASSIGNMENT	☐☐☐☐☐☐☐☐☐☐☐☐☐☐☐

Problem 6–3, page 44

1. ______
2. ______
3. ______
4. ______
5. ______
6. ______
7. ______

Problem 6–4

You are an office worker for a small charter airline company. Part of your job is to enter data about charter flights the company schedules into a scheduled flight file.

Directions

Look at the partial screen shown below, and answer the questions that follow.

FLIGHT RECORD

FLIGHT NUMBER 189

DATE OF FLIGHT 11/02/20--

TIME OF FLIGHT 08:20AM

ORIGINATING FIELD STEWAR

DESTINATION FIELD

PILOT

FIRST OFFICER

Problem 6–4, Concluded

1. The screen shows that you have entered part of the name of the airfield from which the plane is to take off. What key should you press when you finish entering the name?

____

2. How many fields are shown on the partial screen?

____

3. How many spaces have been provided for the Pilot field?

____

4. How many spaces are provided for the Date field?

____

5. To enter the number for flight 45 in the Flight Number field, what would you key into these spaces?

____

6. When you finish keying in data in all the fields on the record, what will appear on the screen?

____

Problem 6–5

You are a personnel clerk for Tollway Shipping Company. Your supervisor has asked you to set up an employee file for the computer. The Personnel Department wants to use the file to keep track of its employees. The employee records in the file must contain these fields:

1. EMPLOYEE NUMBER (6 spaces)
2. EMPLOYEE NAME (20 spaces)
3. JOB TITLE (25 spaces)
4. DEPARTMENT (20 spaces)
5. STREET ADDRESS (25 spaces)
6. CITY (25 spaces)
7. STATE (2 spaces)
8. ZIP CODE (9 spaces)
9. DATE HIRED (8 spaces)

Directions

In the space that follows, draw an employee record as it would appear on a screen. Use "EMPLOYEE RECORD" as a heading for the record. Use one line for each field. Use an open box to show the spaces you put in each of the fields.

Problem 6–6

You are a record clerk for the Maintenance Department of a large firm. One of the responsibilities of the Maintenance Department is to keep track of all furniture and equipment the firm owns. Your supervisor has asked you to set up a furniture and equipment file. The records in the file must contain these fields:

1. EQUIPMENT NUMBER (5 spaces)
2. EQUIPMENT TYPE (15 spaces)
3. DESCRIPTION (25 spaces)
4. BUILDING NUMBER (2 spaces)
5. ROOM NUMBER (3 spaces)
6. VENDOR (15 spaces)
7. CONDITION (20 spaces)

Directions

In the space that follows, draw a furniture and equipment record as it would appear on a screen. Use "FURNITURE AND EQUIPMENT RECORD" as a heading for the record. Use one line for each field. Use an open box to show the spaces you put in each of the fields.

(This page is without text copy.)

Name ______________________________

Score ____________

Sample Problem, page 46

	A	B	C	D	E	F
1						
2						
3						
4						
5						
6						
7						
8						
9						
10						
11						
12						
13						
14						
15						

Problem 7–1, page 52

	A	B	C	D	E	F
1						
2						
3						
4						
5						
6						
7						
8						
9						
10						
11						
12						
13						
14						
15						

Problem 7–2, page 52

	A	B	C	D	E	F
1						
2						
3						
4						
5						
6						
7						
8						
9						
10						
11						
12						
13						
14						
15						

Name ________________________________

Problem 7–3, page 53

	A	B	C	D	E	F
1						
2						
3						
4						
5						
6						
7						
8						
9						
10						
11						
12						
13						
14						
15						

Problem 7–4, page 53

	A	B	C	D	E	F
1						
2						
3						
4						
5						
6						
7						
8						
9						
10						
11						
12						
13						
14						
15						

Problem 7–5

Aaron Donald is an assistant with the Kerryville Screamers baseball team. One of his tasks is to find the average hits for each outfielder and the total hits for the team for a week. The list of outfielders and hits for the week of June 5 is shown below:

Kerryville Screamers
Hits by Outfielders
Week of June 5

Outfielder	**Hits**
B. Denzig	11
R. Morrero	8
L. Czernak	12
C. Riley	2

Directions

a. Run your spreadsheet software.

b. Create a spreadsheet that contains the headings shown above in Cells A1, A2, and A3.

c. Enter the column headings Outfielder and Hits in Cells A5 and B5.

d. Enter the names for each outfielder in Cells A7 through A10.

e. Enter the hits for each outfielder in Cells B7 through B10.

f. Enter Total Hits in Cell A12 and the formula for calculating the total amounts in Cell B12. Use the SUM function in your formula.

g. Enter Average Hits in Cell A13 and the formula for finding the average number of hits for all 4 outfielders in Cell B13. Use the AVERAGE function in your formula.

h. Save your spreadsheet on a floppy diskette. Use the name Job7–5.

i. If your teacher instructs you to, print a copy of your spreadsheet.

	A	B	C	D	E	F
1						
2						
3						
4						
5						
6						
7						
8						
9						
10						
11						
12						
13						
14						
15						

Name ______________________________

Problem 7–6

It is next week, and Aaron Donald is still an assistant with the Kerryville Screamers baseball team (see Problem 7–5). He needs to find the average hits for each outfielder and the total hits for the team for the week of June 12. The list of outfielders and hits for the week of June 12 is shown below:

Outfielder	Hits
B. Denzig	8
R. Morrero	10
L. Czernak	10
C. Riley	4

Directions

a. Run your spreadsheet software.

b. Start the spreadsheet that you created in Problem 7–5.

c. Change the date in Cell A3 to Week of June 12.

d. Enter the hits for each outfielder in Cells B7 through B10 by placing the cell pointer in each cell and keying in the new numbers.

e. Save your spreadsheet on a floppy diskette. Use the name Job7–6.

f. If your teacher instructs you to, print a copy of your spreadsheet.

	A	B	C	D	E	F
1						
2						
3						
4						
5						
6						
7						
8						
9						
10						
11						
12						
13						
14						
15						

(This page is without text copy.)

Name ______________________________

Score ____________

Reinforcement Activities | CHAPTER 1 Jobs 1–7

Check Your Reading, page 54

1. ______________________________

2a. ______________________________

2b. ______________________________

2c. ______________________________

3. ______________________________

Discussion, page 54

1a. ______________________________

1b. ______________________________

2. ______________________________

3a. ______________________________

3b. ______________________________

3c. ______________________________

4a. ______________________________

4b. ______________________________

4c. ______________________________

Ethics in the Workplace, page 54

Communication in the Workplace, page 55

Focus on Careers, page 55

1.
2a.
2b.
2c.
3.
4.

Reviewing What You Have Learned, page 56

1.
2.
3.
4.
5.
6.
7.
8.
9.
10.
11.
12.

Name ______________________

Mastery Problem, page 56

a.–b.

No.	Correct	Error
1		
2		
3		
4		
5		

No.	Correct	Error
6		
7		
8		
9		
10		

c.

d.

Mastery Problem, Concluded

e. 1. ______________________________

2. ______________________________

3. ______________________________

4. ______________________________

5. ______________________________

6. ______________________________

7. ______________________________

8. ______________________________

9. ______________________________

10. ______________________________

f.

Name ______________________________

Reviewing Your Business Vocabulary

Choose the words that match the statements. Write each word you choose next to the statement number it matches. Be careful; some of the words listed should not be used.

Statements

1. Contains the headings, labels, and formulas that will not change in a spreadsheet . . . . ______________
2. The total of a money column written in small figures . . . . . ______________
3. Information . . . . ______________
4. To check for accuracy . . . . ______________
5. Doing something to data to make them more useful . . . . . . ______________
6. Forms from which you get data to enter into the computer . . . . ______________
7. By date . . . . ______________
8. Input and output devices, and a central processing unit . . . . ______________
9. By the alphabet . . . . ______________
10. The computer system part that processes the data . . . . ______________
11. An output device . . . . ______________
12. Instructions the computer follows to process the data . . . . . ______________
13. Used to help find records in a file . . . . ______________
14. Workers trained to store and retrieve data . . . . ______________
15. To find a document . . . . ______________
16. A chronological file of important dates . . . . ______________
17. Arranging the parts of a name so that it can be filed . . . . . . ______________
18. A list of choices on a screen . . . . ______________
19. To enter data using a keyboard . . . . ______________
20. A flashing marker on a screen . . . . ______________
21. Allows pencil marks to be read by special machines . . . . . . ______________
22. A bar code placed on products which can be read by special cash registers . . . . ______________
23. The second step in the data processing cycle . . . . ______________
24. Last name . . . . ______________
25. A group of records . . . . ______________

Words

alphabetically
cell
central processing unit
chronologically
computer program
computer software
computer system
cursor
data

data processing
double rulings
electronically
file
footing
formula
guides
indexing
key

manually
menu
numerically
optical mark recognition
printer
processing
record clerks
retrieve
run

source documents
spreadsheet software
stock clerks
store
surname
template
tickler file
UPC
verify

(This page is without text copy.)

Name ______________________________

Score ____________

Keeping a Personal Budget

CHAPTER 2
Job 8

Sample Problem, page 60

____

____

____

DATE	EXPLANATION (ESTIMATED)	TOTAL RECEIPTS	TOTAL PAYMENTS	TYPE OF PAYMENT			
				LUNCHES	SCHOOL SUPPLIES	ENTER-TAINMENT	COLLEGE SAVINGS

Problem 8–1, page 65

a.–i.

DATE		EXPLANATION (ESTIMATED)	TOTAL RECEIPTS		TOTAL PAYMENTS		TYPE OF PAYMENT							
							LUNCHES		SCHOOL SUPPLIES		ENTER-TAINMENT		SAVINGS	

j. 1.

2.

3.

4.

5.

Name ______________________________

Problem 8–2, page 66

a.–i.

DATE	EXPLANATION (ESTIMATED)	TOTAL RECEIPTS	TOTAL PAYMENTS	TYPE OF PAYMENT: AUTO EXPENSES	LUNCHES	BOOKS AND SUPPLIES	ENTER-TAINMENT	PIANO LESSONS	SAVINGS

j. 1. ______________________________

2. ______________________________

3. ______________________________

4. ______________________________

5. ______________________________

Problem 8–3

Louis Rosenthal attends Los Gatos Vocational School. Louis works part-time as a clerk in a real estate agency in town. He also works on weekends at a fast food store. His estimated receipts and payments for the week of August 21, 20-- are:

Estimated Receipts		Estimated Payments	
From part-time job	$20.00	Auto expenses	$14.00
From weekend job	32.00	Lunches	11.00
		School supplies	4.00
		Entertainment	12.00
		Gifts	4.00
		Savings	7.00
Total estimated receipts	$52.00	Total estimated payments	$52.00

Directions

a. Enter the heading on the top three lines of the receipts and payments record on the next page.

b. Record the estimated budget amounts in parentheses under the column headings.

c. Record the actual receipts and payments:

August	21	Received $21.00 in pay from part-time job.
	22	Received $30.00 in pay from weekend job.
	22	Paid $2.15 for lunch and $7.50 for gasoline.
	23	Paid $2.75 for lunch and $3.00 for school lab supplies.
	24	Paid $2.25 for lunch and $7.00 for a concert ticket.
	25	Paid $1.80 for lunch.
	26	Paid $2.80 for lunch, $5.00 for a gift for a friend, and put $7.00 in savings account.
	27	Paid $6.00 for gasoline and $3.00 for oil for the car.

d. Rule and foot the money columns.

e. Verify the totals by crossfooting.

f. Write the totals below the footings and double rule the money columns.

g. Find the balance of cash on hand by subtracting the total of the Total Payments column from the total of the Total Receipts column.

h. Record the balance of cash on hand on the line below the double rulings. Use August 28 as the date and write "Balance" in the Explanation column.

i. Answer these questions:

1. What amount was spent for lunches?
2. How much was spent for entertainment?
3. On which items did Louis spend more than planned?
4. Did Louis put more or less savings in the bank than planned?
5. Did Louis receive more or less income than planned?

Name ________________________________

Problem 8–3, Concluded

a.–h.

DATE	EXPLANATION (ESTIMATED)	TOTAL RECEIPTS	TOTAL PAYMENTS	TYPE OF PAYMENT					
				AUTO EXPENSES	LUNCHES	SCHOOL SUPPLIES	ENTER-TAINMENT	GIFTS	SAVINGS

i. 1. ________________________________

2. ________________________________

3. ________________________________

4. ________________________________

5. ________________________________

Problem 8–4

Pat Nguyen is a part-time student at Mission Community College. Pat works part-time in an insurance company in his town. He also washes, vacuums, and waxes cars on weekends out of his home during warm weather months. He saves as much as he can to help pay for tuition and other college costs. His estimated receipts and payments for the week of May 14, 20-- are:

Estimated Receipts		Estimated Payments	
From part-time job	$ 48.00	Auto expenses	$ 15.00
From weekend job	70.00	Lunches	11.00
		School supplies and fees	12.00
		Entertainment	15.00
		Car service supplies	5.00
		Savings	60.00
Total estimated receipts	$118.00	Total estimated payments	$118.00

Directions

a. Enter the heading on the top three lines of the receipts and payments record on the next page.

b. Record the estimated budget amounts in parentheses under the column headings.

c. Record the actual receipts and payments:

May	14	Received $65.00 for cleaning and waxing two cars.
	15	Paid $2.53 for lunch.
	16	Paid $2.75 for lunch and $8.29 for gasoline.
	17	Paid $3.02 for lunch and $8.00 for school computer supplies.
	18	Paid $1.87 for lunch and $6.00 for bowling lane fees.
	19	Received $48.00 in pay from part-time job.
	19	Paid $3.72 for lunch, $8.59 for car wax and cleaner, and put $60.00 in savings account.
	20	Paid $7.33 for gasoline.

d. Rule and foot the money columns.

e. Verify the totals by crossfooting.

f. Write the totals below the footings and double rule the money columns.

g. Find the balance of cash on hand by subtracting the total of the Total Payments column from the total of the Total Receipts column.

h. Record the balance of cash on hand on the line below the double rulings. Use May 21 as the date and write "Balance" in the Explanation column.

i. Answer these questions:

1. What amount was spent for auto expenses?
2. How much was spent for lunches?
3. On which items did Pat spend less than planned?
4. Did Pat put more or less savings in the bank than planned?
5. Did Pat receive more or less income than planned?

Name ______________________

Problem 8–4, Concluded

a.–h.

____

____

____

DATE		EXPLANATION (ESTIMATED)	TOTAL RECEIPTS	TOTAL PAYMENTS	TYPE OF PAYMENT					
					AUTO EXPENSES	LUNCHES	SCHOOL SUPPLIES AND FEES	ENTERTAINMENT	CAR SERVICE SUPPLIES	SAVINGS

i. 1. ______________________

2. ______________________

3. ______________________

4. ______________________

5. ______________________

(This page is without text copy.)

Name ______________________

Score ____________

Sample Problem, page 68

DATE	EXPLANATION (ESTIMATED)	TOTAL RECEIPTS	TOTAL PAYMENTS	TYPE OF PAYMENT							
				HOUSEHOLD EXPENSES	CLOTHING	TRANS-PORTATION	HEALTH & PERSONAL	ENTER-TAINMENT	EDUCATION	GIFTS	SAVINGS

Problem 9–1, page 75

DATE	EXPLANATION (ESTIMATED)	TOTAL RECEIPTS	TOTAL PAYMENTS	TYPE OF PAYMENT HOUSEHOLD EXPENSES	CLOTHING	TRANS-PORTATION	HEALTH & PERSONAL	ENTER-TAINMENT	EDUCATION	GIFTS	SAVINGS

Name ______________________________

Problem 9–2, page 76

DATE	EXPLANATION (ESTIMATED)	TOTAL RECEIPTS	TOTAL PAYMENTS	TYPE OF PAYMENT							
				HOUSEHOLD EXPENSES	CLOTHING	TRANS-PORTATION	HEALTH & PERSONAL	ENTER-TAINMENT	EDUCATION	GIFTS	SAVINGS

Problem 9–3

Fiona Washington keeps a monthly record of receipts and payments. Fiona works as an accountant and has two daughters in elementary school.

Directions

a. Complete the heading for the record using the form provided. Use as the heading for your record:

Fiona Washington and Family
Record of Receipts and Payments
For May, 20--

b. Enter these estimated totals:

1. Date
2. Explanation
3. Total Receipts ($2,500.00)
4. Total Payments ($2,500.00)
5. Household Expenses ($1,050.00)
6. Clothing ($225.00)
7. Transportation ($500.00)
8. Health and Personal ($225.00)
9. Entertainment ($125.00)
10. Education ($50.00)
11. Gifts ($75.00)
12. Savings ($250.00)

c. Record the following receipts and payments for May, 20--:

May 1 Balance of cash, $518.26.

5 Fiona received her paycheck for $2,500.00.

7 The payments made since April 30 were:

Groceries	$117.83	Newspapers	6.35
Mortgage payment	640.00	Skating rink fees	6.00
Electric skillet	45.69	School lunches	12.00
Gasoline, oil for car	19.38	Contribution	10.00
Haircuts	15.00		

14 The payments made since last week were:

Groceries	$ 82.01	Beauty salon	25.00
Gas, electric bills	177.22	YMCA swim fee	3.00
Sweaters	44.18	School lunches	12.00
Gasoline for car	15.61	Notebooks, paper	7.88
New tire for car	86.79	Gift for niece's wedding	35.00

21 The payments made since last week were:

Groceries	$115.22	Flu shots	24.00
Telephone bill	41.19	Newspapers	12.70
Gasoline for car	14.73	School lunches	12.00

28 The payments made since last week were:

Groceries	$ 92.46	Movie	13.00
Real estate taxes	225.27	Newspapers, magazines	5.00
Suit	139.95	School lunches	12.00
Gasoline for car	13.11	Savings account deposit	250.00
Cough syrup, cough drops	13.62		

31 The payments made since the 28th were:

Groceries	$ 41.31	YMCA swim fee	3.00
Homeowner's insurance	140.00	School lunches	6.00
Gasoline, oil for car	9.28	Father's day gift	30.00

d. Rule and foot the columns. Verify the totals by crossfooting.

e. Write the totals below the footings and double rule the columns.

f. Record the new balance for June 1.

Name ______________________________

Problem 9–3, Concluded

DATE	EXPLANATION (ESTIMATED)	TOTAL RECEIPTS	TOTAL PAYMENTS	TYPE OF PAYMENT							
				HOUSEHOLD EXPENSES	CLOTHING	TRANS-PORTATION	HEALTH & PERSONAL	ENTER-TAINMENT	EDUCATION	GIFTS	SAVINGS

Problem 9–4

Roger and Jennifer Hopewell have begun to keep a monthly record of receipts and payments. Jennifer operates a service station. Roger is a nurse at a hospital. They have one son attending college.

Directions

a. Complete the heading for their record using the form provided. Enter these estimated totals:

1. Date
2. Explanation
3. Total Receipts ($5,600.00)
4. Total Payments ($5,600.00)
5. Household Expenses ($1,700.00)
6. Clothing ($350.00)
7. Transportation ($1,350.00)
8. Health and Personal ($300.00)
9. Entertainment ($300.00)
10. Education ($1,000.00)
11. Gifts ($200.00)
12. Savings ($400.00)

b. Record the following receipts and payments for February, 20--. Classify the payments carefully.

Feb. 1 Balance of cash, $711.82.

2 Jennifer Hopewell received her paycheck for $865.38.

4 Roger Hopewell received his paycheck for $423.08.

7 The payments made since January 31 were:

Groceries	$122.18	Magazines	10.00
Contribution	20.00	Mortgage payment	1,100.00
Gasoline, oil for cars	36.59	Textbooks	75.42
Beauty salon	15.00	Tuition	500.00
Newspaper subscription	12.88	Savings account deposit	100.00

9 Jennifer Hopewell received her paycheck for $865.38.

11 Roger Hopewell received his paycheck for $423.08.

14 The payments made since last week were:

Utility bill	$215.18	Health insurance	123.17
Hockey game	45.00	Fitness center membership fee	110.00
Ski boots	115.27	Automobile insurance	461.43
Gasoline for cars	32.19	Notebooks, paper	23.78
Groceries	104.04	Savings account deposit	100.00

16 Jennifer Hopewell received her paycheck for $865.38.

18 Roger Hopewell received his paycheck for $423.08.

21 The payments made since last week were:

Groceries	$ 92.18	Magazine subscription	25.76
Car payment	118.25	Gasoline for cars	31.89
Doctor visit, medicine	52.00	Dormitory fees	450.00
Telephone bill	75.11	Dinner out	46.62

23 Jennifer Hopewell received her paycheck for $865.38.

25 Roger Hopewell received his paycheck for $423.08.

28 The payments made since last week were:

College laboratory fees	$ 35.00	Magazines	15.00
New mattress, boxsprings	525.75	Contribution	150.00
Gasoline for cars	29.00	Sports jacket	136.90
Newspapers	12.88	Savings account deposit	200.00
Groceries	115.87		

c. Rule and foot the columns. Verify the totals by crossfooting.

d. Write the totals below the footings and double rule the columns.

e. Record the new balance for March 1.

Problem 9–4, Concluded

DATE	EXPLANATION (ESTIMATED)	TOTAL RECEIPTS	TOTAL PAYMENTS	TYPE OF PAYMENT							
				HOUSEHOLD EXPENSES	CLOTHING	TRANS-PORTATION	HEALTH & PERSONAL	ENTER-TAINMENT	EDUCATION	GIFTS	SAVINGS

(This page is without text copy.)

Name ______________________

Score __________

Keeping a Business Budget

CHAPTER 2
Job 10

Sample Problem, page 79

DESCRIPTION	JANUARY	FEBRUARY	MARCH	TOTAL
Receipts:				
Residential Sales	14 4 0 0 00	15 0 0 0 00	8 8 0 0 00	
Commercial Sales	4 8 0 0 00	5 4 0 0 00	13 6 0 0 00	
Total Receipts				
Payments:				
Wages	11 6 0 0 00	11 6 0 0 00	13 0 0 0 00	
Rent	2 4 0 0 00	2 4 0 0 00	2 4 0 0 00	
Utilities	4 2 0 00	4 2 0 00	3 0 0 00	
Supplies	6 0 0 00	6 0 0 00	1 0 0 0 00	
Office Expenses	1 8 0 00	1 8 0 00	2 0 0 00	
Repairs	4 0 0 00	4 0 0 00	1 1 0 0 00	
Insurance	7 5 0 00	7 5 0 00	7 5 0 00	
Taxes	2 3 2 0 00	2 3 2 0 00	2 6 0 0 00	
Equipment			1 5 0 0 00	
Total Payments				
Balance				

Problem 10–1, page 85

a.

DESCRIPTION	APRIL	MAY	JUNE	TOTAL
Receipts:				
Residential Sales	7,200.00	7,000.00	9,000.00	
Commercial Sales	14,000.00	14,800.00	18,600.00	
Total Receipts				
Payments:				
Wages	13,000.00	13,000.00	14,000.00	
Rent	2,400.00	2,400.00	2,400.00	
Utilities	200.00	200.00	200.00	
Supplies	1,000.00	1,000.00	1,100.00	
Office Expenses	180.00	180.00	180.00	
Repairs	400.00	300.00	300.00	
Insurance	750.00	750.00	750.00	
Taxes	2,600.00	2,600.00	3,000.00	
Equipment		2,200.00		
Total Payments				
Balance				

b. 1. ______

2. ______

3. ______

4. ______

5. ______

6. ______

7. ______

Name ____________________

Problem 10–2, page 86

a.

____

____

____

DESCRIPTION	JANUARY	FEBRUARY	MARCH	TOTAL
Receipts:				
Hospital Sales	13000 00	13000 00	13400 00	
Medical Office Sales	7800 00	8400 00	7600 00	
Total Receipts				
Payments:				
Wages	12400 00	12400 00	12400 00	
Rent	2000 00	2000 00	2000 00	
Insurance	800 00	800 00	800 00	
Telephone	500 00	500 00	500 00	
Utilities	340 00	340 00	260 00	
Taxes	2200 00	2200 00	2700 00	
Equipment	200 00	600 00	600 00	
Supplies	1200 00	1200 00	1200 00	
Other		2200 00		
Total Payments				
Balance				

b. **1.** ____________________

2. ____________________

3. ____________________

4. ____________________

5. ____________________

6. ____________________

7. ____________________

Problem 10–3, page 87

a.

DESCRIPTION	APRIL	MAY	JUNE	TOTAL
Receipts:				
Hospital Sales	14000 00	14400 00	15000 00	
Medical Office Sales	7600 00	7600 00	7600 00	
Total Receipts				
Payments:				
Wages	12400 00	12400 00	12400 00	
Rent	2000 00	2000 00	2000 00	
Insurance	800 00	800 00	800 00	
Telephone	500 00	500 00	500 00	
Utilities	200 00	140 00	100 00	
Taxes	2200 00	2200 00	2700 00	
Equipment	200 00	200 00	1000 00	
Supplies	1200 00	1200 00	1200 00	
Other	4200 00			
Total Payments				
Balance				

b. 1. ______

2. ______

3. ______

4. ______

5. ______

6. ______

7. ______

Problem 10–4

You are the record keeper for Santa Cruz Linen and Uniform Service, which provides and cleans uniforms and linens for industrial and restaurant use. The owner, Amy Cariel, has estimated the cash receipts and cash payments for the company for the first quarter of next year. She has asked you to complete the cash budget.

Directions

a. Complete the cash budget.

DESCRIPTION	JANUARY	FEBRUARY	MARCH	TOTAL
Receipts:				
Industrial Service	1980 00	3200 00	6500 00	
Restaurant Service	1400 00	2100 00	4200 00	
Total Receipts				
Payments:				
Wages	1900 00	1900 00	4500 00	
Rent	1500 00	1500 00	1500 00	
Insurance	350 00	350 00	350 00	
Telephone	45 00	125 00	150 00	
Utilities	120 00	150 00	200 00	
Taxes	400 00	400 00	900 00	
Equipment	50 00	100 00	500 00	
Supplies	100 00	200 00	700 00	
Other			1000 00	
Total Payments				
Balance				

Problem 10–4, Concluded

b. Answer these questions about the completed cash budget:

1. Which cash payments are fixed cash payments?

   ____

2. Which cash payments are variable cash payments?

   ____

3. What are the total estimated cash receipts from restaurant services for the quarter?

   ____

4. What are the total estimated cash payments for equipment for the quarter?

   ____

5. In what month(s) is there a positive cash flow?

   ____

6. In what month(s) is there a negative cash flow?

   ____

7. Is the cash flow for the entire quarter positive or negative?

   ____

Name ______________________

Score __________

Sample Problem, page 90

	BUDGETED	ACTUAL	VARIANCE

Problem 11–1, page 94

a.

	BUDGETED	ACTUAL	VARIANCE
Receipts:			
Corporate Sales	133 600 00	132 560 00	
Government Sales	44 000 00	47 080 00	
Total Receipts	177 600 00		
Payments:			
Wages	109 000 00	109 000 00	
Mortgage Payment	4 780 00	4 780 00	
Gas and Electric	1 500 00	1 360 00	
Supplies	25 000 00	23 800 00	
Office Expenses	1 580 00	1 720 00	
Equipment	3 000 00	2 040 00	
Insurance	4 600 00	4 600 00	
Taxes	25 500 00	25 500 00	
Telephone	700 00	700 00	
Total Payments	175 660 00		
Balance	1 940 00		

b. **1.** ______

2. ______

3. ______

4. ______

5. ______

Name ______________________

Problem 11–2, page 95

a. ______________________

____

____

	BUDGETED	ACTUAL	VARIANCE
Receipts:			
Heating Sales	74 175 00	74 175 00	
Air Conditioning Sales	34 600 00	36 125 00	
Total Receipts	108 775 00		
Payments:			
Wages	55 000 00	57 500 00	
Rent	7 900 00	7 900 00	
Gas and Electric	1 625 00	1 690 00	
Mechanical Parts	22 850 00	23 200 00	
Office Expenses	2 425 00	2 275 00	
Equipment Repair	1 250 00	1 072 50	
Insurance	2 880 00	2 880 00	
Taxes	11 875 00	11 240 00	
Telephone	745 00	780 00	
Total Payments	106 550 00		
Balance	2 225 00		

b. 1. ______________________

2. ______________________

3. ______________________

4. ______________________

5. ______________________

Problem 11–3

You work as an accounting clerk for Almaden Flooring Company. You have been asked to complete the company budget variance report for July:

	BUDGETED	ACTUAL	VARIANCE
Receipts:			
Carpet Sales	31,780.00	32,890.00	
Linoleum Sales	19,800.00	20,750.00	
Total Receipts	51,580.00		
Payments:			
Wages	31,200.00	31,200.00	
Mortgage Payment	2,100.00	2,100.00	
Gas and Electric	850.00	990.00	
Sales Supplies	1,700.00	1,280.00	
Office Expenses	640.00	635.00	
Insurance	1,080.00	1,080.00	
Taxes	9,150.00	9,640.00	
Transportation	1,790.00	1,820.00	
Total Payments	48,510.00		
Balance	3,070.00		

Name ______________________________

Problem 11–3, Concluded

Directions

a. Complete the budget variance report.

b. Answer these questions about your completed budget variance report:

1. Which cash receipts had the smallest variance?

   ____

2. Which cash payments had no variance?

   ____

3. Which cash payments had a negative variance?

   ____

4. Which cash payment had the largest positive variance?

   ____

5. Was the actual cash balance greater or less than the budgeted cash balance?

   ____

Problem 11–4

You are a staff accountant for Techmart Corporation. You have been asked to complete the company budget variance report for May:

	BUDGETED	ACTUAL	VARIANCE
Receipts:			
Hardware Sales	135,600.00	137,880.00	
Software Sales	168,400.00	172,620.00	
Repair Sales	49,250.00	47,750.00	
Total Receipts	353,250.00		
Payments:			
Wages	48,200.00	48,200.00	
Rent	2,390.00	2,390.00	
Gas and Electric	750.00	730.00	
Hardware	155,000.00	153,900.00	
Software	124,320.00	124,850.00	
Transportation	2,450.00	2,160.00	
Insurance	2,800.00	2,800.00	
Taxes	15,750.00	14,350.00	
Telephone	1,250.00	1,150.00	
Total Payments	352,910.00		
Balance	340.00		

Name ______________________________

Problem 11–4, Concluded

Directions

a. Complete the budget variance report.

b. Answer these questions about your completed budget variance report:

1. Which cash receipts had a negative variance?

   ____

2. Which cash payments had no variance?

   ____

3. Which cash payments had a negative variance?

   ____

4. Which cash payment had the largest positive variance?

   ____

5. Was the actual cash balance greater or less than the budgeted cash balance?

   ____

(This page is without text copy.)

Name ______________________________

Score __________

Reinforcement Activities

CHAPTER 2
Jobs 8–11

Check Your Reading, page 96

1. ______________________________

2. ______________________________

3. ______________________________

Discussion, page 96

____

Critical Thinking, page 96

1. ______________________________

2. ______________________________

3. ______________________________

Communication in the Workplace, page 97

1. ______

2. ______

Focus on Careers, page 97

1. First Job: ______

   Second Job: ______

2. ______

3. ______

Reviewing What You Have Learned, page 97

1. ______
2. ______
3. ______
4. ______
5. ______
6. ______
7. ______
8. ______

Mastery Problem, page 98

Phase 1: Budgeting for a Family

DATE	EXPLANATION (ESTIMATED)	TOTAL RECEIPTS	TOTAL PAYMENTS	TYPE OF PAYMENT							
				HOUSEHOLD EXPENSES	CLOTHING	TRANS-PORTATION	HEALTH & PERSONAL	ENTER-TAINMENT	EDUCATION	GIFTS	SAVINGS

Mastery Problem, Continued

Phase 2: Budgeting for a Business

DESCRIPTION	JULY	AUGUST	SEPTEMBER	TOTAL
Receipts:				
Production Services	9000 00	10000 00	10000 00	
Special Events	11000 00	12000 00	13000 00	
Total Receipts				
Payments:				
Wages	11400 00	11400 00	11400 00	
Rent	2400 00	2400 00	2400 00	
Loans	800 00	800 00	800 00	
Insurance	600 00	600 00	600 00	
Utilities	420 00	450 00	350 00	
Telephone	830 00	850 00	900 00	
Repairs	100 00	100 00	100 00	
Supplies	300 00	300 00	300 00	
Taxes	2500 00	2500 00	2500 00	
Total Payments				
Balance				

Name ______________________________

Mastery Problem, Concluded

Phase 3: Analyzing a Budget

	BUDGETED	ACTUAL	VARIANCE
Receipts:			
Production Services	9,000.00	8,460.00	
Special Events	11,000.00	11,680.00	
Total Receipts			
Payments:			
Wages	11,400.00	11,400.00	
Rent	2,400.00	2,400.00	
Loans	800.00	800.00	
Insurance	600.00	600.00	
Utilities	420.00	510.00	
Telephone	830.00	870.00	
Repairs	100.00	150.00	
Supplies	300.00	180.00	
Taxes	2,500.00	2,500.00	
Total Payments			
Balance			

Reviewing Your Business Vocabulary

Choose the words that match the statements. Write each word you choose next to the statement number it matches. Be careful; some of the words listed should not be used.

Statements

1. Making a careful guess . . . . ____________
2. Amounts spent . . . . ____________
3. To record an amount again in a second column . . . . ____________
4. When items that are alike are grouped together . . . . ____________
5. Amounts of money received . . . . ____________
6. Adding a row of figures across a business form . . . . ____________
7. A careful plan, made in advance, of cash receipts and cash payments . . . . ____________
8. Cash payments that change from period to period . . . . . . ____________
9. When cash receipts are greater than cash payments . . . . . ____________
10. A report showing the estimated cash flow of a business . . ____________
11. When cash payments are greater than cash receipts . . . . . ____________
12. Cash payments that are the same from period to period . . ____________
13. A three-month period . . . . ____________
14. A form that compares budgeted amounts with actual amounts . . . . ____________
15. A microcomputer . . . . ____________
16. A computer program that lets you create and enter data into forms . . . . ____________
17. Moving around on a computer screen . . . . ____________
18. A difference . . . . ____________

Words

budget
budget variance report
cash budget
cash flow
classified
crossfooting
estimating
extend an amount
fixed payments
footing
negative cash flow
payments
personal computer
positive cash flow
quarter
receipts
scrolling
spreadsheet
variable payments
variance
verify

Name ______________________

Score __________

Sample Problem, page 106

FNB Flagstone National Bank
VALUCARD

CREDIT APPLICATION FORM

APPLICANT:

1. Name (Last)	(First)	(Initial)	2. Birthdate	3. Social Security No.
4. Address (Street)	(City)		(State)	(Zip)
5. Area Code/Tel. Number	6. Lived At Present Address Years Months	7. ___Own___Rent___Other		8. Monthly Payment
9. Previous Street Address (if less than 2 years at present address)				10. Lived At Previous Address Years Months
11. Present Employer	12. How Long Employed Years Months		13. Job Title	14. Mo. Net Income
15. Employer's Address (Street)	(City)	(State)	(Zip)	16. Area Code/Tel. Number
17. Previous Employer	18. How Long Employed Years Months		19. Job Title	20. Mo. Net Income
21. Employer's Address (Street)	(City)	(State)	(Zip)	22. Area Code/Tel. Number
23. Other Sources Of Income				24. Net Income Per Month

CO-APPLICANT: Complete this section only if a joint account is requested. (Spouse can be a co-applicant.)

25. Name (Last)	(First)	(Initial)	26. Birthdate	27. Social Security No.
28. Address (Street)	(City)	(State)	(Zip)	

CREDIT REFERENCES:

48. Savings Account (Institution Name)	(Account No.)	(Balance)
49. Checking Account (Institution Name)	(Account No.)	(Balance)

LOANS AND OUTSTANDING DEBTS: List all debts owing. Attach additional sheet if necessary.

50. Auto Make, Model, & Year	51. Financed By	52. Account No.	53. Balance	54. Mo. Payment
55. Name of Creditor/Lender		56. Account No.	57. Balance	58. Mo. Payment

The above information is given to obtain credit privileges. I (we) hereby authorize the obtaining of information about any statements made herein, and I (we) agree to be bound by the terms of the National Credit Card agreement. Signers shall be jointly and severally liable.

Applicant's Signature	Date	Authorized User(s)	
Co-Applicant's Signature	Date	Relationship to Applicant	No. of Cards Requested

Problem 12–1, page 109

Name	Weekly Pay	Yearly Pay	Monthly Pay
A. Berle	$550.00		
B. Coster	$452.00		
C. Dazai	$286.90		
D. Espino	$340.60		
E. Frisch	$490.80		

Problem 12–2, page 109

FNB Flagstone National Bank
VALUCARD

CREDIT APPLICATION FORM

APPLICANT:

1. Name (Last)	(First)	(Initial)	2. Birthdate	3. Social Security No.
4. Address (Street)		(City)	(State)	(Zip)
5. Area Code/Tel. Number	6. Lived At Present Address Years Months		7. ___Own___Rent___Other	8. Monthly Payment
9. Previous Street Address (if less than 2 years at present address)				10. Lived At Previous Address Years Months
11. Present Employer	12. How Long Employed Years Months		13. Job Title	14. Mo. Net Income
15. Employer's Address (Street)	(City)	(State)	(Zip)	16. Area Code/Tel. Number
17. Previous Employer	18. How Long Employed Years Months		19. Job Title	20. Mo. Net Income
21. Employer's Address (Street)	(City)	(State)	(Zip)	22. Area Code/Tel. Number
23. Other Sources Of Income				24. Net Income Per Month

CO-APPLICANT: Complete this section only if a joint account is requested. (Spouse can be a co-applicant.)

25. Name (Last)	(First)	(Initial)	26. Birthdate	27. Social Security No.
28. Address (Street)	(City)	(State)	(Zip)	

CREDIT REFERENCES:

48. Savings Account (Institution Name)	(Account No.)	(Balance)
49. Checking Account (Institution Name)	(Account No.)	(Balance)

LOANS AND OUTSTANDING DEBTS: List all debts owing. Attach additional sheet if necessary.

50. Auto Make, Model, & Year	51. Financed By	52. Account No.	53. Balance	54. Mo. Payment
55. Name of Creditor/Lender		56. Account No.	57. Balance	58. Mo. Payment

The above information is given to obtain credit privileges. I (we) hereby authorize the obtaining of information about any statements made herein, and I (we) agree to be bound by the terms of the National Credit Card agreement. Signers shall be jointly and severally liable.

Applicant's Signature	Date	Authorized User(s)	
Co-Applicant's Signature	Date	Relationship to Applicant	No. of Cards Requested

Problem 12–3, page 110

FREDONIA CITY BANK
T O T A L C A R D

CREDIT APPLICATION FORM

APPLICANT:

1. Name (Last)	(First)	(Initial)	2. Birthdate	3. Social Security No.
4. Address (Street)		(City)	(State)	(Zip)
5. Area Code/Tel. Number	6. Lived At Present Address Years Months		7. ___Own___Rent___Other	8. Monthly Payment
9. Previous Street Address (if less than 2 years at present address)				10. Lived At Previous Address Years Months
11. Present Employer	12. How Long Employed Years Months		13. Job Title	14. Mo. Net Income
15. Employer's Address (Street)	(City)	(State)	(Zip)	16. Area Code/Tel. Number
17. Previous Employer	18. How Long Employed Years Months		19. Job Title	20. Mo. Net Income
21. Employer's Address (Street)	(City)	(State)	(Zip)	22. Area Code/Tel. Number
23. Other Sources Of Income				24. Net Income Per Month

CO-APPLICANT: Complete this section only if a joint account is requested. (Spouse can be a co-applicant.)

25. Name (Last)	(First)	(Initial)	26. Birthdate	27. Social Security No.
28. Address (Street)	(City)	(State)	(Zip)	

CREDIT REFERENCES:

48. Savings Account (Institution Name)	(Account No.)	(Balance)
49. Checking Account (Institution Name)	(Account No.)	(Balance)

LOANS AND OUTSTANDING DEBTS: List all debts owing. Attach additional sheet if necessary.

50. Auto Make, Model, & Year	51. Financed By	52. Account No.	53. Balance	54. Mo. Payment
55. Name of Creditor/Lender		56. Account No.	57. Balance	58. Mo. Payment

The above information is given to obtain credit privileges. I (we) hereby authorize the obtaining of information about any statements made herein, and I (we) agree to be bound by the terms of the National Credit Card agreement. Signers shall be jointly and severally liable.

Applicant's Signature	Date	Authorized User(s)	
Co-Applicant's Signature	Date	Relationship to Applicant	No. of Cards Requested

Problem 12–4

Mike Hamilton is applying for a MajorCard from the Tell City National Bank.

Directions

Complete the credit application form for Mike Hamilton using the data provided. Be sure to compute his monthly net pay accurately and to sign and date the form 4/3/--. Mike wants only one card and is the only authorized user.

Applicant Section Data:
Name: Mike Hamilton
Birthdate: 5/6/73
Social Security Number: 347-34-3987
Address: 734 Hartman Street
City: Seattle
State: Washington
Zip Code: 98118-5614
Telephone Number: 206-555-5161
Other Data: Has rented his present apartment for 3 years and 1 month at $450.00 a month
Present Employer: B & G Publishing Co., 2 Glenwood Street, Seattle, WA 98112-6503, telephone 206-555-7812
Present Job: Shipping Clerk for 2 years and 7 months with a weekly net pay of $188.89
Previous Employer: None
Previous Job: None
Other Sources of Income: Part-time security guard for Belmont College with a weekly net pay of $86

Credit References Section Data:
Savings Account: Account No. 107-667 with a balance of $226.87 at Seaview Savings and Loan
Checking Account: Account No. 307-5617 with a balance of $277.13 at Crestwood State Bank

Loans and Outstanding Debts Section Data:
Auto Loan: A balance of $2,891.67, with monthly payments of $189.77, in loan account No. 5478 for a 20-- Ford Truck with Crestwood State Bank
Other Lender: A $307.88 balance, with monthly payments of $45.00, in account No. 608 with Dunwale Music Store

Problem 12–4, Concluded

Tell City MAJORCARD **NATIONAL BANK**

CREDIT APPLICATION FORM

APPLICANT:

1. Name (Last) (First) (Initial) 2. Birthdate 3. Social Security No.

4. Address (Street) (City) (State) (Zip)

5. Area Code/Tel. Number 6. Lived At Present Address Years Months 7. ___Own___Rent___Other 8. Monthly Payment

9. Previous Street Address (if less than 2 years at present address) 10. Lived At Previous Address Years Months

11. Present Employer 12. How Long Employed Years Months 13. Job Title 14. Mo. Net Income

15. Employer's Address (Street) (City) (State) (Zip) 16. Area Code/Tel. Number

17. Previous Employer 18. How Long Employed Years Months 19. Job Title 20. Mo. Net Income

21. Employer's Address (Street) (City) (State) (Zip) 22. Area Code/Tel. Number

23. Other Sources Of Income 24. Net Income Per Month

CO-APPLICANT: Complete this section only if a joint account is requested. (Spouse can be a co-applicant.)

25. Name (Last) (First) (Initial) 26. Birthdate 27. Social Security No.

28. Address (Street) (City) (State) (Zip)

CREDIT REFERENCES:

48. Savings Account (Institution Name) (Account No.) (Balance)

49. Checking Account (Institution Name) (Account No.) (Balance)

LOANS AND OUTSTANDING DEBTS: List all debts owing. Attach additional sheet if necessary.

50. Auto Make, Model, & Year 51. Financed By 52. Account No. 53. Balance 54. Mo. Payment

55. Name of Creditor/Lender 56. Account No. 57. Balance 58. Mo. Payment

The above information is given to obtain credit privileges. I (we) hereby authorize the obtaining of information about any statements made herein, and I (we) agree to be bound by the terms of the National Credit Card agreement. Signers shall be jointly and severally liable.

Applicant's Signature Date Authorized User(s)

Co-Applicant's Signature Date Relationship to Applicant No. of Cards Requested

Name ______________________

Score ____________

Sample Problem, page 113

a. Unauthorized charges listed on statement:

Date	Store	Amount
________	____________________	$__________
________	____________________	$__________

b. Corrections to amounts on statement:

For an overcharge:

Charge on statement $________

Charge on sales slip $________

Amount overcharged $________

For an undercharge:

Charge on sales slip $________

Charge on statement $________

Amount undercharged $________

c. Calculating the correct new balance:

New balance from statement $________

Less: Unauthorized charges $________

Overcharge on statement $________

____

$________

Add: Undercharge on statement $________

Correct new balance $________

Problem 13–1, page 116

	Total of Sales Slip	Amount Charged on Statement	Overcharge	Undercharge
1	$223.87	$223.78		
2	$409.18	$409.81		
3	$ 19.59	$119.59		
4	$ 72.08	$ 72.00		
5	$ 8.93	$ 8.99		

Problem 13–2, page 116

a. Unauthorized charges listed on statement:

Date	Store	Amount
________	________________	$ ________
________	________________	$ ________

b. Corrections to amounts on statement:

For an overcharge:

Charge on statement $________

Charge on sales slip $________

Amount overcharged $________

For an undercharge:

Charge on sales slip $________

Charge on statement $________

Amount undercharged $________

c. Calculating the correct new balance:

New balance from statement $________

Less: Unauthorized charges $________

Overcharge on statement $________

____

$________

Add: Undercharge on statement ________

Correct new balance $________

Problem 13–3, page 118

a. Unauthorized charges listed on statement:

Date	Store	Amount
________	____________________	$ ____________
________	____________________	$ ____________

b. Corrections to amounts on statement:

For an overcharge:

Charge on statement $________

Charge on sales slip $________

Amount overcharged $________

For an undercharge:

Charge on sales slip $________

Charge on statement $________

Amount undercharged $________

c. Calculating the correct new balance:

New balance from statement $________

Less: Unauthorized charges $________

Overcharge on statement $________

____

$________

Add: Undercharge on statement ________

Correct new balance $________

Problem 13–4

Kelly Corrigan has saved each of her credit card sales slips for the month of August. Kelly renews her card membership every August for a fee of $45.00. Her checkbook shows that she made a payment of $273.31 on August 3. She wants to verify her credit card statement for August.

Directions

a. You are given Kelly's credit card statement and the top sections of her sales slips for August. Use a credit card statement work sheet to verify the statement.

b. List the date, store, and amount of every transaction which should not appear on the statement.

c. Compare the "sale amounts" on the sales slips to the amounts on the statement. If an amount is incorrect, find the overcharge or undercharge. Do not compare the "Amount" on the slips with the statement. The "Amount" and "sale amount" may differ because the bottom sections of the slips, showing sales taxes and totals, are not provided.

d. Find the correct new balance for the statement.

Problem 13–4, Continued

ACCOUNT NUMBER 0719 441 309
SALE AMOUNT 00023.38
INVOICE NUMBER 718905
8/X1 8/X3
KELLY CORRIGAN
0033989
VANGUARD PHARMACY

DATE	AUTHORIZATION NO.	SALES CLERK	DEPT.
8/4/--	—	17	4

QUAN.	DESCRIPTION	PRICE	AMOUNT
1	Prescription	23.38	23 38

ANT COPY

ACCOUNT NUMBER 0719 441 309
SALE AMOUNT 00094.49
INVOICE NUMBER 292910
8/X1 8/X3
KELLY CORRIGAN
0084533
TOWER ELECTRONICS

DATE	AUTHORIZATION NO.	SALES CLERK	DEPT.
8/17/--	—	25	8

QUAN.	DESCRIPTION	PRICE	AMOUNT
1	Telephone	89.99	89 99

ANT COPY

ACCOUNT NUMBER 0719 441 309
SALE AMOUNT 00026.04
INVOICE NUMBER 100889
8/X1 8/X3
KELLY CORRIGAN
8880803
OSCAR'S INC.

DATE	AUTHORIZATION NO.	SALES CLERK	DEPT.
8/19/--	—	5	—

QUAN.	DESCRIPTION	PRICE	AMOUNT
—	Dinner	24.80	24 80

ANT COPY

ACCOUNT NUMBER 0719 441 309
SALE AMOUNT 00176.25
INVOICE NUMBER 076852
8/X1 8/X3
KELLY CORRIGAN
0003378
KING OFFICE SUPPLIES

DATE	AUTHORIZATION NO.	SALES CLERK	DEPT.
8/22/--	039788	16	12

QUAN.	DESCRIPTION	PRICE	AMOUNT
1	Computer desk	129.98	129 98
1	Computer chair	37.88	37 88

ANT COPY

ACCOUNT NUMBER 0719 441 309
SALE AMOUNT 00228.65
INVOICE NUMBER 755732
8/X1 8/X3
KELLY CORRIGAN
1108916
DILLON'S DECOR, INC.

DATE	AUTHORIZATION NO.	SALES CLERK	DEPT.
8/27/--	448009	23	16

QUAN.	DESCRIPTION	PRICE	AMOUNT
2	Table lamps	45.89	91 78
1	Table	125.98	125 98

ANT COPY

ACCOUNT NUMBER 0719 441 309
SALE AMOUNT 00184.05
INVOICE NUMBER 097884
8/X1 8/X3
KELLY CORRIGAN
2279824
VASSON ANTIQUES

DATE	AUTHORIZATION NO.	SALES CLERK	DEPT.
8/28/--	199732	—	—

QUAN.	DESCRIPTION	PRICE	AMOUNT
1	Antique clock	175.29	175 29

ANT COPY

Problem 13–4, Concluded

VISA **ALAMO Commercial Bank** MasterCard

Transaction Date	Reference	Transaction Description		New Loans, Fees, & Purchases	Payments & Credits
08/03/--	12120943	Payment -- Thank You			273.31
08/04/--	37238809	Vanguard Pharmacy	Boston, MA	28.33	
08/05/--	74574531	El Paso Tires, Inc.	El Paso, TX	255.89	
08/10/--		Annual Fee		45.00	
08/17/--	00708917	Tower Electronics	Boston, MA	94.49	
08/19/--	67083328	Oscar's, Inc.	Boston, MA	26.04	
08/22/--	49082314	King Office Supplies	Boston, MA	176.25	
08/27/--	46210805	Dillon's Decor, Inc.	Boston, MA	228.65	
08/28/--	10781102	Vasson Antiques	Albany, NY	184.05	

How We Arrived At Your Finance Charge	Monthly Rate	Annual Percentage Rate	Balance to Which Monthly Rate Applied	Finance Charge

Previous Balance	Payments & Credits	New Loans, Fees, & Purchases	Finance Charge	New Balance	Minimum Payment Due
273.31	273.31	1038.70	0.00	1038.70	75.00

Billing Date	Date Payment Due	Credit Line	Account Number	In case of billing error, write to this address: P.O. Box 25255, Boston, MA 02140-3308
08/31/--	09/25/--	2500	0719 441 309	Direct telephone inquiries to 1-800-555-9200

a. Unauthorized charges listed on statement:

Date	Store	Amount
______	______	$______
______	______	$______

b. Corrections to amounts on statement:

For an overcharge:

Charge on statement $______

Charge on sales slip $______

Amount overcharged $______

For an undercharge:

Charge on sales slip $______

Charge on statement $______

Amount undercharged $______

c. Calculating the correct new balance:

New balance from statement $______

Less: Unauthorized charges $______

Overcharge on statement $______

______

$______

Add: Undercharge on statement ______

Correct new balance $______

Name ______________________

Score __________

Sample Problem, page 122

IN TUNE MUSIC STORE, INC.
2100 LINCOLN PLAZA
PHILADELPHIA, PA 19118-5671
Retail Installment Contract

Contract No.: 197822 Item: Compact Disk Player, Model No. 56A34

Buyer's Name: Felicia Peters

Buyer's Address: 4512 Ferndoan Street

City: Philadelphia State: PA Zip: 19148-4478

1.	Cash Price	$ 537.50
2.	Down Payment	107.50
3.	Amount Financed	430.00
4.	Installment Price	647.02
5.	Finance Charge	109.52
6.	Annual Percentage Rate	18%

Buyer agrees to pay In Tune Music Store, Inc., at their offices, the installment price shown above in 24 monthly installments of $ 22.48. The first installment is payable on June 6, 20 --, and all subsequent payments are to be made on the same day of each consecutive month until the installment price is paid in full, subject to the conditions on the reverse side of this contract.

Signed *Felicia Peters*

Step 1 Find the amount of the down payment.

Step 2 Find the amount financed.

Step 3 Find the installment price.

Step 4 Find the finance charge.

Problem 14–1, page 125

SEARLES EQUIPMENT COMPANY
241 GARDENIA STREET
WARWICK, RI 02888-2978
Retail Installment Contract

Contract No.: 34078 Item: Electronic Keyboard, Model TR-3411

Buyer's Name: Ellen Berman

Buyer's Address: 23 Cordell Avenue

City: Warwick State: RI Zip: 02886-6598

1.	Cash Price	$ 312.50
2.	Down Payment	62.50
3.	Amount Financed	250.00
4.	Installment Price	333.46
5.	Finance Charge	29.60
6.	Annual Percentage Rate	15%

Buyer agrees to pay Searles Equipment Company, at their offices, the installment price shown above in 12 monthly installments of $ 22.58 . The first installment is payable on August 12 , 20 -- , and all subsequent payments are to be made on the same day of each consecutive month until the installment price is paid in full, subject to the conditions on the reverse side of this contract.

Signed ______________________________

Space for calculations:

Problem 14–2, page 125

ORTIZ OFFICE EQUIPMENT COMPANY
1212 RICHARDS BOULEVARD
CINCINNATI, OH 45244-0288
Retail Installment Contract

Contract No.: 918022 Item: Desktop Copier, Model No. 44508-1

Buyer's Name: Barry Young

Buyer's Address: 14-78 Locale Road

City: Cincinnati State: OH Zip: 45247-3361

1.	Cash Price	$ 3000.00
2.	Down Payment	300.00
3.	Amount Financed	2700.00
4.	Installment Price	3554.00
5.	Finance Charge	554.00
6.	Annual Percentage Rate	17%

Buyer agrees to pay Ortiz Office Equipment Company, at their offices, the installment price shown above in 24 monthly installments of $133.50. The first installment is payable on February 2, 20--, and all subsequent payments are to be made on the same day of each consecutive month until the installment price is paid in full, subject to the conditions on the reverse side of this contract.

Signed ______________________

Space for calculations:

Problem 14–3

Adele Zahn bought a van priced at $13,000.00 from Saga Motors, Inc. Saga asked her to pay 10% down and the rest in monthly payments of $391.41 for three years. The company also asked her to sign the installment contract shown in this problem.

Directions

a. Verify the down payment, the amount financed, the installment price, and the finance charge on the contract. If you find an error, cross out the incorrect amount and write the correct amount to the right of it. Correct any subsequent amounts on lines 1–5 of the contract in the same way.

b. If you find no errors in the amounts, sign Adele's name to the contract.

SAGA MOTORS, INC.
300 GRIFFIE AVENUE
SYRACUSE, NY 13207-4114
Retail Installment Contract

Contract No.: 12-8904 Item: Van, Model LX2

Buyer's Name: Adele Zahn

Buyer's Address: Apt. 5, Mervin Street

City: Syracuse State: NY Zip: 13202-8493

1.	Cash Price	$ 13000.00
2.	Down Payment	1300.00
3.	Amount Financed	11700.00
4.	Installment Price	15390.76
5.	Finance Charge	2390.76
6.	Annual Percentage Rate	12½%

Buyer agrees to pay Saga Motors, Inc., at their offices, the installment price shown above in 36 monthly installments of $ 391.41. The first installment is payable on March 27, 20--, and all subsequent payments are to be made on the same day of each consecutive month until the installment price is paid in full, subject to the conditions on the reverse side of this contract.

Signed ______________________

Space for calculations:

Problem 14–4

Sol Epstein bought a laser printer for his business computer system priced at $4,156.25 from Jansen Office Supply Company. The company asked him to pay 20% down and the rest in monthly payments of $132.41 for two and one-half years. The company also asked him to sign the installment contract shown in this problem.

Directions

a. Verify the down payment, the amount financed, the installment price, and the finance charge on the contract. If you find an error, cross out the incorrect amount and write the correct amount to the right of it. Correct any subsequent amounts on lines 1–5 of the contract in the same way.

b. If you find no errors in the amounts, sign Sol's name to the contract.

JANSEN OFFICE SUPPLY COMPANY
3307 HERBERT STREET
GREEN BAY, WI 54302-3327
Retail Installment Contract

Contract No.: 134-7980 Item: Laser Printer, Model No. LPM-3389A

Buyer's Name: Sol Epstein

Buyer's Address: 145 West Orley Street

City: Green Bay State: WI Zip: 54301-8652

1.	Cash Price	$ 4156.25
2.	Down Payment	872.81
3.	Amount Financed	3283.44
4.	Installment Price	4845.11
5.	Finance Charge	688.86
6.	Annual Percentage Rate	14¼%

Buyer agrees to pay Jansen Office Supply Company, at their offices, the installment price shown above in 30 monthly installments of $ 132.41 . The first installment is payable on May 29 , 20 -- , and all subsequent payments are to be made on the same day of each consecutive month until the installment price is paid in full, subject to the conditions on the reverse side of this contract.

Signed ______________________

Space for calculations:

(This page is without text copy.)

Name ______________________

Score __________

Sample Problem, page 128

$ 9,500.00 Springfield, IL May 15, 20 X2

Two years AFTER DATE I PROMISE TO PAY TO

THE ORDER OF First Division Bank

Nine thousand, five hundred 00/100 --------------- DOLLARS

PAYABLE AT First Division Bank

FOR VALUE RECEIVED WITH INTEREST AT 12 %

NO. 33897 DUE May 15, 20 X4 Ai Fen Lin

I = P × R × T

I = __________ × __________ × __________

I = __________

Problem 15–1, page 130

1. __________
2. __________
3. __________
4. __________
5. __________

Problem 15–2, page 131

1. __________
2. __________
3. __________
4. __________
5. __________

Problem 15–3, page 131

1. __________
2. __________
3. __________
4. __________
5. __________

Problem 15–4

Maria Berrios wants to borrow money for her business using the promissory note shown below.

$ 23,550.00	Jackson, MS	November 18, 20 X3

Three months AFTER DATE I PROMISE TO PAY TO

THE ORDER OF River Bend National Bank

Twenty-three thousand, five hundred fifty and no/100 DOLLARS

PAYABLE AT River Bend National Bank

FOR VALUE RECEIVED WITH INTEREST AT 17 %

NO. 34-981 DUE February 18, 20 X4 *Maria Berrios*

Answer these questions:

1. What is the annual rate of interest?

____

2. What is the due date of the note?

____

3. What is the time of the note?

____

4. How much interest must be paid when the note is due?

____

5. What is the amount due on the due date?

____

Problem 15–5

Timothy Mallory wants to borrow money for his business using the promissory note shown below.

$ 44,200.00   Helena, MT   March 11, 20 X4

2 1/2 years AFTER DATE I PROMISE TO PAY TO

THE ORDER OF Great Mountain Trust Company

Forty-four thousand, two hundred and no/100------- DOLLARS

PAYABLE AT Great Mountain Trust Company

FOR VALUE RECEIVED WITH INTEREST AT 9 %

NO. 8972-5 DUE September 11, 20 X6 Timothy Mallory

Answer these questions:

1. What is the annual rate of interest?

   ____

2. What is the due date of the note?

   ____

3. What is the time of the note?

   ____

4. How much interest must be paid when the note is due?

   ____

5. What is the amount due on the due date?

   ____

(This page is without text copy.)

Name ______________________________

Score ____________

Reinforcement Activities

CHAPTER 3
Jobs 12–15

Check Your Reading, page 132

1a. ______________________________

1b. ______________________________

1c. ______________________________

2. ______________________________

3. ______________________________

4. ______________________________

Discussion, page 132

1. ______________________________

2. ______________________________

3. ______________________________

Ethics in the Workplace, page 132

ADVANTAGES	DISADVANTAGES

Communication in the Workplace, page 133

Focus on Careers, page 133

1. ____________________
2. ____________________
3. ____________________
4. ____________________
5. ____________________

Global Business: International Telephone Calling Activity, page 134

Your corporation has now opened offices around the world. In this exercise, assume that all the sales offices have the same local seven-digit telephone number, 555-9876. Based on the following country codes and city codes, write out the numbers you would dial to call the sales office in each city.

City	Country Code	City Code	International Number
Bangkok, Thailand	66	2	____________
Berlin, Germany	49	30	____________
Calcutta, India	91	33	____________
Helsinki, Finland	358	9	____________
Moscow, Russia	7	095	____________
Rio de Janiero, Brazil	55	21	____________

Reviewing What You Have Learned, page 134

1. ____________________
2. ____________________
3. ____________________
4. ____________________
5. ____________________
6. ____________________
7. ____________________

Mastery Problem, page 135

Phase 1: Checking a Credit Card Statement

a. Unauthorized charges listed on statement:

Date	Store	Amount
________	________________	$________
________	________________	$________

b. Corrections to amounts on statement:

For an overcharge:		For an undercharge:	
Charge on statement	$________	Charge on sales slip	$________
Charge on sales slip	$________	Charge on statement	$________
Amount overcharged	$________	Amount undercharged	$________

c. Calculating the correct new balance:

New balance from statement		$________
Less: Unauthorized charges	$________	
Overcharge on statement	$________	
		________
		$________
Add: Undercharge on statement		________
Correct new balance		$________

Mastery Problem, Continued

Phase 2: Checking an Installment Contract

LOCKHART ELECTRONICS, INC.
1388 BORDEN STREET
TULSA, OK 74103-8278
Retail Installment Contract

Contract No.: 13933 Item: Ballow TV, Model LS-1200

Buyer's Name: Rose Stroud

Buyer's Address: 245 West Bostonian Boulevard

City: Tulsa State: OK Zip: 74107-3617

1.	Cash Price	$ 4250.00
2.	Down Payment	850.00
3.	Amount Financed	3400.00
4.	Installment Price	4682.56
5.	Finance Charge	1282.56
6.	Annual Percentage Rate	15½%

Buyer agrees to pay Lockhart Electronics, Inc., at their offices, the installment price shown above in 18 monthly installments of $212.92. The first installment is payable on July 24, 20--, and all subsequent payments are to be made on the same day of each consecutive month until the installment price is paid in full, subject to the conditions on the reverse side of this contract.

Signed ______________________

Phase 3: Borrowing on a Promissory Note

1. ______________________
2. ______________________
3. ______________________
4. ______________________
5. ______________________

Reviewing Your Business Vocabulary

Choose the words that match the statements. Write each word you choose next to the statement number it matches. Be careful; some of the words listed should not be used.

Statements

1. When you buy now and pay later . . . . ________
2. A source of credit; lender . . . . ________
3. A form of credit offered by stores . . . . ________
4. A credit card issued by banks . . . . ________
5. To approve . . . . ________
6. Yearly . . . . ________
7. A written record of a sale . . . . ________
8. A form showing the transactions and balances for a credit card account . . . . ________
9. Something that happens in a business that is recorded . . . ________
10. When you are charged more than you should be . . . . ________
11. A form of credit in which you pay for an item in monthly payments . . . . ________
12. The difference between the cash and installment prices of an item . . . . ________
13. The part of the installment price paid at the time an item is bought . . . . ________
14. The down payment plus the total of all monthly payments . . . . ________
15. The annual finance charge shown as a rate or percent . . . . ________
16. A written promise to pay . . . . ________
17. Money paid for the use of money . . . . ________
18. The amount borrowed on a note . . . . ________
19. The date a note must be paid . . . . ________
20. Principal plus interest owed on the due date of a promissory note . . . . ________
21. Installment price less down payment; amount borrowed . . . . ________
22. Identifies the person buying on credit . . . . ________
23. People likely to pay off their debts . . . . ________
24. An account for two people . . . . ________
25. Printed in raised characters . . . . ________

Words

amount due
amount financed
annual
annual percentage rate
authorize
bank credit card
cash price
charge account
credit
credit card
credit card statement
creditor
date of note
down payment
due date
embossed
finance charge
good credit risks
installment plan
installment price
interest
joint account
overcharged
principal
promissory note
sales slip
transaction
undercharged

Name ______________________________

Score ____________

Comprehensive Project 1 | **CHAPTERS 1–3**

You are an office assistant to Tien Sun, who owns and manages Prime Data, Inc. Tien has identified and written down the 10 customers with the highest sales for last year. She has also written down when those customers were last visited by a salesperson. Another office clerk has keyed and printed the information.

Phase 1: Verify the Printed/Keyboarded Data

Directions

Compare the printed data to the handwritten data for each customer. If both the handwritten and printed data are the same, put a check mark in the Correct column of the check list below. If they are not exactly the same, put a check mark in the Error column.

Handwritten Customer Data

1. Lynn R. Barr
   August 14, 2001
   $75,890
2. Barr Stores, Inc.
   October 1, 2001
   $138,833
3. L. R. Barr, Inc.
   September 28, 2001
   $89,472
4. Kelley Markets, Inc.
   October 6, 2001
   $92,398
5. Gorman Enterprises, Inc.
   October 16, 2001
   $122,516
6. Kelly Gorman, Inc.
   October 21, 2001
   $187,905
7. Jay Kelly Company
   November 6, 2001
   $135,671
8. Lynn's Shops, Inc.
   November 7, 2001
   $107,761
9. Barry Gorman, Inc.
   December 3, 2001
   $107,900
10. Jay Discount Stores, Inc.
    December 9, 2001
    $171,900

Printed Customer Data

1. Lynn R. Barr
   August 14, 2001
   $75,890
2. Barr Stores, Inc.
   October 1, 2001
   $188,833
3. L. R. Barr, Inc.
   September 28, 2001
   $89,472
4. Kelly Markets, Inc.
   October 6, 2001
   $92,398
5. Gorman Enterprises, Inc.
   October 16, 2001
   $122,516
6. Kelly Gorman, Inc.
   October 12, 2001
   $187,905
7. Jay Kelly Company
   November 6, 2001
   $135,671
8. Lynn's Shops, Inc.
   November 7, 2001
   $107,671
9. Barry Gorman, Inc.
   December 3, 2001
   $107,900
10. Jay Discount Stores, Inc.
    December 9, 2001
    $171,900

No.	Correct	Error
1.	________	________
2.	________	________
3.	________	________
4.	________	________
5.	________	________

No.	Correct	Error
6.	________	________
7.	________	________
8.	________	________
9.	________	________
10.	________	________

Phase 2: Sort the Data Numerically, Chronologically, and Alphabetically

Directions

Tien asks you to make three new lists of the customer data. On List No. 1, she wants the customer data listed in numerical order using the sales amount. On List No. 2, she wants the data shown in chronological order using the date the customer was visited last. On List No. 3, she wants the data shown in alphabetical order by customer name. Use the handwritten data prepared by Tien for your lists.

Comprehensive Project 1, Continued

a. List No. 1: Print the data below so that the customers are listed in descending numerical order by sales amount. List the customer with the highest sales first. The first line for each customer should contain the amount of sales; the second line, the customer name; the third line, the date.

b. List No. 2: Print the data below so that the customers are listed in chronological order by the date they were visited. List the customer who was visited *most recently* first. The first line for each customer should contain the date; the second line, the customer name; the third line, the amount of sales.

Name ______________________________

Comprehensive Project 1, Continued

c. Before you prepare List No. 3, print the customer names in indexing order in the spaces below.

1. ______________________________
2. ______________________________
3. ______________________________
4. ______________________________
5. ______________________________
6. ______________________________
7. ______________________________
8. ______________________________
9. ______________________________
10. ______________________________

d. List No. 3: Print the data so that the customers are listed in alphabetical order by name. The first line should contain the customer name in *indexing* order. The second line should contain the date, and the third line the sale amount.

____

____

____

____

____

____

____

____

____

____

____

____

____

____

____

____

____

____

____

____

____

____

____

____

____

____

____

____

____

____

Comprehensive Project 1, Continued

Phase 3: Preparing a Budget

Tien Sun also wants to plan the budget for her business for the first quarter of 2002. She has estimated the firm's receipts and payments for January, February, and March, 2002. Complete the cash budget.

DESCRIPTION	JANUARY	FEBRUARY	MARCH	TOTAL
Receipts:				
Systems	88,300.00	75,000.00	125,000.00	
Training	35,500.00	36,000.00	16,500.00	
Total Receipts				
Payments:				
Wages	87,300.00	87,300.00	87,300.00	
Rent	2,500.00	2,500.00	2,500.00	
Insurance	500.00	500.00	500.00	
Utilities	475.00	425.00	375.00	
Telephone	550.00	550.00	550.00	
Travel	300.00	400.00	600.00	
Supplies	300.00	300.00	400.00	
Taxes	12,500.00	12,500.00	12,500.00	
Total Payments				
Balance				

Name ______________________________

Comprehensive Project 1, Continued

Phase 4: Analyzing a Budget

Tien Sun has entered the budgeted and actual receipts and payments for December, 2001. Complete the report.

	BUDGETED	ACTUAL	VARIANCE
Receipts:			
Systems	89 750 00	92 570 00	
Training	24 500 00	27 650 00	
Total Receipts			
Payments:			
Wages	82 500 00	83 700 00	
Rent	2 500 00	2 500 00	
Insurance	500 00	500 00	
Utilities	400 00	475 00	
Telephone	400 00	525 00	
Travel	250 00	275 00	
Supplies	250 00	300 00	
Taxes	11 250 00	12 500 00	
Total Payments			
Balance			

Comprehensive Project 1, Continued

Phase 5: Checking Your Credit Card Statement

Tien Sun has a BuyerCard from Merchant's Bank, which she uses for her business purchases. She has saved each of her credit card sales slips for the month of December. Tien renews her card membership every December for a $40.00 fee. The business checkbook shows that she made a payment of $627.18 on December 14. She wants to verify her credit card statement for December.

Directions

a. You are given Tien's credit card statement and the top sections of her sales slips for December. Use a credit card statement work sheet to verify the statement.

b. List the date, store, and amount of every transaction which should not appear on the statement.

c. Compare the "sale amounts" on the sales slips to the amounts on the statement. If an amount is incorrect, find the overcharge or undercharge. Do not compare the "Amount" on the slips with the statement. The "Amount" and "sale amount" may differ because the bottom sections of the slips, showing sales taxes and totals, are not provided.

d. Find the correct new balance for the statement.

Comprehensive Project 1, Continued

ACCOUNT NUMBER 1982 551 042
12/2001 12/2002
TIEN SUN
1029378
TERON'S SUPPLIES

SALE AMOUNT 00075.90
INVOICE NUMBER 229810

DATE	AUTHORIZATION NO.	SALES CLERK	DEPT.
12/02/01	229812	13	4

QUAN.	DESCRIPTION	PRICE	AMOUNT

ANT COPY

ACCOUNT NUMBER 1982 551 042
12/2001 12/2002
TIEN SUN
2109116
SEAVIEW MOTEL

SALE AMOUNT 00055.98
INVOICE NUMBER 882197

DATE	AUTHORIZATION NO.	SALES CLERK	DEPT.
12/05/01	197811	2	—

QUAN.	DESCRIPTION	PRICE	AMOUNT

ANT COPY

ACCOUNT NUMBER 1982 551 042
12/2001 12/2002
TIEN SUN
3109885
OLLIE'S INN

SALE AMOUNT 00041.88
INVOICE NUMBER 981828

DATE	AUTHORIZATION NO.	SALES CLERK	DEPT.
12/09/01	—	15	—

QUAN.	DESCRIPTION	PRICE	AMOUNT

ANT COPY

ACCOUNT NUMBER 1982 551 042
12/2001 12/2002
TIEN SUN
3652653
VISTA RESTAURANT

SALE AMOUNT 00025.11
INVOICE NUMBER 088197

DATE	AUTHORIZATION NO.	SALES CLERK	DEPT.
12/19/01	—	8	—

QUAN.	DESCRIPTION	PRICE	AMOUNT

ANT COPY

ACCOUNT NUMBER 1982 551 042
12/2001 12/2002
TIEN SUN
6676221
SANDWICH SHOP

SALE AMOUNT 00012.15
INVOICE NUMBER 007377

DATE	AUTHORIZATION NO.	SALES CLERK	DEPT.
12/20/01	—	15	—

QUAN.	DESCRIPTION	PRICE	AMOUNT

ANT COPY

ACCOUNT NUMBER 1982 551 042
12/2001 12/2002
TIEN SUN
1029378
TERON'S SUPPLIES

SALE AMOUNT 00147.80
INVOICE NUMBER 232178

DATE	AUTHORIZATION NO.	SALES CLERK	DEPT.
12/28/01	991185	7	2

QUAN.	DESCRIPTION	PRICE	AMOUNT

ANT COPY

Comprehensive Project 1, Continued

VISA **merchant's-bank** MasterCard

Transaction Date	Reference	Transaction Description		New Loans, Fees, & Purchases	Payments & Credits
12/02/2001	78172833	Teron's Supplies	Oakland, CA	75.90	
12/05/2001	39712564	Seaview Motel	Santa Rosa, CA	55.98	
12/09/2001	71282255	Ollie's Inn	San Jose, CA	41.88	
12/14/2001	33307922	Payment -- Thank You			627.18
12/16/2001		Annual Membership Fee		40.00	
12/19/2001	89989112	Vista Restaurant	San Diego, CA	25.11	
12/20/2001	70029812	Sandwich Shop	San Diego, CA	12.75	
12/24/2001	00879806	Crest Hotel	Denver, CO	79.68	
12/28/2001	85769123	Teron's Supplies	Oakland, CA	147.80	

How We Arrived At Your Finance Charge	Monthly Rate	Annual Percentage Rate	Balance to Which Monthly Rate Applied	Finance Charge

Previous Balance	Payments & Credits	New Loans, Fees, & Purchases	Finance Charge	New Balance	Minimum Payment Due
627.18	627.18	479.10	0.00	479.10	25.00

Billing Date	Date Payment Due	Credit Line	Account Number	In case of billing error, write to this address: P.O. Box 200, Oakland, CA, 94604-4141
12/31/2001	01/25/2002	2000	1982 551 042	Direct telephone inquiries to 1-800-555-1800

a. Unauthorized charges listed on statement:

Date	Store	Amount
________	____________________	$________
________	____________________	$________

b. Corrections to amounts on statement:

For an overcharge:		For an undercharge:	
Charge on statement	$________	Charge on sales slip	$________
Charge on sales slip	$________	Charge on statement	$________
Amount overcharged	$________	Amount undercharged	$________

c. Calculating the correct new balance:

New balance from statement		$________
Less: Unauthorized charges	$________	
Overcharge on statement	$________	
		________
		$________
Add: Undercharge on statement		________
Correct new balance		$________

Comprehensive Project 1, Concluded

Phase 6: Borrowing on a Promissory Note

Tien borrowed money to expand her business using the promissory note shown below.

$ 35,800.00   Oakland, CA   December 4, 20 01

Six months AFTER DATE I PROMISE TO PAY TO

THE ORDER OF Merchant's Bank

Thirty-five thousand, eight hundred and no/100---- DOLLARS

PAYABLE AT Merchant's Bank

FOR VALUE RECEIVED WITH INTEREST AT 12 %

NO. 89126 DUE June 4, 20 02   Tien Sun

Answer these questions:

1. What is the principal of the note?

   ____

2. What is the time of the note?

   ____

3. What is the due date of the note?

   ____

4. How much interest must be paid when the note is due?

   ____

5. What is the amount due on the due date?

   ____

(This page is without text copy.)

Name ______________________

Score ______________

Sample Problem, page 141

No. 1078	**Gorbea Vending Company** No. 1078
Date:	Date: ______ __
Received from:	Received from: ______ $ ______
	______ Dollars
Route:	Route: ______ For: ______
Amount: $	______ Cashier

GORBEA VENDING COMPANY

Record of Cashier's Collections

Cashier ______________________ Week of ______________ 20 __

Route	Employee	Monday		Tuesday		Wednesday		Thursday		Friday		Totals	
						856	25						
								997	50				
				524	75					846	25		
						10,028	75			12,037	75		
				709	50			915	75				
						594	25			684	25		
						840	25			867	75		
						512	75			648	50		
				335	75			691	50				
						511	75			679	75		
	TOTALS												

Problem 16–1, page 145

b.

No. ______	**Gorbea Vending Company**
Date: ______	No. ____
Received from: ______	Date: ______ ____
______	Received from: ______ $ ______
Route: ______	______ Dollars
Amount: $ ______	Route: ______ For: ______
	______ Cashier

No. ______	**Gorbea Vending Company**
Date: ______	No. ____
Received from: ______	Date: ______ ____
______	Received from: ______ $ ______
Route: ______	______ Dollars
Amount: $ ______	Route: ______ For: ______
	______ Cashier

No. ______	**Gorbea Vending Company**
Date: ______	No. ____
Received from: ______	Date: ______ ____
______	Received from: ______ $ ______
Route: ______	______ Dollars
Amount: $ ______	Route: ______ For: ______
	______ Cashier

No. ______	**Gorbea Vending Company**
Date: ______	No. ____
Received from: ______	Date: ______ ____
______	Received from: ______ $ ______
Route: ______	______ Dollars
Amount: $ ______	Route: ______ For: ______
	______ Cashier

Name ______________________________

Problem 16–1, Concluded

a., c.–h.

GORBEA VENDING COMPANY

Record of Cashier's Collections

Cashier ______________________________ Week of ______________ 20 __

Route	Employee	Monday		Tuesday		Wednesday		Thursday		Friday		Totals	
	TOTALS												

i. 1. ______________________________

2. ______________________________

3. ______________________________

4. ______________________________

Problem 16–2, page 146

b.

No. ______
Date: ______
Received from: ______
______
Route: ______
Amount: $ ______

City of Glen Carbon
No. ______
Date: ______ ___
Received from: ______ $ ______
______ Dollars
Route: ______ For: ______
______
Cashier

No. ______
Date: ______
Received from: ______
______
Route: ______
Amount: $ ______

City of Glen Carbon
No. ______
Date: ______ ___
Received from: ______ $ ______
______ Dollars
Route: ______ For: ______
______
Cashier

No. ______
Date: ______
Received from: ______
______
Route: ______
Amount: $ ______

City of Glen Carbon
No. ______
Date: ______ ___
Received from: ______ $ ______
______ Dollars
Route: ______ For: ______
______
Cashier

No. ______
Date: ______
Received from: ______
______
Route: ______
Amount: $ ______

City of Glen Carbon
No. ______
Date: ______ ___
Received from: ______ $ ______
______ Dollars
Route: ______ For: ______
______
Cashier

Problem 16–2, Concluded

a., c.–h.

CITY OF GLEN CARBON

Record of Cashier's Collections

Cashier ______________________ Week of ______________ 20 __

Route	Collector	Monday		Tuesday		Wednesday		Thursday		Friday		Totals	

i. **1.** ______________________

2. ______________________

3. ______________________

4. ______________________

Problem 16–3

You are the cashier for R & D Arcade Company. The company operates video game arcades in a two-city area. The arcades are open five days a week. Some close on Sunday and Monday. Others close on Monday and Tuesday. Your job is to count the money collected daily from the arcade operators and to keep a weekly record of the collections.

Directions

a. Use the record of cashier's collections form provided. Complete the heading by using your name as cashier and June 16 as the week. Use the headings Arcade and Operator instead of Route No. and Employee. Head the last seven columns for the days Tuesday through Sunday and Totals. Record the Arcade numbers 1–8 in numerical order in the Arcade column.

Problem 16–3, Continued

b. You received money on Tuesday, June 16, as shown below.

Arcade No.	Operator	Amount
1	M. Barr	$312.25
2	T. Cray	456.45
3	B. Vine	590.10
4	D. Zelor	971.25

Make a receipt for each operator. Be sure to fill out the stub first. The starting number for your receipts will be 401. Sign your own name as cashier.

c. Enter the information found on the stubs in the record of cashier's collections.

d. Foot, verify, and enter the total for the column headed Tuesday.

e. Fill in the record of cashier's collections for the rest of the week in the same way using the information given below. You are not required to make any more receipts.

Wednesday, June 17

Arcade	Operator	Amount
1	M. Barr	$208.60
2	T. Cray	175.65
3	B. Vine	124.85
4	D. Zelor	225.90
5	F. Cheng	301.35
6	R. Bell	409.20
7	E. Mendez	100.70
8	N. Stein	78.85

Thursday, June 18

Arcade	Operator	Amount
1	M. Barr	$240.90
2	T. Cray	357.35
3	B. Vine	288.65
4	D. Zelor	510.30
5	F. Cheng	410.40
6	R. Bell	220.20
7	E. Mendez	328.55
8	N. Stein	435.75

Friday, June 19

Arcade	Operator	Amount
1	M. Barr	$563.25
2	T. Cray	500.20
3	B. Vine	449.50
4	D. Zelor	473.45
5	F. Cheng	680.90
6	R. Bell	594.45
7	E. Mendez	450.10
8	N. Stein	710.25

Saturday, June 20

Arcade	Operator	Amount
1	M. Barr	$585.55
2	T. Cray	520.80
3	B. Vine	486.65
4	D. Zelor	495.30
5	F. Cheng	695.85
6	R. Bell	605.15
7	E. Mendez	475.60
8	N. Stein	700.05

Sunday, June 21

Arcade	Operator	Amount
5	F. Cheng	$135.80
6	R. Bell	89.45
7	E. Mendez	45.60
8	N. Stein	73.55

f. Find the total collected from each arcade for the week by crossfooting.

g. Foot the grand total for the week by adding the amounts in the Totals column.

h. Check your addition by crossfooting the totals for each day. The answer should agree with the grand total found in direction "g." If the answer agrees, write the grand total below the footing. If the totals do not agree, find the error by re-adding all the columns.

i. Answer these questions about the completed record:

1. From which arcade was the most money collected for the week?
2. From which arcade was the least money collected for the week?
3. On which day was the most money collected?
4. On which day was the least money collected?

Problem 16–3, Continued

b.

No. ______	R & D Arcade Company
Date: ______	No. ____
Received from: ______	Date: ______________ ___
______	Received from: ______________ $ ______
Arcade: ______	______________ Dollars
Amount: $ ______	Arcade: ______ For: ______________
	______ Cashier

No. ______	R & D Arcade Company
Date: ______	No. ____
Received from: ______	Date: ______________ ___
______	Received from: ______________ $ ______
Arcade: ______	______________ Dollars
Amount: $ ______	Arcade: ______ For: ______________
	______ Cashier

No. ______	R & D Arcade Company
Date: ______	No. ____
Received from: ______	Date: ______________ ___
______	Received from: ______________ $ ______
Arcade: ______	______________ Dollars
Amount: $ ______	Arcade: ______ For: ______________
	______ Cashier

No. ______	R & D Arcade Company
Date: ______	No. ____
Received from: ______	Date: ______________ ___
______	Received from: ______________ $ ______
Arcade: ______	______________ Dollars
Amount: $ ______	Arcade: ______ For: ______________
	______ Cashier

Problem 16–3, Concluded

a., c.–h.

R & D ARCADE COMPANY

Record of Cashier's Collections

Cashier ______________________________ Week of ______________ 20 __

Arcade	Operator	Tuesday	Wednesday	Thursday	Friday	Saturday	Sunday	Totals

i. **1.** ______________________________

2. ______________________________

3. ______________________________

4. ______________________________

Problem 16–4

You are the cashier for Woodlawn Laundromats, Inc. The company operates clothes washing and drying shops in a large city. The laundromats are open five days a week. Some close on Sunday and Monday. Others close on Monday and Tuesday. Your job is to count the money collected daily from the laundromat operators and to keep a weekly record of the collections.

Directions

a. Use the record of cashier's collections form provided. Complete the heading by using your name as cashier and August 8 as the week. Enter the laundromat numbers in numerical order with the operator names.

Problem 16–4, Continued

b. You received money on Tuesday, August 8, as shown below.

Laundromat	Operator	Amount
1	A. Cone	$426.80
4	D. Arden	580.45
5	E. Nair	370.20
8	H. Mann	488.65

Make a receipt for each operator. Be sure to fill out the stub first. The starting number for your receipts will be 601. Sign your own name as cashier.

c. Enter the information found on the stubs in the record of cashier's collections.

d. Foot, verify, and enter the total for the column headed Tuesday.

e. Fill in the record of cashier's collections for the rest of the week in the same way using the information given below. You are not required to make any more receipts.

Wednesday, August 9			Thursday, August 10			Friday, August 11		
Laundromat	**Operator**	**Amount**	**Laundromat**	**Operator**	**Amount**	**Laundromat**	**Operator**	**Amount**
1	A. Cone	$208.60	1	A. Cone	$240.90	1	A. Cone	$563.25
2	L. Torres	175.65	2	L. Torres	357.35	2	L. Torres	500.20
3	P. Grey	124.85	3	P. Grey	288.65	3	P. Grey	449.50
4	D. Arden	225.90	4	D. Arden	510.30	4	D. Arden	473.45
5	E. Nair	301.35	5	E. Nair	410.40	5	E. Nair	680.90
6	V. Bode	409.20	6	V. Bode	220.20	6	V. Bode	594.45
7	T. Moran	100.70	7	T. Moran	328.55	7	T. Moran	450.10
8	H. Mann	78.85	8	H. Mann	435.75	8	H. Mann	710.25

Saturday, August 12			Sunday, August 13		
Laundromat	**Operator**	**Amount**	**Laundromat**	**Operator**	**Amount**
1	A. Cone	$585.55	2	L. Torres	$145.80
2	L. Torres	520.80	3	P. Grey	79.45
3	P. Grey	486.65	6	V. Bode	55.60
4	D. Arden	495.30	7	T. Moran	63.55
5	E. Nair	695.85			
6	V. Bode	605.15			
7	T. Moran	475.60			
8	H. Mann	700.05			

f. Find the total collected from each laundromat for the week by crossfooting.

g. Foot the grand total for the week by adding the amounts in the Totals column.

h. Check your addition by crossfooting the totals for each day. The answer should agree with the grand total found in direction "g." If the answer agrees, write the grand total below the footing. If the totals do not agree, find the error by re-adding all the columns.

Problem 16–4, Continued

b.

	Woodlawn Laundromats, Inc.
No. ____	No. ____
Date: ____	Date: ____ ____
Received from: ____	Received from: ____ $ ____
____	____ Dollars
Laundromat: ____	Laundromat: ____ For: ____
Amount: $ ____	____ Cashier

	Woodlawn Laundromats, Inc.
No. ____	No. ____
Date: ____	Date: ____ ____
Received from: ____	Received from: ____ $ ____
____	____ Dollars
Laundromat: ____	Laundromat: ____ For: ____
Amount: $ ____	____ Cashier

	Woodlawn Laundromats, Inc.
No. ____	No. ____
Date: ____	Date: ____ ____
Received from: ____	Received from: ____ $ ____
____	____ Dollars
Laundromat: ____	Laundromat: ____ For: ____
Amount: $ ____	____ Cashier

	Woodlawn Laundromats, Inc.
No. ____	No. ____
Date: ____	Date: ____ ____
Received from: ____	Received from: ____ $ ____
____	____ Dollars
Laundromat: ____	Laundromat: ____ For: ____
Amount: $ ____	____ Cashier

Problem 16–4, Concluded

a., c.–h.

WOODLAWN LAUNDROMATS, INC.

Record of Cashier's Collections

Cashier ______________________ Week of ______________ 20 __

Laundromat	Operator	Tuesday	Wednesday	Thursday	Friday	Saturday	Sunday	Totals

i. Answer these questions about the completed record:

1. From which laundromat was the most money collected for the week?

____

2. From which laundromat was the least money collected for the week?

____

3. On which day was the most money collected?

____

4. On which day was the least money collected?

____

(This page is without text copy.)

Name ______________________________

Score __________

Using a Cash Register

CHAPTER 4
Job 17

Sample Problem, page 150

Step 1 [ ] [ ] [ ] [ ]

Step 2 [ ]
[ ]
[ ]

Step 3 [ ] [ ]

Problem 17–1, page 153

a.

	Items Bought	Department Keys Used
$2.99	AA Batteries	________
$4.71	Meat	________
$1.69	Shredded cheese	________
$2.98	Apples	________
$3.49	Cold tablets	________

b.

Bills and Coins	Number Used
Pennies	________
Dimes	________
Dollars	________

Problem 17–2, page 153

a.

	Items Bought	Department Keys Used
$ .95	Sweet potatoes	________
$2.89	Pumpkin pie	________
$ .29	Canned corn	________
$2.39	Dish detergent	________
$5.89	Whole turkey	________

b.

Bills and Coins	Number Used
Pennies	________
Nickels	________
Half-dollars	________
Dollars	________

Problem 17–3

Ed Rivers is the cashier at Karl's Market. He uses a cash register with the keys shown in Illustration 17C in the text.

Directions

a. A customer buys the items shown below. Next to each item, write the name of the department key Ed would use to enter the item into his cash register.

b. After entering each item, the register shows a total sale of $17.44. The amount tendered by the customer is a twenty-dollar bill. List the bills or coins Ed should give the customer for change.

1)

Items Bought		Department Keys Used
$4.35	Frying pan	____________
$2.95	Chicken parts	____________
$3.78	Cherry pie	____________
$2.38	Milk	____________
$3.98	Shampoo	____________

2)

Bills and Coins	Number Used
Pennies	______
Nickels	______
Dimes	______
Quarters	______
Half-dollars	______
Dollars	______
Five dollars	______
Ten dollars	______

Problem 17–4

You are the cashier at the Vextor Market. You use a cash register with the keys shown in Illustration 17C in the text.

Directions

a. A customer buys the items shown below. Next to each item, write the name of the department key you would use to enter the item into your cash register.

b. After entering each item, the register shows a total sale of $8.71. The amount tendered by the customer is a twenty-dollar bill. List the bills or coins you should give the customer for change.

1)

Items Bought		Department Keys Used
$2.42	Cereal	____________
$ .49	Margarine	____________
$2.56	Ice cream	____________
$ .79	Masking tape	____________
$2.45	Aspirin	____________

2)

Bills and Coins	Number Used
Pennies	______
Nickels	______
Dimes	______
Quarters	______
Half-dollars	______
Dollars	______
Five dollars	______
Ten dollars	______

Name ______________________________

Problem 17–5

You are the cashier at the Market Basket Food Store. You use a cash register with the keys shown in Illustration 17C in the text.

Directions

a. A customer buys the items shown below. Next to each item, write the name of the department key you would use to enter the item into your cash register.

b. After entering each item, the register shows a total sale of $21.80. The amount tendered by the customer is thirty dollars. List the bills or coins you should give the customer for change.

1)

Items Bought		Department Keys Used
$7.49	Shrimp	____________
$2.79	Peanuts	____________
$2.18	Salami	____________
$8.45	Dust mop	____________
$0.89	Canned soup	____________

2)

Bills and Coins	Number Used
Pennies	______
Nickels	______
Dimes	______
Quarters	______
Half-dollars	______
Dollars	______
Five dollars	______
Ten dollars	______

(This page is without text copy.)

Name ______________________

Score __________

Sample Problem, page 155

Step 1

Step 2

Step 3

Sample Problem, Concluded

Step 4

DREW LANSING
1645 Abel Street
Allentown, PA 18104-0423

No. 1063

Date July 19 20--

3-332
2784

PAY TO THE ORDER OF RiteBuy Supermarket $ 10.00

Ten 00/100 Dollars

For Classroom Use Only

HILLSTON BANK
Allentown, PA 18103-8890

Drew Lansing

⑆027840745⑆ 308⑈455⑈

Step 5

Change: Pennies ____________
Half-dollar ____________
Dollars ____________
Five dollars ____________

Name ________________________________

Problem 18–1, page 159

Customer 1:

a. **CHECK-CASHING POLICIES**

_____ **1.** (The customer's name or address is not printed on the check.)
_____ **2.** (The name, address, or customer signature on the card does not match the name, address, or signature on the check.)
_____ **3.** (The amount of the check in writing is not the same as the amount in figures.)
_____ **4.** (The date on the check is a future date.)
_____ **5.** (The check is not from a local bank.)
_____ **6.** (The check is for more than $25 over the total sale.)
_____ **7.** (The check is not made out to RiteBuy Supermarket.)

b.

Bills and Coins	**Number Used**
Pennies	________
Dimes	________
Dollars	________
Ten dollars	________

Customer 2:

a. **CHECK-CASHING POLICIES**

_____ **1.** (The customer's name or address is not printed on the check.)
_____ **2.** (The name, address, or customer signature on the card does not match the name, address, or signature on the check.)
_____ **3.** (The amount of the check in writing is not the same as the amount in figures.)
_____ **4.** (The date on the check is a future date.)
_____ **5.** (The check is not from a local bank.)
_____ **6.** (The check is for more than $25 over the total sale.)
_____ **7.** (The check is not made out to RiteBuy Supermarket.)

b.

Bills and Coins	**Number Used**
Pennies	________
Dimes	________
Quarters	________
Half-dollars	________
Dollars	________
Ten dollars	________

Problem 18–1, Continued

Customer 3:

After entering each item bought by Lisa McDonald, your register displayed a total sale of $80.98. Lisa gave you the following check-cashing privilege card and check.

RiteBuy Supermarket

No. 0712

Check-Cashing Privilege Card

This card allows: Lisa McDonald
1001 Lake Road
Allentown, PA 18104-8811

To cash checks for purchases according to the restrictions printed on the back of this card.

Customer Signature *Lisa McDonald* Date *Feb. 19,* 20--

Vince Howard
1001 Lake Road
Allentown, PA 18104-8811

No. 1082

Date *May 17,* 20-- 3-332/2075

PAY TO THE ORDER OF *RiteBuy Supermarket* $ *100.00*

One hundred 00/100 Dollars

For Classroom Use Only

RIVERBEND BANK
Allentown, PA 18105-3108

Vince Howard

⑆0207507454⑆ 067⑈113⑈

Name ______________________________

Problem 18–1, Continued

Directions

a. Verify the check against these seven policies by placing a check mark next to any policy found to be true.

b. List the type and number of each bill or coin you should give the customer for change if you accept the check or if it is authorized by the supervisor.

CHECK-CASHING POLICIES

_______ **1.** (The customer's name or address is not printed on the check.)

_______ **2.** (The name, address, or customer signature on the card does not match the name, address, or signature on the check.)

_______ **3.** (The amount of the check in writing is not the same as the amount in figures.)

_______ **4.** (The date on the check is a future date.)

_______ **5.** (The check is not from a local bank.)

_______ **6.** (The check is for more than $25 over the total sale.)

_______ **7.** (The check is not made out to RiteBuy Supermarket.)

Bills and Coins	**Number Used**
Pennies	_______
Nickels	_______
Dimes	_______
Quarters	_______
Half-dollars	_______
Dollars	_______
Five dollars	_______
Ten dollars	_______

Problem 18–1, Continued

Customer 4:

After entering each item bought by Bob Fern, your register displayed a total sale of $12.09. Bob gave you the following check-cashing privilege card and check.

RiteBuy Supermarket

No. 1008

Check-Cashing Privilege Card

This card allows: Bob Fern
107 Senate Drive
Allentown, PA 18102-7637

To cash checks for purchases according to the restrictions printed on the back of this card.

Customer Signature *Bob Fern* Date *Dec. 4,* 20--

Bob Fern
107 Senate Drive
Allentown, PA 18102-7637

No. 2007

Date *May 17,* 20--   3-332/1122

PAY TO THE ORDER OF *RiteBuy Supermarket* $ *25.00*

Twenty 00/100 Dollars

For Classroom Use Only

Forge Bank & Trust Co.
Allentown, PA 18103-2088

Bob Fern

⑆011220745⑆ 323⑈767⑈

Problem 18–1, Continued

Directions

a. Verify the check against these seven policies by placing a check mark next to any policy found to be true.

b. List the type and number of each bill or coin you should give the customer for change if you accept the check or if it is authorized by the supervisor. Legally, the written amount (twenty) is the amount you must use for this check.

CHECK-CASHING POLICIES

________ **1.** (The customer's name or address is not printed on the check.)

________ **2.** (The name, address, or customer signature on the card does not match the name, address, or signature on the check.)

________ **3.** (The amount of the check in writing is not the same as the amount in figures.)

________ **4.** (The date on the check is a future date.)

________ **5.** (The check is not from a local bank.)

________ **6.** (The check is for more than $25 over the total sale.)

________ **7.** (The check is not made out to RiteBuy Supermarket.)

Bills and Coins	Number Used
Pennies	________
Nickels	________
Dimes	________
Quarters	________
Half-dollars	________
Dollars	________
Five dollars	________
Ten dollars	________

Problem 18–1, Continued

Customer 5:

After entering each item bought by Edwin Cleary, your register displayed a total sale of $81.78. Edwin gave you the following check-cashing privilege card and check.

RiteBuy Supermarket

No. 0975

Check-Cashing Privilege Card

This card allows: Edwin Cleary
Concordia Lane
Allentown, PA 18104-5675

To cash checks for purchases according to the restrictions printed on the back of this card.

Customer Signature *Edwin Cleary* Date *Oct. 10,* 20--

Edwin Cleary

No. 297

Date *May 17,* 20--

3-332/1122

PAY TO THE ORDER OF *RiteBuy Supermarket* $ *85.00*

Eighty-five 00/100 Dollars

For Classroom Use Only

Forge Bank & Trust Co.
Allentown, PA 18103-2088

Edwin Cleary

⑆011220745⑆ 141⑈286⑈

Problem 18–1, Concluded

Directions

a. Verify the check against these seven policies by placing a check mark next to any policy found to be true.

b. List the type and number of each bill or coin you should give the customer for change if you accept the check or if it is authorized by the supervisor.

CHECK-CASHING POLICIES

________ **1.** (The customer's name or address is not printed on the check.)

________ **2.** (The name, address, or customer signature on the card does not match the name, address, or signature on the check.)

________ **3.** (The amount of the check in writing is not the same as the amount in figures.)

________ **4.** (The date on the check is a future date.)

________ **5.** (The check is not from a local bank.)

________ **6.** (The check is for more than $25 over the total sale.)

________ **7.** (The check is not made out to RiteBuy Supermarket.)

Bills and Coins	Number Used
Pennies	________
Nickels	________
Dimes	________
Quarters	________
Half-dollars	________
Dollars	________
Five dollars	________
Ten dollars	________

(This page is without text copy.)

Name ______________________

Score ____________

Sample Problem, page 162

UPLAND STORES, INC.

Cash Count Report

Date: ______________________ 20--

Cashier No.: ______________ Register No.: ______________

Quantity	Denomination	Amount	
	$20.00 Bills		
	$10.00 Bills		
	$5.00 Bills		
	$1.00 Bills		
	$0.50 Coins		
	$0.25 Coins		
	$0.10 Coins		
	$0.05 Coins		
	$0.01 Coins		
	Checks		
Total Cash in Cash Drawer			

Signature: ______________________

Sample Problem, Concluded

UPLAND STORES, INC.
Cash Proof Form

Date ______________________ 20--

Change fund		
Add total cash sales from audit tape		
Total		
Less cash paid out from audit tape		
Cash that should be in register		
Cash actually in register		
Cash short		
Cash over		

Cash Register No.:______ Cashier No.: ______

Signature: ____________________________

Cash that should be in register		
Cash actually in register		
Cash short		

Cash that should be in register		
Cash actually in register		
Cash short		
Cash over		

Name ______________________________

Problem 19–1, page 166

ALLIED FOOD STORES, INC.

Cash Count Report

Date: ______________________________ 20--

Cashier No.: ______________________ Register No.: ______________

Quantity	Denomination	Amount	
	$20.00 Bills		
	$10.00 Bills		
	$5.00 Bills		
	$1.00 Bills		
	$0.50 Coins		
	$0.25 Coins		
	$0.10 Coins		
	$0.05 Coins		
	$0.01 Coins		
	Checks		
Total Cash in Cash Drawer			

Signature: ______________________________________

Problem 19–2, page 166

ALLIED FOOD STORES, INC.

Cash Proof Form

Date ______________________ 20--

Change fund		
Add total cash sales from audit tape		
Total		
Less cash paid out from audit tape		
Cash that should be in register		
Cash actually in register		
Cash short		
Cash over		

Cash Register No.: ________ Cashier No.: ________

Signature: ______________________

Problem 19–3, page 166

BUY-WISE DISCOUNT STORE

Cash Count Report

Date: ______________________ 20--

Cashier No.: ______________ Register No.: ______________

Quantity	Denomination	Amount	
	$20.00 Bills		
	$10.00 Bills		
	$5.00 Bills		
	$1.00 Bills		
	$0.50 Coins		
	$0.25 Coins		
	$0.10 Coins		
	$0.05 Coins		
	$0.01 Coins		
	Checks		
Total Cash in Cash Drawer			

Signature: ______________________

BUY-WISE DISCOUNT STORE

Cash Proof Form

Date ______________ 20--

Change fund		
Add total cash sales from audit tape		
Total		
Less cash paid out from audit tape		
Cash that should be in register		
Cash actually in register		
Cash short		
Cash over		

Cash Register No.: ______ Cashier No.: ______

Signature: ______________________

Problem 19–4

You are cashier no. 16 at cash register no. 3 for Bell's Lumber Company. On May 6, 20--, you started the day with a change fund of $150.00. At the end of the day, your register's detailed audit tape showed total cash sales of $2,763.91 and total cash paid out of $73.88. You counted $975.00 in checks and this cash in the drawer:

Quantity	Denomination
41	$20.00 bills
72	$10.00 bills
28	$ 5.00 bills
110	$ 1.00 bills
85	$ 0.50 coins
92	$ 0.25 coins
37	$ 0.10 coins
28	$ 0.05 coins
231	$ 0.01 coins

Directions

a. Prepare a cash count report, using the form provided.

BELL'S LUMBER COMPANY

Cash Count Report

Date: ______________________________ 20--

Cashier No.: ______________________ Register No.: ______________

Quantity	Denomination	Amount	
	$20.00 Bills		
	$10.00 Bills		
	$5.00 Bills		
	$1.00 Bills		
	$0.50 Coins		
	$0.25 Coins		
	$0.10 Coins		
	$0.05 Coins		
	$0.01 Coins		
	Checks		
Total Cash in Cash Drawer			

Signature: ______________________________

Problem 19–4, Concluded

b. Prepare a proof of cash, using the form provided.

BELL'S LUMBER COMPANY
Cash Proof Form

Date ______________________ 20--

Change fund		
Add total cash sales from audit tape		
Total		
Less cash paid out from audit tape		
Cash that should be in register		
Cash actually in register		
Cash short		
Cash over		

Cash Register No.:_______ Cashier No.: _______

Signature: ______________________________

Problem 19–5

You are cashier no. 2 at cash register no. 4 for A & R Hardware, Inc. On June 7, 20--, you started the day with a change fund of $100.00. At the end of the day, your register's detailed audit tape showed total cash sales of $1,389.74 and total cash paid out of $31.25. You counted $241.10 in checks and this cash in the drawer:

Quantity	Denomination
22	$20.00 bills
45	$10.00 bills
48	$ 5.00 bills
39	$ 1.00 bills
56	$ 0.50 coins
61	$ 0.25 coins
24	$ 0.10 coins
12	$ 0.05 coins
88	$ 0.01 coins

Directions

a. Prepare a cash count report, using the form provided.

A & R HARDWARE, INC.

Cash Count Report

Date: ______________________________ 20--

Cashier No.: ______________________ Register No.: ______________

Quantity	Denomination	Amount	
	$20.00 Bills		
	$10.00 Bills		
	$5.00 Bills		
	$1.00 Bills		
	$0.50 Coins		
	$0.25 Coins		
	$0.10 Coins		
	$0.05 Coins		
	$0.01 Coins		
	Checks		
Total Cash in Cash Drawer			

Signature: ______________________________

Problem 19–5, Concluded

b. Prepare a proof of cash, using the form provided.

A & R HARDWARE, INC.
Cash Proof Form

Date ______________________ 20--

Change fund		
Add total cash sales from audit tape		
Total		
Less cash paid out from audit tape		
Cash that should be in register		
Cash actually in register		
Cash short		
Cash over		

Cash Register No.:_______ Cashier No.: _______

Signature: ______________________________

Problem 19–6

You are cashier no. 9 at cash register no. 2 for Tully's Snappy Shop. On August 3, 20--, you started the day with a change fund of $75.00. At the end of the day, your register's detailed audit tape showed total cash sales of $755.43 and total cash paid out of $15.50. You counted $45.00 in checks and this cash in the drawer:

Quantity	Denomination
18	$20.00 bills
21	$10.00 bills
19	$ 5.00 bills
47	$ 1.00 bills
80	$ 0.50 coins
37	$ 0.25 coins
63	$ 0.10 coins
92	$ 0.05 coins
236	$ 0.01 coins

Directions

a. Prepare a cash count report, using the form provided.

TULLY'S SNAPPY SHOP

Cash Count Report

Date: ______________________ 20--

Cashier No.: ______________________ Register No.: ______________

Quantity	Denomination	Amount	
	$20.00 Bills		
	$10.00 Bills		
	$5.00 Bills		
	$1.00 Bills		
	$0.50 Coins		
	$0.25 Coins		
	$0.10 Coins		
	$0.05 Coins		
	$0.01 Coins		
	Checks		
Total Cash in Cash Drawer			

Signature: ______________________

Problem 19–6, Concluded

b. Prepare a proof of cash, using the form provided.

TULLY'S SNAPPY SHOP
Cash Proof Form

Date ______________________ 20--

Change fund		
Add total cash sales from audit tape		
Total		
Less cash paid out from audit tape		
Cash that should be in register		
Cash actually in register		
Cash short		
Cash over		

Cash Register No.:_______ Cashier No.: _______

Signature: ______________________________

Name ______________________________

Score ____________

Sample Problem, page 168

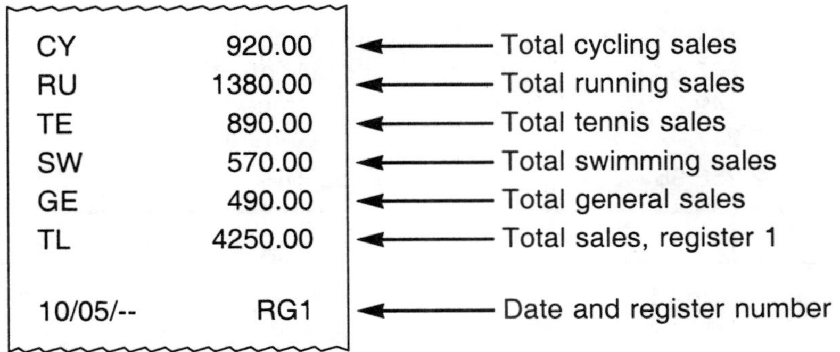

MAIN STREET SPORTING GOODS
Departmental Sales Report

Cashier No.: 4 Register No.: 1

Department	Total
Cycling	$ 920.00
Running	1,380.00
Tennis	980.00
Swimming	570.00
General	490.00
Total	$4,250.00

Signature: Tyrone Williams

Date: March 5, 20--

MAIN STREET SPORTING GOODS
Summary of Departmental Sales
March 5, 20--

Department	Registers 1			2			3			4			Department Total		
Cycling					345	89		651	98		201	90			
Running					448	99		812	43		209	34			
Tennis				2	009	58		312	45	2	298	33			
Swimming					128	12		498	53		509	63			
General					798	39		408	66		976	42			
Totals				3 3	730 730	97 97	2 2	684 684	05 05	4 4	195 195	62 62			

Problem 20–1, page 171

Cashier No.: 4 Register No.: 1

Department	Total
Meat	$ 879.23
Produce	407.21
Dairy	303.67
Grocery	449.21
General	217.82
Total	$2,256.96

Signature: Victor Bell

Date: July 6, 20--

ME	879.23
PR	407.12
DA	303.67
GR	449.12
GE	217.82
TL	2256.96
07/06/--	RG1

Cashier No.: 2 Register No.: 2

Department	Total
Meat	$ 699.29
Produce	310.06
Dairy	607.88
Grocery	421.87
General	439.76
Total	$2,478.86

Signature: Ana Lopez

Date: July 6, 20--

ME	699.29
PR	310.06
DA	607.88
GR	421.87
GE	439.76
TL	2478.86
07/06/--	RG2

Cashier No.: 1 Register No.: 3

Department	Total
Meat	$ 809.98
Produce	531.54
Dairy	688.12
Grocery	708.34
General	433.80
Total	$3,171.78

Signature: Ed Tieg

Date: July 6, 20--

ME	809.98
PR	531.54
DA	688.12
GR	708.34
GE	433.80
TL	3171.78
07/06/--	RG3

Cashier No.: 3 Register No.: 4

Department	Total
Meat	$2,003.39
Produce	698.23
Dairy	823.19
Grocery	399.31
General	729.11
Total	$4,653.23

Signature: Louise Clark

Date: July 6, 20--

ME	2003.39
PR	698.23
DA	823.19
GR	399.31
GE	729.11
TL	4653.23
07/06/--	RG4

Problem 20–1, Concluded

KEY FOOD MART
Summary of Departmental Sales
July 6, 20--

Department	Registers 1	2	3	4	Department Total
Meat					
Produce					
Dairy					
Grocery					
General					
Totals					

Problem 20–2, page 172

Cashier No.: 2 Register No.: 1

Department	Total
Video Systems	$ 2,801.34
Sound Systems	5,228.91
Computer Systems	11,010.99
Communication Systems	3,078.43
General	1,851.76
Total	$23,071.43

Signature: Charles Turner

Date: April 12, 20--

Cashier No.: 4 Register No.: 2

Department	Total
Video Systems	$ 3,211.31
Sound Systems	8,145.98
Computer Systems	10,208.23
Communication Systems	1,897.45
General	2,301.87
Total	$25,773.84

Signature: Leslie Sykes

Date: April 12, 20--

VS	2801.34
SS	5228.91
CO	11010.99
CS	3078.43
GE	1851.76
TL	23971.43
04/12/--	RG1

VS	3211.31
SS	8154.98
CO	10208.23
CS	1897.45
GE	2301.87
TL	25773.84
04/12/--	RG2

Problem 20–2, Concluded

Cashier No.: 3 Register No.: 3

Department	Total
Video Systems	$ 6,389.01
Sound Systems	3,207.98
Computer Systems	8,114.41
Communication Systems	3,781.31
General	1,506.82
Total	$22,999.53

Signature: John Kriege

Date: April 12, 20--

Cashier No.: 1 Register No.: 4

Department	Total
Video Systems	$ 8,301.22
Sound Systems	4,109.99
Computer Systems	7,981.98
Communication Systems	2,113.01
General	1,556.65
Total	$24,062.85

Signature: Eva O'Brien

Date: April 12, 20--

VS	6389.01
SS	3207.98
CO	8114.41
CS	3781.31
GE	1506.82
TL	22999.53
04/12/--	RG3

VS	8301.22
SS	4109.99
CO	7981.98
CS	2113.01
GE	1556.65
TL	24062.85
04/12/--	RG4

STAR ELECTRONICS, INC.
Summary of Departmental Sales
April 12, 20--

Department	Registers				Department Total
	1	2	3	4	
Video Systems					
Sound Systems					
Computer Systems					
Communication Systems					
General					
Totals					

Problem 20–3

You are a clerk in the manager's office at the Second Street Pharmacy. The manager has asked you to prepare a summary of departmental sales report for August 2, 20--.

Directions

a. Verify each departmental sales report by comparing it to the detailed audit tape shown below it or on the following page. Correct any departmental sales reports which contain errors.

Cashier No.: 2 Register No.: 1

Department	Total
Prescriptions	$ 941.66
Nonprescription medicines	731.88
Health equipment	1,783.77
Medical supplies	412.90
Miscellaneous	331.87
Total	$4,202.08

Signature: Louis Earls

Date: August 2, 20--

PR	941.66
NP	731.88
HE	1783.77
MS	412.90
MI	331.87
TL	4202.08
08/02/--	RG1

Cashier No.: 4 Register No.: 2

Department	Total
Prescriptions	$ 393.45
Nonprescription medicines	889.92
Health equipment	501.44
Medical supplies	739.91
Miscellaneous	481.82
Total	$3,006.54

Signature: Farah Turner

Date: August 2, 20--

PR	393.45
NP	889.92
HE	501.44
MS	739.91
MI	481.82
TL	3006.54
08/02/--	RG2

Cashier No.: 3 Register No.: 3

Department	Total
Prescriptions	$ 713.86
Nonprescription medicines	583.64
Health equipment	2,620.77
Medical supplies	472.91
Miscellaneous	406.07
Total	$4,797.25

Signature: Richard Dukes

Date: August 2, 20--

Cashier No.: 1 Register No.: 4

Department	Total
Prescriptions	$1,030.44
Nonprescription medicines	481.24
Health equipment	887.90
Medical supplies	405.69
Miscellaneous	277.71
Total	$3,012.98

Signature: Alma Richards

Date: August 2, 20--

Problem 20–3, Concluded

PR	713.86
NP	583.64
HE	2620.77
MS	472.91
MI	406.07
TL	4797.25
08/02/--	RG3

PR	1030.44
NP	481.24
HE	887.90
MS	405.69
MI	207.71
TL	3012.98
08/02/--	RG4

b. Copy the amounts from the departmental sales report for each register to the summary of departmental sales report for the whole store.

c. Find the column, line, and grand totals. Verify them by crossfooting, and double rule the report.

SECOND STREET PHARMACY
Summary of Departmental Sales
August 2, 20--

Department	Registers 1	Registers 2	Registers 3	Registers 4	Department Total
Prescriptions					
Nonprescription Medicines					
Health Equipment					
Medical Supplies					
Miscellaneous					
Totals					

Name ______________________

Score ____________

Sample Problem, page 174

TALLY SHEET	Date ____________ 20--					
No.	**Bills**					
	Packages of $100 bills × $10,000.00					
	Loose $100 bills					
	Packages of $50 bills × $5,000.00					
	Loose $50 bills					
	Packages of $20 bills × $2,000.00					
	Loose $20 bills					
	Packages of $10 bills × $1,000.00					
	Loose $10 bills					
	Packages of $5 bills × $500.00					
	Loose $5 bills					
	Packages of $1 bills × $100.00					
	Loose $1 bills					
	Total bills to be deposited					
No.	**Coins**					
	Rolls of half-dollars × $10.00					
	Loose half-dollars					
	Rolls of quarters × $10.00					
	Loose quarters					
	Rolls of dimes × $5.00					
	Loose dimes					
	Rolls of nickels × $2.00					
	Loose nickels					
	Rolls of pennies × $0.50					
	Loose pennies					
	Total coins to be deposited					
	Total cash to be deposited					

Sample Problem, Concluded

For DEPOSIT to the Account of

1-5/210

RIKO'S CASH AND CARRY STORE

DATE ______________ 20____

ALBRY STATE BANK

New York, New York

Subject to the Terms and Conditions of this Bank's Collection Agreement

⑆0210 0625⑆ 2418⑈639⑈

	Dollars	Cents
BILLS		
COINS		
Checks as Follows Properly Endorsed		
TOTAL DEPOSIT		

Name ______________________________

Problem 21–1, page 179

	TALLY SHEET	Date __________ 20--
No.	**Bills**	
	Packages of $100 bills × $10,000.00	
	Loose $100 bills	
	Packages of $50 bills × $5,000.00	
	Loose $50 bills	
	Packages of $20 bills × $2,000.00	
	Loose $20 bills	
	Packages of $10 bills × $1,000.00	
	Loose $10 bills	
	Packages of $5 bills × $500.00	
	Loose $5 bills	
	Packages of $1 bills × $100.00	
	Loose $1 bills	
	Total bills to be deposited	
No.	**Coins**	
	Rolls of half-dollars × $10.00	
	Loose half-dollars	
	Rolls of quarters × $10.00	
	Loose quarters	
	Rolls of dimes × $5.00	
	Loose dimes	
	Rolls of nickels × $2.00	
	Loose nickels	
	Rolls of pennies × $0.50	
	Loose pennies	
	Total coins to be deposited	
	Total cash to be deposited	

For DEPOSIT to the Account of

5th ST. QUICK SHOP

96-514
1210

DATE ______________________ 20____

FARMER'S STATE BANK

Portland, Oregon

Subject to the Terms and Conditions of this Bank's Collection Agreement

⑆121004431⑆ 1092⑈652⑈

	Dollars	Cents
BILLS		
COINS		
Checks as Follows Properly Endorsed		
TOTAL DEPOSIT		

Problem 21–1, Continued

TALLY SHEET Date ______________ 20--

No.	Bills	Amount
	Packages of $100 bills × $10,000.00	
	Loose $100 bills	
	Packages of $50 bills × $5,000.00	
	Loose $50 bills	
	Packages of $20 bills × $2,000.00	
	Loose $20 bills	
	Packages of $10 bills × $1,000.00	
	Loose $10 bills	
	Packages of $5 bills × $500.00	
	Loose $5 bills	
	Packages of $1 bills × $100.00	
	Loose $1 bills	
	Total bills to be deposited	
No.	**Coins**	
	Rolls of half-dollars × $10.00	
	Loose half-dollars	
	Rolls of quarters × $10.00	
	Loose quarters	
	Rolls of dimes × $5.00	
	Loose dimes	
	Rolls of nickels × $2.00	
	Loose nickels	
	Rolls of pennies × $0.50	
	Loose pennies	
	Total coins to be deposited	
	Total cash to be deposited	

For DEPOSIT to the Account of

5th ST. QUICK SHOP

96-514
1210

DATE ______________________ 20____

FARMER'S STATE BANK

Portland, Oregon

Subject to the Terms and Conditions of this Bank's Collection Agreement

⑆121004431⑆ 1092⑈652⑈

	Dollars	Cents
BILLS		
COINS		
Checks as Follows Properly Endorsed		
TOTAL DEPOSIT		

Name ____________________________

Problem 21–1, Concluded

TALLY SHEET **Date** ______________ **20--**

No.	Bills						
	Packages of $100 bills × $10,000.00						
	Loose $100 bills						
	Packages of $50 bills × $5,000.00						
	Loose $50 bills						
	Packages of $20 bills × $2,000.00						
	Loose $20 bills						
	Packages of $10 bills × $1,000.00						
	Loose $10 bills						
	Packages of $5 bills × $500.00						
	Loose $5 bills						
	Packages of $1 bills × $100.00						
	Loose $1 bills						
	Total bills to be deposited						
No.	**Coins**						
	Rolls of half-dollars × $10.00						
	Loose half-dollars						
	Rolls of quarters × $10.00						
	Loose quarters						
	Rolls of dimes × $5.00						
	Loose dimes						
	Rolls of nickels × $2.00						
	Loose nickels						
	Rolls of pennies × $0.50						
	Loose pennies						
	Total coins to be deposited						
	Total cash to be deposited						

For DEPOSIT to the Account of

5th ST. QUICK SHOP

96-514
1210

DATE ______________________ 20____

FARMER'S STATE BANK

Portland, Oregon

Subject to the Terms and Conditions of this Bank's Collection Agreement

⑆121004431⑆ 1092⑈652⑈

	Dollars	Cents
BILLS		
COINS		
Checks as Follows Properly Endorsed		
TOTAL DEPOSIT		

Problem 21–2

Eve is a cashier for Tom's Allied Grocery. The store has an account at Elisson Bank and Trust Co. At the close of each day, Eve must sort the cash in her cash register and prepare the money for deposit.

Directions

The cash to be tallied and deposited for three days of the week are listed in this problem. For each day:

a. Prepare a tally sheet.

b. Prepare a deposit slip.

February 15:

Quantity	Denomination
121	$50.00 bills
81	$20.00 bills
255	$10.00 bills
68	$ 5.00 bills
209	$ 1.00 bills
51	$ 0.50 coins
92	$ 0.25 coins
27	$ 0.10 coins
19	$ 0.05 coins
117	$ 0.01 coins

February 16:

Quantity	Denomination
219	$100.00 bills
302	$ 50.00 bills
28	$ 20.00 bills
108	$ 10.00 bills
64	$ 5.00 bills
153	$ 1.00 bills
66	$ 0.50 coins
78	$ 0.25 coins
37	$ 0.10 coins
49	$ 0.05 coins
287	$ 0.01 coins

February 17:

Quantity	Denomination
212	$50.00 bills
83	$20.00 bills
337	$10.00 bills
83	$ 5.00 bills
132	$ 1.00 bills
32	$ 0.50 coins
85	$ 0.25 coins
98	$ 0.10 coins
21	$ 0.05 coins
314	$ 0.01 coins

Name ____________________

Problem 21–2, Continued

	TALLY SHEET	Date ____________ 20--
No.	**Bills**	
	Packages of $100 bills × $10,000.00	
	Loose $100 bills	
	Packages of $50 bills × $5,000.00	
	Loose $50 bills	
	Packages of $20 bills × $2,000.00	
	Loose $20 bills	
	Packages of $10 bills × $1,000.00	
	Loose $10 bills	
	Packages of $5 bills × $500.00	
	Loose $5 bills	
	Packages of $1 bills × $100.00	
	Loose $1 bills	
	Total bills to be deposited	
No.	**Coins**	
	Rolls of half-dollars × $10.00	
	Loose half-dollars	
	Rolls of quarters × $10.00	
	Loose quarters	
	Rolls of dimes × $5.00	
	Loose dimes	
	Rolls of nickels × $2.00	
	Loose nickels	
	Rolls of pennies × $0.50	
	Loose pennies	
	Total coins to be deposited	
	Total cash to be deposited	

For DEPOSIT to the Account of

Tom's Allied Grocery
12 Wicjer Boulevard
Houston, TX 77080-3653

35-1242
1189

DATE ____________________ 20____

Elisson Bank
AND TRUST COMPANY
Houston, Texas

Subject to the Terms and Conditions of this Bank's Collection Agreement

⑆118905181⑆ 6725⑈098⑈

	Dollars	Cents
BILLS		
COINS		
Checks as Follows Properly Endorsed		
TOTAL DEPOSIT		

Problem 21–2, Continued

TALLY SHEET		Date ______ 20--					
No.	**Bills**						
	Packages of $100 bills × $10,000.00						
	Loose $100 bills						
	Packages of $50 bills × $5,000.00						
	Loose $50 bills						
	Packages of $20 bills × $2,000.00						
	Loose $20 bills						
	Packages of $10 bills × $1,000.00						
	Loose $10 bills						
	Packages of $5 bills × $500.00						
	Loose $5 bills						
	Packages of $1 bills × $100.00						
	Loose $1 bills						
	Total bills to be deposited						
No.	**Coins**						
	Rolls of half-dollars × $10.00						
	Loose half-dollars						
	Rolls of quarters × $10.00						
	Loose quarters						
	Rolls of dimes × $5.00						
	Loose dimes						
	Rolls of nickels × $2.00						
	Loose nickels						
	Rolls of pennies × $0.50						
	Loose pennies						
	Total coins to be deposited						
	Total cash to be deposited						

For DEPOSIT to the Account of

Tom's Allied Grocery
12 Wicjer Boulevard
Houston, TX 77080-3653

35-1242
1189

DATE ______ 20___

Elisson Bank
AND TRUST COMPANY
Houston, Texas

Subject to the Terms and Conditions of this Bank's Collection Agreement

⑆118905181⑆ 6725⑈098⑈

	Dollars	Cents
BILLS		
COINS		
Checks as Follows Properly Endorsed		
TOTAL DEPOSIT		

Problem 21–2, Concluded

TALLY SHEET	Date ____________ 20--					
No.	**Bills**					
	Packages of $100 bills × $10,000.00					
	Loose $100 bills					
	Packages of $50 bills × $5,000.00					
	Loose $50 bills					
	Packages of $20 bills × $2,000.00					
	Loose $20 bills					
	Packages of $10 bills × $1,000.00					
	Loose $10 bills					
	Packages of $5 bills × $500.00					
	Loose $5 bills					
	Packages of $1 bills × $100.00					
	Loose $1 bills					
	Total bills to be deposited					
No.	**Coins**					
	Rolls of half-dollars × $10.00					
	Loose half-dollars					
	Rolls of quarters × $10.00					
	Loose quarters					
	Rolls of dimes × $5.00					
	Loose dimes					
	Rolls of nickels × $2.00					
	Loose nickels					
	Rolls of pennies × $0.50					
	Loose pennies					
	Total coins to be deposited					
	Total cash to be deposited					

For DEPOSIT to the Account of

35-1242
1189

Tom's Allied Grocery
12 Wicjer Boulevard
Houston, TX 77080-3653

DATE ______________________ 20____

Elisson Bank
AND TRUST COMPANY
Houston, Texas

Subject to the Terms and Conditions of this Bank's Collection Agreement

⑆118905181⑆ 6725⑈098⑈

	Dollars	Cents
BILLS		
COINS		
Checks as Follows Properly Endorsed		
TOTAL DEPOSIT		

(This page is without text copy.)

Name ______________________

Score __________

Reinforcement Activities | CHAPTER 4 Jobs 16–21

Check Your Reading, page 180

1. ______________________

2. ______________________

3. ______________________

Discussion, page 180

1. a. ______________________

1. b. ______________________

1. c. ______________________

2. ______________________

Critical Thinking, page 180

____

Communication in the Workplace, page 180

1. ______

2. ______

Focus on Careers, page 181

1. a. ______

1. b. ______

1. c. ______

2. ______

Reviewing What You Have Learned, page 181

1. ______
2. ______
3. ______
4. ______
5. ______
6. ______
7. ______
8. ______
9. ______
10. ______

Mastery Problem, page 182

Phase 1: Making Change

a.

Items Bought		Department Keys Used
$8.19	Roast turkey	______
$3.98	Oranges	______
$1.09	Cake frosting	______
$2.89	Light bulbs	______
$2.88	Milk	______

b.

Bills and Coins	Number Used
Pennies	______
Nickels	______
Dimes	______
Quarters	______
Half-dollars	______
Dollars	______
Five dollars	______
Ten dollars	______

Mastery Problem, Continued

Phase 2: Proving Cash

a.

KORTE SUPER MARKETS

Cash Count Report

Date: ______________________ 20--

Cashier No.: ______________________ Register No.: ______________

Quantity	Denomination	Amount	
	$50.00 Bills		
	$20.00 Bills		
	$10.00 Bills		
	$5.00 Bills		
	$1.00 Bills		
	$0.50 Coins		
	$0.25 Coins		
	$0.10 Coins		
	$0.05 Coins		
	$0.01 Coins		
	Checks		
Total Cash in Cash Drawer			

Signature: ______________________

Mastery Problem, Continued

b.

KORTE SUPER MARKETS
Cash Proof Form

Date ________________ 20--

Change fund		
Add total cash sales from audit tape		
Total		
Less cash paid out from audit tape		
Cash that should be in register		
Cash actually in register		
Cash short		
Cash over		

Cash Register No.: ________ Cashier No.: ________

Signature: ________________________

Phase 3: Preparing a Summary of Departmental Sales Report

Cashier No.: 5 Register No.: 1

Department	Total
Meat	$ 512.89
Dairy	307.14
Produce	222.76
Bakery	202.18
Grocery	217.89
Health and beauty	310.69
General merchandise	305.28
Total	$2,078.83

Signature: Elsa Stern

Date: July 9, 20--

Cashier No.: 8 Register No.: 2

Department	Total
Meat	$ 721.25
Dairy	417.12
Produce	388.98
Bakery	315.22
Grocery	289.99
Health and beauty	448.12
General merchandise	376.98
Total	$2,957.66

Signature: Alan Dempsey

Date: July 9, 20--

ME	512.89
DA	307.14
PR	222.76
BA	202.18
GR	217.89
HE	310.69
GE	305.28
TL	2078.83
07/09/--	RG1

ME	721.25
DA	417.12
PR	388.98
BA	315.22
GR	289.99
HE	448.12
GE	376.98
TL	2957.66
07/09/--	RG2

Mastery Problem, Continued

Cashier No.: 2 Register No.: 3

Department	Total
Meat	$ 641.41
Dairy	315.11
Produce	387.01
Bakery	130.66
Grocery	333.51
Health and beauty	278.87
General merchandise	448.91
Total	$2,535.48

Signature: Eve Lucco

Date: July 9, 20--

Cashier No.: 4 Register No.: 4

Department	Total
Meat	$ 801.68
Dairy	390.09
Produce	412.81
Bakery	200.18
Grocery	339.98
Health and beauty	100.98
General merchandise	414.54
Total	$2,668.27

Signature: Lisa Bolger

Date: July 9, 20--

ME	641.41
DA	315.11
PR	387.01
BA	130.66
GR	333.51
HE	278.87
GE	448.91
TL	2535.48
07/09/--	RG3

ME	801.68
DA	390.09
PR	412.81
BA	200.18
GR	339.98
HE	108.99
GE	414.54
TL	2668.27
07/09/--	RG4

KORTE SUPER MARKETS
Summary of Departmental Sales
July 9, 20--

Department	Registers				Department Total
	1	2	3	4	
Meat					
Dairy					
Produce					
Bakery					
Grocery					
Health and Beauty					
General Merchandise					
Totals					

Mastery Problem, Concluded

Phase 4: Tallying and Depositing the Cash

a.

TALLY SHEET Date ____________ 20--

No.	Bills						
	Packages of $100 bills × $10,000.00						
	Loose $100 bills						
	Packages of $50 bills × $5,000.00						
	Loose $50 bills						
	Packages of $20 bills × $2,000.00						
	Loose $20 bills						
	Packages of $10 bills × $1,000.00						
	Loose $10 bills						
	Packages of $5 bills × $500.00						
	Loose $5 bills						
	Packages of $1 bills × $100.00						
	Loose $1 bills						
	Total bills to be deposited						
No.	**Coins**						
	Rolls of half-dollars × $10.00						
	Loose half-dollars						
	Rolls of quarters × $10.00						
	Loose quarters						
	Rolls of dimes × $5.00						
	Loose dimes						
	Rolls of nickels × $2.00						
	Loose nickels						
	Rolls of pennies × $0.50						
	Loose pennies						
	Total coins to be deposited						
	Total cash to be deposited						

b.

For DEPOSIT to the Account of

KORTE SUPER MARKETS
3016 JASON LANE
INDIANAPOLIS, IN 46227-3874

DATE ______________________ 20____

MARINE BANK & TRUST CO.
Indianapolis, IN

Subject to the Terms and Conditions of this Bank's Collection Agreement

⑆074020891⑆ 1185⑈541⑈

20-25/740

	Dollars	Cents
BILLS		
COINS		
Checks as Follows Properly Endorsed		
TOTAL DEPOSIT		

Reviewing Your Business Vocabulary

Choose the words that match the statements. Write each word you choose next to the statement number it matches. Be careful; some of the words listed should not be used.

Statements

1. The part of the receipt which stays in the book . . . . ______
2. A form issued for cash received . . . . ______
3. A form used to find the amount of cash on hand . . . . ______
4. A person who receives and pays out money . . . . ______
5. An exact copy . . . . ______
6. A total of other totals . . . . ______
7. A machine used to reduce errors and safeguard money . . . . ______
8. A special bar code read by electronic cash registers . . . . . ______
9. A total on which other calculations will be made . . . . ______
10. Allows payments to be made from checking accounts immediately . . . . ______
11. Money given back to a customer for returned bottles or merchandise . . . . ______
12. Rules or procedures . . . . ______
13. Checks from people other than customers . . . . ______
14. The value of a coin or bill . . . . ______
15. A record of all cash register transactions . . . . ______
16. A form on which you compare how much cash you are supposed to have with what you actually have in the drawer . . . . ______
17. An amount given to a cashier at the beginning of the day for making change . . . . ______
18. When there is less cash in the register at the end of the day than there should be . . . . ______
19. The amount of cash given to the cashier by the customer . . . . ______
20. Bills that do not fill their wrappers . . . . ______
21. A checklist of money to be deposited . . . . ______
22. A form which lists the money deposited in a bank account . . . . ______

Words

amount tendered	cashier	duplicate	refund
cash box	change fund	grand total	stub
cash count report	debit card	loose bills	subtotal
cash overage	denomination	policies	tally sheet
cash register	deposit slip	proof of cash	third-party checks
cash shortage	detailed audit tape	receipt	Universal Product Code (or UPC)

(This page is without text copy.)

Name ____________________

Score __________

Opening a Bank Checking Account

CHAPTER 5
Job 22

Sample Problem, page 187

Monterey Bank
of Commerce
411 Peachtree Road NE, Atlanta, GA 30303-0411

ACCOUNT ________

AUTHORIZED SIGNATURE FOR:

NAME ____________________

ADDRESS ____________________

TELEPHONE ____________________

SIGNATURE ____________________

DATE ____________________

For DEPOSIT to the Account of

37–502
0810

Marty's Computer and Fax Repair Service
212 Dobbs Ct.
Atlanta, GA 30304-0212

Date ____________ 20___

Monterey Bank
of Commerce
Atlanta, GA

Subject to the Terms and Conditions of this Bank's Collection Agreement

⑆081001351⑆ 1568⑈ 284⑈

	Dollars	Cents
BILLS		
COINS		
Checks as Follows Properly Endorsed		
TOTAL DEPOSIT		

	Dollars	Cents
BILLS		
COINS		
Checks as Follows Properly Endorsed		
TOTAL DEPOSIT		

Problem 22–1, page 190

ACCOUNT ____________

AUTHORIZED SIGNATURE FOR:

NAME ____________________

ADDRESS ____________________

TELEPHONE ____________________

SIGNATURE ____________________

DATE ____________________

Problem 22–2, page 190

For DEPOSIT to the Account of

5–110/1351

Eastern Floral
309 Carter Road
Passaic, NJ 07055-0309

DATE ____________ 20___

ATLANTIC NATIONAL BANK
Passaic, New Jersey

Subject to the Terms and Conditions of this Bank's Collection Agreement

⑆135121016⑆ 317⑈ 2619⑈

	Dollars	Cents
BILLS		
COINS		
Checks as Follows Properly Endorsed		
TOTAL DEPOSIT		

Problem 22–3, page 190

For DEPOSIT to the Account of

41–19/1631

Bolaris Lock and Key
121 Division Street
Elko, NV 89801-0121

DATE ____________ 20___

Quicksilver Savings and Loan Elko, Nevada

Subject to the Terms and Conditions of this Bank's Collection Agreement

⑆163110014⑆ 596⑈ 26588⑈

	Dollars	Cents
BILLS		
COINS		
Checks as Follows Properly Endorsed		
TOTAL DEPOSIT		

Problem 22–4

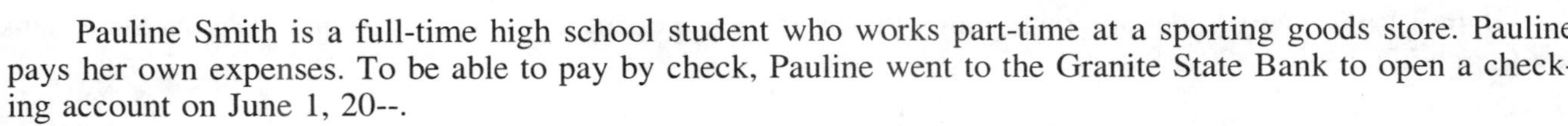

Pauline Smith is a full-time high school student who works part-time at a sporting goods store. Pauline pays her own expenses. To be able to pay by check, Pauline went to the Granite State Bank to open a checking account on June 1, 20--.

Directions

1. Prepare a signature card for Pauline. Assume that you are Pauline, so sign her name. Her address is 108 Pleasant Street, Hooksett, NH 03106-0108. Her phone number is (603) 555-9999. The bank assigns account number 147-1003 to Pauline.
2. Her initial deposit on June 1, 20--, consists of the following:

		Checks:	ABA No.	Amount
Bills:	$76.00		4-17	$ 87.50
Coins:	$ 9.75		21-177	$142.67
			19-03	$ 9.95

Prepare her deposit slip.

ACCOUNT ____________

AUTHORIZED SIGNATURE FOR:

NAME ____________________

ADDRESS ____________________

TELEPHONE ____________________

SIGNATURE ____________________

DATE ____________________

For DEPOSIT to the Account of

5–19/2117

Pauline Smith
108 Pleasant Street
Hooksett, NH 03106-0108

DATE ____________ 20___

Granite STATE BANK
Manchester, New Hampshire

Subject to the Terms and Conditions of this Bank's Collection Agreement

⑆211713162⑆ 147⑈1003⑈

	Dollars	Cents
BILLS		
COINS		
Checks as Follows Properly Endorsed		
TOTAL DEPOSIT		

Problem 22–5

James Vo is an art dealer and owns Jimmy's Art Store. He opens a checking account at Dakota State Bank on March 27, 20--.

Directions

Prepare James's deposit slip on March 27 for the following items:

Bills:			**Coins:**		
	2	$50 bills		7	$0.50 coins
	4	$20 bills		15	$0.25 coins
	11	$10 bills		39	$0.10 coins
	6	$ 5 bills		27	$0.05 coins
	17	$ 1 bills		14	$0.01 coins

Checks:	**ABA NO.**	**Amount**
	4-21	$450.00
	13-109	$203.16
	6-92	$ 91.18
	4-11	$102.44

For DEPOSIT to the Account of

16–044 / 5117

Jimmy's Art Store
215 65th Ave., N.
Fargo, ND 58102-0215

DATE ________________ 20___

DAKOTA
STATE BANK
Fargo, North Dakota

Subject to the Terms and Conditions of this Bank's Collection Agreement

⑆511741010⑆ 312⑈4115⑈

	Dollars	**Cents**
BILLS		
COINS		
Checks as Follows Properly Endorsed		
TOTAL DEPOSIT		

Name ____________________

Score __________

Sample Problem, page 192

No. 1 $ ________
Date ________
To ________
For ________

	Dollars	Cents
Bal. Bro't. For'd.		
Amt. Deposited		
Total		
Amt. This Check		
Bal. Car'd. For'd.		

Marty's Computer and Fax Repair Service
212 Dobbs Ct.
Atlanta, GA 30304-0212

No. **1**

Date ____________ 20__ 37-502/0810

PAY TO THE ORDER OF ____________ $ ________

For Classroom Use Only

____________ Dollars

Monterey Bank of Commerce
Atlanta, GA

⑆081001351⑆ 1568⑈ 284⑈

No. 2 $ ________
Date ________
To ________
For ________

	Dollars	Cents
Bal. Bro't. For'd.		
Amt. Deposited		
Total		
Amt. This Check		
Bal. Car'd. For'd.		

Marty's Computer and Fax Repair Service
212 Dobbs Ct.
Atlanta, GA 30304-0212

No. **2**

Date ____________ 20__ 37-502/0810

PAY TO THE ORDER OF ____________ $ ________

For Classroom Use Only

____________ Dollars

Monterey Bank of Commerce
Atlanta, GA

⑆081001351⑆ 1568⑈ 284⑈

No. 3 $ ________
Date ________
To ________
For ________

	Dollars	Cents
Bal. Bro't. For'd.		
Amt. Deposited		
Total		
Amt. This Check		
Bal. Car'd. For'd.		

Marty's Computer and Fax Repair Service
212 Dobbs Ct.
Atlanta, GA 30304-0212

No. **3**

Date ____________ 20__ 37-502/0810

PAY TO THE ORDER OF ____________ $ ________

For Classroom Use Only

____________ Dollars

Monterey Bank of Commerce
Atlanta, GA

⑆081001351⑆ 1568⑈ 284⑈

Problem 23–1, page 197

1. ______________________________ Dollars

2. ______________________________ Dollars

3. ______________________________ Dollars

4. ______________________________ Dollars

5. ______________________________ Dollars

6. ______________________________ Dollars

7. ______________________________ Dollars

8. ______________________________ Dollars

9. ______________________________ Dollars

10. ______________________________ Dollars

Name ______________________

Problem 23–2, page 198

No. 1	$ ______
Date	
To	
For	

	Dollars	Cents
Bal. Bro't. For'd.		
Amt. Deposited		
Total		
Amt. This Check		
Bal. Car'd. For'd.		

WESTMONT SKATEBOARD PARK No. **1**
4012 Brown Street
Little Rock, AR 72204-3899 Date ______________ 20__ 81-35/820

PAY TO THE ORDER OF ______________________ $ ______
For Classroom Use Only

______________________________ Dollars

Midwest
STATE BANK
89 Commerce Street • Little Rock, AR 72201-2992 ______________

⑆0820104570⑆ 361⑈0412⑈

No. 2	$ ______
Date	
To	
For	

	Dollars	Cents
Bal. Bro't. For'd.		
Amt. Deposited		
Total		
Amt. This Check		
Bal. Car'd. For'd.		

WESTMONT SKATEBOARD PARK No. **2**
4012 Brown Street
Little Rock, AR 72204-3899 Date ______________ 20__ 81-35/820

PAY TO THE ORDER OF ______________________ $ ______
For Classroom Use Only

______________________________ Dollars

Midwest
STATE BANK
89 Commerce Street • Little Rock, AR 72201-2992 ______________

⑆0820104570⑆ 361⑈0412⑈

No. 3	$ ______
Date	
To	
For	

	Dollars	Cents
Bal. Bro't. For'd.		
Amt. Deposited		
Total		
Amt. This Check		
Bal. Car'd. For'd.		

WESTMONT SKATEBOARD PARK No. **3**
4012 Brown Street
Little Rock, AR 72204-3899 Date ______________ 20__ 81-35/820

PAY TO THE ORDER OF ______________________ $ ______
For Classroom Use Only

______________________________ Dollars

Midwest
STATE BANK
89 Commerce Street • Little Rock, AR 72201-2992 ______________

⑆0820104570⑆ 361⑈0412⑈

Problem 23–3, page 198

No. 1 $ ________
Date ________
To ________
For ________

	Dollars	Cents
Bal. Bro't. For'd.		
Amt. Deposited		
Total		
Amt. This Check		
Bal. Car'd. For'd.		

MESA AUTO PARTS AND ACCESSORIES
1120 Aspen Avenue, East
Mesa, AZ 85204-4025

No. **1**

Date ________ 20__ 91-411/1221

PAY TO THE ORDER OF ________ $ ________

For Classroom Use Only

________ Dollars

Sedona
National Bank 700 Ingram Street, East
Mesa, AZ 85203-5973

⑆122103761⑆ 1172045⑈

No. 2 $ ________
Date ________
To ________
For ________

	Dollars	Cents
Bal. Bro't. For'd.		
Amt. Deposited		
Total		
Amt. This Check		
Bal. Car'd. For'd.		

MESA AUTO PARTS AND ACCESSORIES
1120 Aspen Avenue, East
Mesa, AZ 85204-4025

No. **2**

Date ________ 20__ 91-411/1221

PAY TO THE ORDER OF ________ $ ________

For Classroom Use Only

________ Dollars

Sedona
National Bank 700 Ingram Street, East
Mesa, AZ 85203-5973

⑆122103761⑆ 1172045⑈

No. 3 $ ________
Date ________
To ________
For ________

	Dollars	Cents
Bal. Bro't. For'd.		
Amt. Deposited		
Total		
Amt. This Check		
Bal. Car'd. For'd.		

MESA AUTO PARTS AND ACCESSORIES
1120 Aspen Avenue, East
Mesa, AZ 85204-4025

No. **3**

Date ________ 20__ 91-411/1221

PAY TO THE ORDER OF ________ $ ________

For Classroom Use Only

________ Dollars

Sedona
National Bank 700 Ingram Street, East
Mesa, AZ 85203-5973

⑆122103761⑆ 1172045⑈

Problem 23–4

You are a record keeper for Dan Slater Construction Company, a builder of fine custom homes. On April 1, Dan opens a checking account at the Second National Bank with a deposit of $1,968.00. He puts you in charge of keeping the checkbook. You are authorized to sign the checks with your own name.

Directions

a. On April 1, enter the opening deposit of $1,968.00 in the space for "Amt. Deposited" on the stub of Check No. 1. Fill in the total.

b. On April 2, write Check No. 1 for $114.85 to the United Insurance Company for auto insurance.

c. On April 4, write Check No. 2 for $42.50 to the Bluff City Printing Company for office stationery.

d. On April 7, write Check No. 3 for $219.00 to MicroPower Company for computer service. (If you worked accurately, the balance carried forward on the stub of Check No. 3 should be $1,591.65.)

No. **1** $ ________

Date ________

To ________

For ________

	Dollars	Cents
Bal. Bro't. For'd.		
Amt. Deposited		
Total		
Amt. This Check		
Bal. Car'd. For'd.		

DAN SLATER CONSTRUCTION COMPANY No. **1**
3721 Rosewood Drive
Louisville, KY 40229-5318 Date ________ 20__ 21-14/830

PAY TO THE ORDER OF ________ $ ________
For Classroom Use Only

________ Dollars

Second National Bank 702 Congress Street Louisville, KY 40203-3021 ________

⑆083010441⑆ 21629111⑈

No. **2** $ ________

Date ________

To ________

For ________

	Dollars	Cents
Bal. Bro't. For'd.		
Amt. Deposited		
Total		
Amt. This Check		
Bal. Car'd. For'd.		

DAN SLATER CONSTRUCTION COMPANY No. **2**
3721 Rosewood Drive
Louisville, KY 40229-5318 Date ________ 20__ 21-14/830

PAY TO THE ORDER OF ________ $ ________
For Classroom Use Only

________ Dollars

Second National Bank 702 Congress Street Louisville, KY 40203-3021 ________

⑆083010441⑆ 21629111⑈

Problem 23–4, Concluded

No. 3 $______
Date ______
To ______

For ______

	Dollars	Cents
Bal. Bro't. For'd.		
Amt. Deposited		
Total		
Amt. This Check		
Bal. Car'd. For'd.		

DAN SLATER CONSTRUCTION COMPANY
3721 Rosewood Drive
Louisville, KY 40229-5318

No. 3

Date ______ 20__

21-14/830

PAY TO THE ORDER OF ______ $______

For Classroom Use Only

______ Dollars

Second National Bank
702 Congress Street
Louisville, KY 40203-3021

⑆083010441⑆ 2162911⑈

Problem 23–5

You are a record keeper for Amy Juarez, who owns a landscape service. On July 1, Amy opens a checking account at the Andrews National Bank with a deposit of $2,500.00. She puts you in charge of keeping the checkbook. You are authorized to sign the checks with your own name.

Directions

a. Enter the July 1 deposit in the correct place.

b. On July 3, write Check No. 1 for $205.75 to Central Lawn Supply for lawn chemicals.

c. On July 6, write Check No. 2 for $310.96 to Atlantic Fuel Company for oil and lubricants.

d. On July 10, write Check No. 3 for $300.00 to Amy Juarez for personal expenses. (If you worked accurately, the balance carried forward on the stub of Check No. 3 should be $1,683.29.)

No. 1 $______
Date ______
To ______

For ______

	Dollars	Cents
Bal. Bro't. For'd.		
Amt. Deposited		
Total		
Amt. This Check		
Bal. Car'd. For'd.		

AMY JUAREZ LANDSCAPE AND DESIGN
496 Coyle Road
Portland, ME 04103-3421

No. 1

Date ______ 20__

52-7225/2112

PAY TO THE ORDER OF ______ $______

For Classroom Use Only

______ Dollars

Andrews NATIONAL BANK
527 Park Avenue, Portland, ME 04102-9053

⑆211211631⑆ 4271034⑈

Problem 23–5, Concluded

No. 2 $ ________
Date ________
To ________
For ________

	Dollars	Cents
Bal. Bro't. For'd.		
Amt. Deposited		
Total		
Amt. This Check		
Bal. Car'd. For'd.		

AMY JUAREZ LANDSCAPE AND DESIGN
496 Coyle Road
Portland, ME 04103-3421

No. 2

Date ________ 20__ 52-7225/2112

PAY TO THE ORDER OF ________ $________

For Classroom Use Only

________ Dollars

Andrews
NATIONAL BANK
527 Park Avenue, Portland, ME 04102-9053

⑆211211631⑆ 4271034⑈

No. 3 $ ________
Date ________
To ________
For ________

	Dollars	Cents
Bal. Bro't. For'd.		
Amt. Deposited		
Total		
Amt. This Check		
Bal. Car'd. For'd.		

AMY JUAREZ LANDSCAPE AND DESIGN
496 Coyle Road
Portland, ME 04103-3421

No. 3

Date ________ 20__ 52-7225/2112

PAY TO THE ORDER OF ________ $________

For Classroom Use Only

________ Dollars

Andrews
NATIONAL BANK
527 Park Avenue, Portland, ME 04102-9053

⑆211211631⑆ 4271034⑈

(This page is without text copy.)

Name ______________________________

Score ______________

Sample Problem, page 200

For DEPOSIT to the Account of

37–502
0810

Marty's Computer and Fax Repair Service
212 Dobbs Ct.
Atlanta, GA 30304-0212

Date ______________________ 20___

Monterey Bank of Commerce
Atlanta, GA

Subject to the Terms and Conditions of this Bank's Collection Agreement

⑆081001351⑆ 1568⑈284⑈

	Dollars	Cents
BILLS		
COINS		
Checks as Follows Properly Endorsed		
TOTAL DEPOSIT		

No. **3** $ ____________
Date ____________
To ____________
____
For ____________

	Dollars	Cents
Bal. Bro't. For'd.		
Amt. Deposited		
Total		
Amt. This Check		
Bal. Car'd. For'd.		

No. **5** $ ____________
Date ____________
To ____________
____
For ____________

	Dollars	Cents
Bal. Bro't. For'd.		
Amt. Deposited		
Total		
Amt. This Check		
Bal. Car'd. For'd.		

No. **4** $ ____________
Date ____________
To ____________
____
For ____________

	Dollars	Cents
Bal. Bro't. For'd.		
Amt. Deposited		
Total		
Amt. This Check		
Bal. Car'd. For'd.		

Problem 24–1, page 204

No. **83** $ ________
Date ________
To ________
____
For ________

	Dollars	Cents
Bal. Bro't. For'd.		
Amt. Deposited		
Total		
Amt. This Check		
Bal. Car'd. For'd.		

No. **84** $ ________
Date ________
To ________
____
For ________

	Dollars	Cents
Bal. Bro't. For'd.		
Amt. Deposited		
Total		
Amt. This Check		
Bal. Car'd. For'd.		

No. **85** $ ________
Date ________
To ________
____
For ________

	Dollars	Cents
Bal. Bro't. For'd.		
Amt. Deposited		
Total		
Amt. This Check		
Bal. Car'd. For'd.		

Problem 24–2, page 204

No. **212** $ ________
Date ________
To ________
____
For ________

	Dollars	Cents
Bal. Bro't. For'd.		
Amt. Deposited		
Total		
Amt. This Check		
Bal. Car'd. For'd.		

No. **213** $ ________
Date ________
To ________
____
For ________

	Dollars	Cents
Bal. Bro't. For'd.		
Amt. Deposited		
Total		
Amt. This Check		
Bal. Car'd. For'd.		

No. **214** $ ________
Date ________
To ________
____
For ________

	Dollars	Cents
Bal. Bro't. For'd.		
Amt. Deposited		
Total		
Amt. This Check		
Bal. Car'd. For'd.		

Name ______________________________

Problem 24–3, page 204

No. **101** $ ________
Date ________
To ________
____
For ________

	Dollars	Cents
Bal. Bro't. For'd.		
Amt. Deposited		
Total		
Amt. This Check		
Bal. Car'd. For'd.		

HERITAGE FURNITURE COMPANY
82 SW Westland Drive
Knoxville, TN 37919-3871

No. **101**

Date ____________ 20___ 63-710/1044

PAY TO THE ORDER OF ____________________ $ ________

For Classroom Use Only

____________________________________ Dollars

TENNESSEE NATIONAL BANK
35 NW Oak Hill Road
Knoxville, TN 37917-4638

____

⑆1044 2177⑆ 3622595⑈

No. **102** $ ________
Date ________
To ________
____
For ________

	Dollars	Cents
Bal. Bro't. For'd.		
Amt. Deposited		
Total		
Amt. This Check		
Bal. Car'd. For'd.		

HERITAGE FURNITURE COMPANY
82 SW Westland Drive
Knoxville, TN 37919-3871

No. **102**

Date ____________ 20___ 63-710/1044

PAY TO THE ORDER OF ____________________ $ ________

For Classroom Use Only

____________________________________ Dollars

TENNESSEE NATIONAL BANK
35 NW Oak Hill Road
Knoxville, TN 37917-4638

____

⑆1044 2177⑆ 3622595⑈

No. **103** $ ________
Date ________
To ________
____
For ________

	Dollars	Cents
Bal. Bro't. For'd.		
Amt. Deposited		
Total		
Amt. This Check		
Bal. Car'd. For'd.		

HERITAGE FURNITURE COMPANY
82 SW Westland Drive
Knoxville, TN 37919-3871

No. **103**

Date ____________ 20___ 63-710/1044

PAY TO THE ORDER OF ____________________ $ ________

For Classroom Use Only

____________________________________ Dollars

TENNESSEE NATIONAL BANK
35 NW Oak Hill Road
Knoxville, TN 37917-4638

____

⑆1044 2177⑆ 3622595⑈

Problem 24–3, Concluded

For DEPOSIT to the Account of		Dollars	Cents
HERITAGE FURNITURE COMPANY 82 SW Westland Drive Knoxville, TN 37919-3871	BILLS		
Date ______________ 20___	COINS		
	Checks as Follows Properly Endorsed		
TENNESSEE NATIONAL BANK Knoxville, Tennessee			
Subject to the Terms and Conditions of this Bank's Collection Agreement			
⑆104412177⑆ 362⑈2595⑈	TOTAL DEPOSIT		

63-710/1044

Problem 24–4

You are a record keeper for Shreveport Jewelry. On May 1, Shreveport Jewelry opened a checking account at the Fairfield Bank with a deposit of $6,000.00. You are placed in charge of keeping the checkbook. You are authorized to sign the checks with your own name.

Directions

a. On May 1, enter the opening deposit on the stub of Check No. 101.

b. On May 4, write Check No. 101 for $1,200.00 to Glavine Realty for office rent.

c. On May 10, write Check No. 102 for $371.94 to Smoltz Company for office supplies.

d. On May 12, you make the following deposit:

Cash:	Quantity	Denomination
	6	$20.00 bills
	12	$10.00 bills
	17	$ 5.00 bills
	37	$ 1.00 bills
	35	$ 0.50 coins
	34	$ 0.25 coins
	57	$ 0.10 coins
	36	$ 0.05 coins
	17	$ 0.01 coins
Checks:	**ABA Number**	**Amount**
	4-17	$ 46.75
	31-12	$391.18
	19-106	$477.12

Prepare the deposit slip. Enter the total amount of the deposit on the stub of Check No. 103 and enter the new balance on the Total line.

e. On May 21, write Check No. 103 for $2,150.00 to Boever Computer Company for a computer.

Name ______________________

Problem 24–4, Continued

No. 101 $ ________
Date ________
To ________
For ________

	Dollars	Cents
Bal. Bro't. For'd.		
Amt. Deposited		
Total		
Amt. This Check		
Bal. Car'd. For'd.		

SHREVEPORT JEWELRY
8102 Fulton Street
Shreveport, LA 71103-5514

No. **101**

Date ________ 20__ 84-296/1111

PAY TO THE ORDER OF ________ $ ________

For Classroom Use Only

________ Dollars

Fairfield Bank
1002 Fairfield Avenue, Shreveport, LA 71101-1033

⑆111129651⑆ 24 2581⑈

No. 102 $ ________
Date ________
To ________
For ________

	Dollars	Cents
Bal. Bro't. For'd.		
Amt. Deposited		
Total		
Amt. This Check		
Bal. Car'd. For'd.		

SHREVEPORT JEWELRY
8102 Fulton Street
Shreveport, LA 71103-5514

No. **102**

Date ________ 20__ 84-296/1111

PAY TO THE ORDER OF ________ $ ________

For Classroom Use Only

________ Dollars

Fairfield Bank
1002 Fairfield Avenue, Shreveport, LA 71101-1033

⑆111129651⑆ 24 2581⑈

No. 103 $ ________
Date ________
To ________
For ________

	Dollars	Cents
Bal. Bro't. For'd.		
Amt. Deposited		
Total		
Amt. This Check		
Bal. Car'd. For'd.		

SHREVEPORT JEWELRY
8102 Fulton Street
Shreveport, LA 71103-5514

No. **103**

Date ________ 20__ 84-296/1111

PAY TO THE ORDER OF ________ $ ________

For Classroom Use Only

________ Dollars

Fairfield Bank
1002 Fairfield Avenue, Shreveport, LA 71101-1033

⑆111129651⑆ 24 2581⑈

Problem 24–4, Concluded

For DEPOSIT to the Account of

84–296
1111

SHREVEPORT JEWELRY
8102 Fulton Street
Shreveport, LA 71103-5514

Date ____________________ 20___

Fairfield Bank
Shreveport, Louisiana

Subject to the Terms and Conditions of this Bank's Collection Agreement

⑆111129651⑆ 242⑈5181⑈

	Dollars	Cents
BILLS		
COINS		
Checks as Follows Properly Endorsed		
TOTAL DEPOSIT		

Name ______________________________

Score ____________

Using a Check Register

CHAPTER 5
Job 25

Sample Problem, page 207

RECORD ALL CHARGES OR CREDITS THAT AFFECT YOUR ACCOUNT

NUMBER	DATE	DESCRIPTION OF TRANSACTION	PAYMENT/ DEBIT (−)		✓ T	FEE (IF ANY) (−)	DEPOSIT/ CREDIT (+)		BALANCE	
		TO								
		FOR								
		TO								
		FOR								
		TO								
		FOR								
		TO								
		FOR								
		TO								
		FOR								
		TO								
		FOR								

Manuel Sousa
1520 Heron Dr.
Atlanta, GA 30301-0519

No. **327**

Date ____________________ 20___

64-61/0715

PAY TO THE ORDER OF ______________________________ $__________

For Classroom Use Only

____ Dollars

GREAT SOUTHERN
SAVINGS AND LOAN
519 Axel Road, Atlanta, GA 30301-0519

____

⑆071051361 2⑆ 4112073⑈

Problem 25–1, page 209

$ 45/100 ____________

1. ____ Dollars

$ 82/100 ____________

2. ____ Dollars

$ 63/100 ____________

3. ____ Dollars

$ 51/100 ____________

4. ____ Dollars

$ 20/100 ____________

5. ____ Dollars

$ 97/100 ____________

6. ____ Dollars

$ 19/100 ____________

7. ____ Dollars

$ 55/100 ____________

8. ____ Dollars

$ 78/100 ____________

9. ____ Dollars

$ 09/100 ____________

10. ____ Dollars

Name ______________________________

Problem 25–2, page 210

RECORD ALL CHARGES OR CREDITS THAT AFFECT YOUR ACCOUNT

NUMBER	DATE	DESCRIPTION OF TRANSACTION	PAYMENT/ DEBIT (−)	✓ T	FEE (IF ANY) (−)	DEPOSIT/ CREDIT (+)	BALANCE
		TO					
		FOR					
		TO					
		FOR					
		TO					
		FOR					
		TO					
		FOR					
		TO					
		FOR					
		TO					
		FOR					

Problem 25–3, page 210

RECORD ALL CHARGES OR CREDITS THAT AFFECT YOUR ACCOUNT

NUMBER	DATE	DESCRIPTION OF TRANSACTION	PAYMENT/ DEBIT (−)	✓ T	FEE (IF ANY) (−)	DEPOSIT/ CREDIT (+)	BALANCE
		TO					
		FOR					
		TO					
		FOR					
		TO					
		FOR					
		TO					
		FOR					
		TO					
		FOR					
		TO					
		FOR					

Problem 25–4

You have a personal checking account at the Menlo Park Federal Bank. You use a check register to keep an up-to-date balance of your account. On April 1, you have a balance of $685.56 in your account.

Directions

a. Enter the April 1 balance on the first line of the check register in the column headed "Balance."

b. On April 7, issue Check No. 151 for $45.00 to Sound World for compact discs. Enter the check in the check register and find the new balance. Write the check.

c. On April 9, enter the deposit of $359.58 in the check register. Label the deposit "Salary." Find the new balance.

d. On April 10, issue Check No. 152 for $0.85 to the Sun Printing Company for a map. Enter the check in the check register and find the new balance. Write the check.

e. On April 18, issue Check No. 153 for $125.00 to Varsity Clothing Store for a blazer. Enter the check in the check register and find the new balance. Write the check.

f. On April 22, Varsity Clothing Store tells you that Check No. 153, sent on April 18, should have been for $125.95 instead of $125.00. You decide to issue Check No. 154 for $0.95 to correct the error. Enter the check in the check register and find the new balance. Write the check.

RECORD ALL CHARGES OR CREDITS THAT AFFECT YOUR ACCOUNT

NUMBER	DATE	DESCRIPTION OF TRANSACTION	PAYMENT/ DEBIT (−)	✓ T	FEE (IF ANY) (−)	DEPOSIT/ CREDIT (+)	BALANCE
		TO					
		FOR					
		TO					
		FOR					
		TO					
		FOR					
		TO					
		FOR					
		TO					
		FOR					
		TO					
		FOR					

STUDENT'S NAME
STUDENT'S ADDRESS

No. **151**

Date ______________ 20___ 55-11/3066

PAY TO THE ORDER OF ______________________ $________

For Classroom Use Only

____ Dollars

Menlo Park
FEDERAL BANK
617 EDISON AVENUE • CHARLESTON, SC 29406-7133

____

⑆306631790⑆ 518⑈ 2044⑈

Name ______________________________

Problem 25–4, Concluded

STUDENT'S NAME
STUDENT'S ADDRESS

No. 152

Date ______________________ 20___ 55-11/3066

PAY TO THE ORDER OF ______________________________ $__________

For Classroom Use Only

____ Dollars

Menlo Park
FEDERAL BANK
617 EDISON AVENUE • CHARLESTON, SC 29406-7133

____

⑆306631790⑆ 518⑈ 2044⑈

STUDENT'S NAME
STUDENT'S ADDRESS

No. 153

Date ______________________ 20___ 55-11/3066

PAY TO THE ORDER OF ______________________________ $__________

For Classroom Use Only

____ Dollars

Menlo Park
FEDERAL BANK
617 EDISON AVENUE • CHARLESTON, SC 29406-7133

____

⑆306631790⑆ 518⑈ 2044⑈

STUDENT'S NAME
STUDENT'S ADDRESS

No. 154

Date ______________________ 20___ 55-11/3066

PAY TO THE ORDER OF ______________________________ $__________

For Classroom Use Only

____ Dollars

Menlo Park
FEDERAL BANK
617 EDISON AVENUE • CHARLESTON, SC 29406-7133

____

⑆306631790⑆ 518⑈ 2044⑈

(This page is without text copy.)

Name ______________________________

Score ____________

Sample Problem 1, page 213

Trailing Edge

ENDORSE HERE

X ______________________________

____

____

DO NOT WRITE, SIGN, OR STAMP BELOW THIS LINE
RESERVED FOR FINANCIAL INSTITUTION USE*

*FEDERAL RESERVE BOARD OF GOVERNORS REG. CC

Leading Edge

Sample Problem 2, page 215

ENDORSE HERE

X ______________________________

____

____

DO NOT WRITE, SIGN, OR STAMP BELOW THIS LINE
RESERVED FOR FINANCIAL INSTITUTION USE*

For DEPOSIT to the Account of

64–61/0715

Manuel Sousa
1520 Heron Dr.
Atlanta, GA 30301-0519

Date ______________________ 20___

Great Southern Savings and Loan
ATLANTA, GA

Subject to the Terms and Conditions of this Bank's Collection Agreement

⑆071513612⑆ 411⑈2073⑈

	Dollars	Cents
BILLS		
COINS		
Checks as Follows Properly Endorsed		
TOTAL DEPOSIT		

RECORD ALL CHARGES OR CREDITS THAT AFFECT YOUR ACCOUNT

NUMBER	DATE	DESCRIPTION OF TRANSACTION	PAYMENT/ DEBIT (−)	✓ T	FEE (IF ANY) (−)	DEPOSIT/ CREDIT (+)	BALANCE
		TO					
		FOR					
		TO					
		FOR					
		TO					
		FOR					
		TO					
		FOR					
		TO					
		FOR					
		TO					
		FOR					

Name ______________________________

Sample Problem 3, page 217

	Dollars	Cents
BILLS		
COINS		
Checks as Follows Properly Endorsed		
TOTAL DEPOSIT		

ENDORSE HERE

X ______________________________

____

____

DO NOT WRITE, SIGN, OR STAMP BELOW THIS LINE
RESERVED FOR FINANCIAL INSTITUTION USE*

Problem 26–1, page 218

ENDORSE HERE

X ______________________________

____

____

DO NOT WRITE, SIGN, OR STAMP BELOW THIS LINE
RESERVED FOR FINANCIAL INSTITUTION USE*

CHECK 1

ENDORSE HERE

X ______________________________

____

____

DO NOT WRITE, SIGN, OR STAMP BELOW THIS LINE
RESERVED FOR FINANCIAL INSTITUTION USE*

CHECK 2

ENDORSE HERE

X ______________________________

____

____

DO NOT WRITE, SIGN, OR STAMP BELOW THIS LINE
RESERVED FOR FINANCIAL INSTITUTION USE*

CHECK 3

Problem 26–2, page 218

ENDORSE HERE
X ______

DO NOT WRITE, SIGN, OR STAMP BELOW THIS LINE
RESERVED FOR FINANCIAL INSTITUTION USE*

CHECK 1

ENDORSE HERE
X ______

DO NOT WRITE, SIGN, OR STAMP BELOW THIS LINE
RESERVED FOR FINANCIAL INSTITUTION USE*

CHECK 2

ENDORSE HERE
X ______

DO NOT WRITE, SIGN, OR STAMP BELOW THIS LINE
RESERVED FOR FINANCIAL INSTITUTION USE*

CHECK 3

ENDORSE HERE
X ______

DO NOT WRITE, SIGN, OR STAMP BELOW THIS LINE
RESERVED FOR FINANCIAL INSTITUTION USE*

CHECK 4

Problem 26–3, page 219

ENDORSE HERE
X ______

DO NOT WRITE, SIGN, OR STAMP BELOW THIS LINE
RESERVED FOR FINANCIAL INSTITUTION USE*

CHECK 1

ENDORSE HERE
X ______

DO NOT WRITE, SIGN, OR STAMP BELOW THIS LINE
RESERVED FOR FINANCIAL INSTITUTION USE*

CHECK 2

For DEPOSIT to the Account of

7–9
104

Khalid Meta
56 Rhodes Street
Abilene, TX 79602-0056

Date ______ 20___

North Street
Abilene, Texas BANK

Subject to the Terms and Conditions of this Bank's Collection Agreement

⑆0104277221⑆ 151⑈3170⑈

	Dollars	Cents
BILLS		
COINS		
Checks as Follows Properly Endorsed		
TOTAL DEPOSIT		

Name ________________________________

Problem 26–4

Myra Bertram is preparing a bank deposit on July 9, 20--. She is depositing cash and two checks:

Cash:	Quantity	Denomination
	6	$10.00 bills
	12	$ 5.00 bills
	19	$ 1.00 bills
	4	$ 0.50 coins
	26	$ 0.25 coins
	17	$ 0.10 coins
	12	$ 0.05 coins
	16	$ 0.01 coins

Checks:	ABA Number	Amount
1	5-12	$141.16
2	21-10	$ 87.35

Directions

a. Prepare the endorsements that Myra will write on the back of each check to deposit them.

b. Complete the deposit slip.

c. Record a balance brought forward of $406.10 on Check Stub No. 116. Then, record the deposit on the check stub and total.

ENDORSE HERE

X ________________________________

____

____

DO NOT WRITE, SIGN, OR STAMP BELOW THIS LINE
RESERVED FOR FINANCIAL INSTITUTION USE*

CHECK 1

ENDORSE HERE

X ________________________________

____

____

DO NOT WRITE, SIGN, OR STAMP BELOW THIS LINE
RESERVED FOR FINANCIAL INSTITUTION USE*

CHECK 2

For DEPOSIT to the Account of

MYRA BERTRAM
2517 North Market Street
San Jose, CA 95110-3953

Date ____________________ 20___

6–12/4112

FNB
First National Bank
San Jose, California

Subject to the Terms and Conditions of this Bank's Collection Agreement

⑆411235177⑆ 171⑈23274⑈

	Dollars	Cents
BILLS		
COINS		
Checks as Follows Properly Endorsed		
TOTAL DEPOSIT		

Problem 26–4, Concluded

No. **116** $______

Date ______

To ______

______

For ______

	Dollars	Cents
Bal. Bro't. For'd.		
Amt. Deposited		
Total		
Amt. This Check		
Bal. Car'd. For'd.		

Problem 26–5

Hector Ramirez is preparing a bank deposit on November 30, 20--. He is depositing cash and one check and cashing a second check. All checks are salary checks from his job.

Cash:	Quantity	Denomination
	4	$20.00 bills
	9	$10.00 bills
	11	$ 5.00 bills
	15	$ 1.00 bills
	11	$ 0.25 coins
	21	$ 0.10 coins
	16	$ 0.05 coins
	23	$ 0.01 coins

Checks:	ABA Number	Amount
1	4-6	$150.00
2	4-7	$ 95.00

Directions

a. Prepare the endorsements that Hector will write on the back of each check. Check 1 will be deposited. Check 2 will be cashed.

b. Complete the deposit slip.

c. Record a balance of $611.28 in his check register. Then, record the deposit, labeling it "Salary and other." Find the total.

Name ______________________

Problem 26–5, Concluded

ENDORSE HERE

X ______________________

____

____

DO NOT WRITE, SIGN, OR STAMP BELOW THIS LINE
RESERVED FOR FINANCIAL INSTITUTION USE*

CHECK 1

ENDORSE HERE

X ______________________

____

____

DO NOT WRITE, SIGN, OR STAMP BELOW THIS LINE
RESERVED FOR FINANCIAL INSTITUTION USE*

CHECK 2

For DEPOSIT to the Account of

$\frac{11-6}{0172}$

Hector Ramirez
7535 King Street
Denver, CO 80221-6173

Date ______________ 20___

ROCKY
MOUNTAIN BANK
Denver, Colorado

Subject to the Terms and Conditions of this Bank's Collection Agreement

⑆0172160141⑆ 102⑈20116⑈

	Dollars	Cents
BILLS		
COINS		
Checks as Follows Properly Endorsed		
TOTAL DEPOSIT		

RECORD ALL CHARGES OR CREDITS THAT AFFECT YOUR ACCOUNT

NUMBER	DATE	DESCRIPTION OF TRANSACTION	PAYMENT/ DEBIT (−)		✓ T	FEE (IF ANY) (−)	DEPOSIT/ CREDIT (+)		BALANCE	
		TO								
		FOR								
		TO								
		FOR								

(This page is without text copy.)

Name ______________________

Score __________

Sample Problem, page 221

LIBERTY
National Savings
1600 Harbor Lane
Erie, PA 16502-1712

Account No. ______________

AUTHORIZED SIGNATURE FOR:

Name ______________________

Address ______________________

Telephone ______________________

Account Type ______________ Mother's Maiden Name ______________

Soc. Sec. No. ______________ I.D. ______________

Birthdate and Place ______________________

Signature ______________________

Date ______________________

SAVINGS DEPOSIT

ACCOUNT NO.: _ _ _ _ _ _

DATE ______________________

NAME (please print) ______________________

ADDRESS ______________________

CITY STATE ZIP CODE ______________________

X ______________________
Please sign in teller's presence for cash received

LIBERTY
National Savings

List checks by bank no.	Dollars	Cents
BILLS		
COINS		
CHECKS		
Subtotal		
Less cash received		
TOTAL DEPOSIT		

Problem 27–1, page 225

SAVINGS DEPOSIT

ACCOUNT NO.: __ __ __ __ __ __

DATE

NAME (please print)

ADDRESS

CITY STATE ZIP CODE

X

Please sign in teller's presence for cash received

Cupertino Federal Bank

List checks by bank no.	Dollars	Cents
BILLS	36	
COINS	9	12
CHECKS	222	44
Subtotal	267	56
Less cash received		
TOTAL DEPOSIT	267	56

SAVINGS DEPOSIT

ACCOUNT NO.: __ __ __ __ __ __

DATE

NAME (please print)

ADDRESS

CITY STATE ZIP CODE

X

Please sign in teller's presence for cash received

Cupertino Federal Bank

List checks by bank no.	Dollars	Cents
BILLS	10	00
COINS	8	62
CHECKS	207	42
Subtotal	225	04
Less cash received		
TOTAL DEPOSIT	225	04

SAVINGS DEPOSIT

ACCOUNT NO.: __ __ __ __ __ __

DATE

NAME (please print)

ADDRESS

CITY STATE ZIP CODE

X

Please sign in teller's presence for cash received

Cupertino Federal Bank

List checks by bank no.	Dollars	Cents
BILLS		
COINS		
CHECKS	380	34
Subtotal	380	34
Less cash received	50	00
TOTAL DEPOSIT	330	34

Name ____________________

Problem 27–2, page 226

SAVINGS WITHDRAWAL

ACCOUNT NO.: ___ ___ - ___ ___ ___ ___

DATE

DOLLARS $

For Classroom Use Only

X

Please sign in teller's presence for cash received

NAME (please print)

ADDRESS

CITY STATE ZIP CODE

Glendale Bank of Wisconsin

SAVINGS WITHDRAWAL

ACCOUNT NO.: ___ ___ - ___ ___ ___ ___

DATE

DOLLARS $

For Classroom Use Only

X

Please sign in teller's presence for cash received

NAME (please print)

ADDRESS

CITY STATE ZIP CODE

Glendale Bank of Wisconsin

Problem 27–3, page 226

No. **603** $ ______

Date ______

To ______

______

For ______

	Dollars	Cents
Bal. Bro't. For'd.		
Amt. Deposited		
Total		
Amt. This Check		
Bal. Car'd. For'd.		

No. **604** $ ______

Date ______

To ______

______

For ______

	Dollars	Cents
Bal. Bro't. For'd.		
Amt. Deposited		
Total		
Amt. This Check		
Bal. Car'd. For'd.		

No. **605** $ ______

Date ______

To ______

______

For ______

	Dollars	Cents
Bal. Bro't. For'd.		
Amt. Deposited		
Total		
Amt. This Check		
Bal. Car'd. For'd.		

Name ________________________________

Problem 27–4

You have a checking account and an ATM access card. You use your check stubs to record your checking account entries.

a. Enter a balance brought forward of $241.79 on Check Stub No. 238.

b. Record each of the following events on your check stubs:

November	11	Deposited $521.42.
	12	Issued Check No. 238 for $109.50 to Galaxy Insurance for car insurance.
	15	Withdrew $100.00 using your ATM access card.
	17	Issued Check No. 239 for $67.64 to TMC Sporting Goods for tennis shoes.
	16	Issued Check No. 240 for $17.23 to Spencer Audio for a compact disc.

No. **238** $ ____________

Date ____________

To ____________

For ____________

	Dollars	Cents
Bal. Bro't. For'd.		
Amt. Deposited		
Total		
Amt. This Check		
Bal. Car'd. For'd.		

No. **240** $ ____________

Date ____________

To ____________

For ____________

	Dollars	Cents
Bal. Bro't. For'd.		
Amt. Deposited		
Total		
Amt. This Check		
Bal. Car'd. For'd.		

No. **239** $ ____________

Date ____________

To ____________

For ____________

	Dollars	Cents
Bal. Bro't. For'd.		
Amt. Deposited		
Total		
Amt. This Check		
Bal. Car'd. For'd.		

(This page is without text copy.)

Name ______________________

Score __________

Sample Problem, page 228

No. 1 $ 820.00 ✓
Date March 6, 20--
To DTS Computer
For specialty tools

	Dollars	Cents
Bal. Bro't. For'd.		00
3/1 Amt. Deposited	6,200	00 ✓
Total	6,200	00
Amt. This Check	820	00
Bal. Car'd. For'd.	5,380	00

No. 2 $ 122.45 ✓
Date March 12, 20--
To Pacific Stationery & Supply
For supplies

	Dollars	Cents
Bal. Bro't. For'd.	5,380	00
Amt. Deposited		
Total	5,380	00
Amt. This Check	122	45
Bal. Car'd. For'd.	5,257	55

No. 3 $ 476.00 ✓
Date March 15, 20--
To Photo Max
For combination fax, printer, and copier machine

	Dollars	Cents
Bal. Bro't. For'd.	5,257	55
3/13 Amt. Deposited	637	50 ✓
Total	5,895	05
Amt. This Check	476	00
Bal. Car'd. For'd.	5,419	05

No. 4 $ 315.00
Date March 17, 20--
To Peninsula Supply House
For electronic parts and components

	Dollars	Cents
Bal. Bro't. For'd.	5,419	05
Amt. Deposited		
Total	5,419	05
Amt. This Check	315	00
Bal. Car'd. For'd.	5,104	05

No. 5 $ 750.00 ✓
Date March 24, 20--
To Cash
For personal use

	Dollars	Cents
Bal. Bro't. For'd.	5,104	05
3/21 Amt. Deposited	900	00 ✓
Total	6,004	05
Amt. This Check	750	00
Bal. Car'd. For'd.	5,254	05

No. 6 $ 100.00
Date March 28, 20--
To Furniture Mart
For used office furniture

	Dollars	Cents
Bal. Bro't. For'd.	5,254	05
Amt. Deposited		
Total	5,254	05
Amt. This Check	100	00
Bal. Car'd. For'd.	5,154	05

Sample Problem, Concluded

Problem 28–1, page 232

Problem 28–2, page 232

Problem 28–3, page 232

Problem 28–4

You are the record keeper for Avalon Security Systems. Part of your job is to keep the checkbook and prepare the bank reconciliation statement. The check stubs show that the following checks were issued during August:

#619	$161.18	#623	$ 26.80	#626	$211.15
#620	204.05	#624	174.10	#627	46.18
#621	4.95	#625	10.99	#628	64.60
#622	71.60				

On August 31, the checkbook balance is $3,177.64. The bank statement shows a balance of $3,487.94. The following canceled checks were returned with the bank statement:

#619	$161.18	#623	$26.80	#626	$211.15
#620	204.05	#625	10.99	#627	46.18
#621	4.95				

Directions

Prepare a bank reconciliation statement as of August 31.

(This page is without text copy.)

Name ______________________________

Score ____________

Sample Problem, page 234

Sample Problem, Concluded

CHECKING ACCOUNT RECONCILIATION

CHECKS OUTSTANDING		
NUMBER	AMOUNT	
TOTAL		

ENTER BALANCE THIS STATEMENT $ ____________

ADD DEPOSITS NOT CREDITED ON THIS STATEMENT 1 ____________

2 ____________

3 ____________

TOTAL ____________

SUBTRACT CHECKS OUTSTANDING ____________

BALANCE $ ____________

SHOULD AGREE WITH YOUR CHECKBOOK BALANCE

IF YOUR ACCOUNT DOES NOT BALANCE

- HAVE YOU CORRECTLY ENTERED THE AMOUNT OF EACH CHECK IN YOUR CHECK REGISTER?
- DO THE AMOUNTS OF YOUR DEPOSITS ENTERED IN YOUR CHECK REGISTER AGREE WITH YOUR STATEMENT?
- HAVE ALL CHECKS BEEN DEDUCTED FROM YOUR CHECK REGISTER BALANCE?
- HAVE YOU CARRIED THE CORRECT BALANCE FORWARD FROM ONE CHECK REGISTER STUB TO THE NEXT?
- HAVE YOU CHECKED ALL ADDITIONS AND SUBTRACTIONS IN YOUR CHECK REGISTER?
- HAVE YOU REVIEWED LAST MONTH'S RECONCILEMENT TO MAKE SURE ANY DIFFERENCES WERE CORRECTED?

ANY ERRORS OR EXCEPTIONS SHOULD BE REPORTED IMMEDIATELY TO THE BANK

Name ______________________________

Problem 29–1, page 236

Problem 29–2, page 236

Problem 29–3, page 237

CHECKING ACCOUNT RECONCILIATION

CHECKS OUTSTANDING		
NUMBER	AMOUNT	
TOTAL		

ENTER BALANCE THIS STATEMENT $ ____________

ADD DEPOSITS NOT CREDITED ON THIS STATEMENT 1 ____________

2 ____________

3 ____________

TOTAL ____________

SUBTRACT CHECKS OUTSTANDING ____________

BALANCE $ ____________

SHOULD AGREE WITH YOUR CHECKBOOK BALANCE

IF YOUR ACCOUNT DOES NOT BALANCE

- HAVE YOU CORRECTLY ENTERED THE AMOUNT OF EACH CHECK IN YOUR CHECK REGISTER?
- DO THE AMOUNTS OF YOUR DEPOSITS ENTERED IN YOUR CHECK REGISTER AGREE WITH YOUR STATEMENT?
- HAVE ALL CHECKS BEEN DEDUCTED FROM YOUR CHECK REGISTER BALANCE?
- HAVE YOU CARRIED THE CORRECT BALANCE FORWARD FROM ONE CHECK REGISTER STUB TO THE NEXT?
- HAVE YOU CHECKED ALL ADDITIONS AND SUBTRACTIONS IN YOUR CHECK REGISTER?
- HAVE YOU REVIEWED LAST MONTH'S RECONCILEMENT TO MAKE SURE ANY DIFFERENCES WERE CORRECTED?

ANY ERRORS OR EXCEPTIONS SHOULD BE REPORTED IMMEDIATELY TO THE BANK

Name ______________________________

Problem 29–4

You are preparing your own bank reconciliation statement.

Directions

Use the following information to prepare a December 31 statement. You are using a bank-supplied form.

Checkbook balance	$1,021.75
Bank statement balance	909.95
Outstanding deposit	257.36
Outstanding checks:	
#411	11.60
#412	104.19
#415	29.77

CHECKING ACCOUNT RECONCILIATION

CHECKS OUTSTANDING		
NUMBER	AMOUNT	
TOTAL		

ENTER BALANCE THIS STATEMENT $ ____________

ADD DEPOSITS NOT CREDITED ON THIS STATEMENT
1 ____________
2 ____________
3 ____________

TOTAL ____________

→SUBTRACT CHECKS OUTSTANDING ____________

BALANCE $ ____________
SHOULD AGREE WITH YOUR CHECKBOOK BALANCE

IF YOUR ACCOUNT DOES NOT BALANCE

- HAVE YOU CORRECTLY ENTERED THE AMOUNT OF EACH CHECK IN YOUR CHECK REGISTER?
- DO THE AMOUNTS OF YOUR DEPOSITS ENTERED IN YOUR CHECK REGISTER AGREE WITH YOUR STATEMENT?
- HAVE ALL CHECKS BEEN DEDUCTED FROM YOUR CHECK REGISTER BALANCE?
- HAVE YOU CARRIED THE CORRECT BALANCE FORWARD FROM ONE CHECK REGISTER STUB TO THE NEXT?
- HAVE YOU CHECKED ALL ADDITIONS AND SUBTRACTIONS IN YOUR CHECK REGISTER?
- HAVE YOU REVIEWED LAST MONTH'S RECONCILEMENT TO MAKE SURE ANY DIFFERENCES WERE CORRECTED?

ANY ERRORS OR EXCEPTIONS SHOULD BE REPORTED IMMEDIATELY TO THE BANK

Problem 29–5

You are record keeper for Dynex Computer Company. Part of your job is to keep the checkbook and prepare the bank reconciliation statement. The check stubs show that the following checks were issued during May:

#361	$56.11	#364	$ 29.98	#367	$26.10
#362	12.05	#365	101.60	#368	19.65
#363	8.90	#366	47.11	#369	91.40

Your records also show the following deposits during May:

May	12	$411.10
	21	308.15
	31	175.60

On May 31, the checkbook balance is $1,172.45. The bank statement shows a balance of $1,046.48. The following canceled checks were returned with the bank statement:

#361	$56.11	#365	$101.60	#369	$91.40
#362	12.05	#366	47.11		
#363	8.90	#367	26.10		

The bank statement shows the following deposits:

May	12	$411.10
	21	308.15

Directions

a. Find the outstanding deposit by comparing your record of deposits with the bank statement.

b. Find the outstanding checks by comparing the list of checks issued with the list of canceled checks.

c. Prepare a bank reconciliation statement as of May 31. Use Illustration 29A in the text as a model.

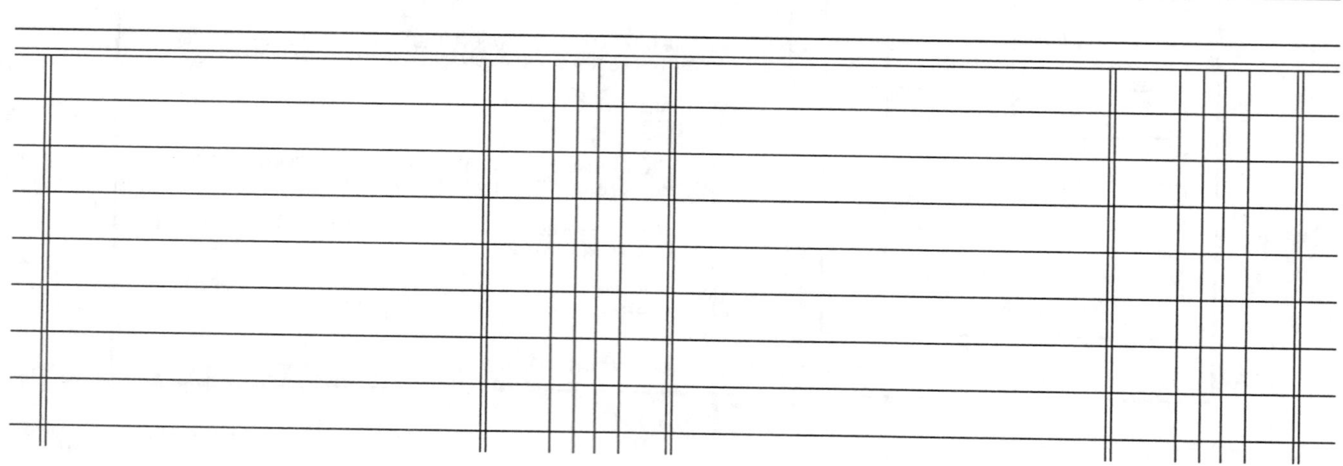

Name ____________________

Score ____________

Sample Problem, page 239

No. **60** $ ________

Date ________

To ________

For ________

	Dollars	Cents
Bal. Bro't. For'd.	6,350	40
Amt. Deposited		
Total		
Amt. This Check		
Bal. Car'd. For'd.		

RECORD ALL CHARGES OR CREDITS THAT AFFECT YOUR ACCOUNT

NUMBER	DATE	DESCRIPTION OF TRANSACTION	PAYMENT/ DEBIT (−)	✓ T	FEE (IF ANY) (−)	DEPOSIT/ CREDIT (+)	BALANCE
		TO					
		FOR					
		TO					
		FOR					
		TO					
		FOR					
		TO					
		FOR					

Problem 30–1, page 242

Problem 30–2, page 243

Name ______________________________

Problem 30–3, page 243

RECORD ALL CHARGES OR CREDITS THAT AFFECT YOUR ACCOUNT

NUMBER	DATE	DESCRIPTION OF TRANSACTION	PAYMENT/ DEBIT (−)	✓ T	FEE (IF ANY) (−)	DEPOSIT/ CREDIT (+)	BALANCE
		TO					
		FOR					
		TO					
		FOR					
		TO					
		FOR					
		TO					
		FOR					
		TO					
		FOR					
		TO					
		FOR					

Problem 30–4

You are a senior bookkeeper for El Camino Lighting. Part of your job is to keep the checkbook and prepare a bank reconciliation statement.

Directions

a. Prepare a bank reconciliation statement as of March 31 from the following information:

Checkbook balance	$2,677.12
Bank statement balance	2,644.52
Service charge	5.00
Interest earned	10.50
Outstanding deposit	371.19
Outstanding checks:	
#149	18.05
#150	104.16
#152	210.88

b. Enter a balance brought forward of $2,677.12 in the check register.

c. Record the service charge and the interest earned in the check register. Find the new balance each time. Your final balance should agree with the adjusted checkbook balance. (Use Illustration 30D in the text as a model.)

Name ________________________________

Problem 30–4, Concluded

RECORD ALL CHARGES OR CREDITS THAT AFFECT YOUR ACCOUNT

NUMBER	DATE	DESCRIPTION OF TRANSACTION	PAYMENT/ DEBIT (−)	✓ T	FEE (IF ANY) (−)	DEPOSIT/ CREDIT (+)	BALANCE
		TO FOR					
		TO FOR					
		TO FOR					
		TO FOR					
		TO FOR					
		TO FOR					

Problem 30–5

You are a junior staff accountant for the Elite Pool Company. Part of your job is to keep the checkbook and prepare a bank reconciliation statement.

Directions

a. Prepare a bank reconciliation statement as of June 30 from the following information:

Checkbook balance	$3,166.11
Bank statement balance	3,353.91
Service charge	7.50
Interest earned	15.05
Outstanding deposit	411.10
Outstanding checks:	
#111	46.90
#112	137.85
#114	415.60

You also discover that Check No. 109 for $87.00 was recorded in your checkbook as $78.00. (You must add back the wrong payment and subtract the right payment.)

b. Enter a balance of $3,166.11 in your check register.

c. Enter the service charge, the interest earned, and the error correction in your check register. Use Illustration 30D in the text as your guide.

Problem 30–5, Concluded

RECORD ALL CHARGES OR CREDITS THAT AFFECT YOUR ACCOUNT

NUMBER	DATE	DESCRIPTION OF TRANSACTION	PAYMENT/ DEBIT (−)	✓ T	FEE (IF ANY) (−)	DEPOSIT/ CREDIT (+)	BALANCE
		TO					
		FOR					
		TO					
		FOR					
		TO					
		FOR					
		TO					
		FOR					
		TO					
		FOR					
		TO					
		FOR					

Name ____________________

Score __________

Reinforcement Activities

CHAPTER 5
Jobs 22–30

Check Your Reading, page 244

1.

2.

3.

4.

5.

6.

7.

Discussion, page 244

Ethics in the Workplace, page 244

Communication in the Workplace, page 244

Focus on Careers, page 244

1.
2.
3.
4.

Reviewing What You Have Learned, page 245

1.
2.
3.
4.
5.
6.
7.
8.
9.
10.
11.
12.
13.
14.
15.
16.
17.
18.
19.
20.

Name ______________________

Mastery Problem, page 246

For DEPOSIT to the Account of

4-126/4811

WRIGHT AVIATION COMPANY
110 NE Oddfellows Road
Bainbridge Island, WA 98110-5055

DATE ______________ 20___

kitty hawk NATIONAL BANK
Seattle, Washington

Subject to the Terms and Conditions of this Bank's Collection Agreement

⑆4811017351⑆ 1364289⑈

	Dollars	Cents
BILLS		
COINS		
Checks as Follows Properly Endorsed		
TOTAL DEPOSIT		

No. 352 $ ______
Date ______
To ______
For ______

	Dollars	Cents
Bal. Bro't. For'd.		
Amt. Deposited		
Total		
Amt. This Check		
Bal. Car'd. For'd.		

WRIGHT AVIATION COMPANY
110 NE Oddfellows Road
Bainbridge Island, WA 98110-5055

No. 352

Date ______________ 20___ 4-126/4811

PAY TO THE ORDER OF ______________ $______

For Classroom Use Only

______________ Dollars

kitty hawk NATIONAL BANK
17801 Yester Way, Seattle, WA 98104-0010

⑆4811017351⑆ 1364289⑈

No. 353 $ ______
Date ______
To ______
For ______

	Dollars	Cents
Bal. Bro't. For'd.		
Amt. Deposited		
Total		
Amt. This Check		
Bal. Car'd. For'd.		

WRIGHT AVIATION COMPANY
110 NE Oddfellows Road
Bainbridge Island, WA 98110-5055

No. 353

Date ______________ 20___ 4-126/4811

PAY TO THE ORDER OF ______________ $______

For Classroom Use Only

______________ Dollars

kitty hawk NATIONAL BANK
17801 Yester Way, Seattle, WA 98104-0010

⑆4811017351⑆ 1364289⑈

Mastery Problem, Continued

No. 354 $ ______
Date ______
To ______
______
For ______

	Dollars	Cents
Bal. Bro't. For'd.		
Amt. Deposited		
Total		
Amt. This Check		
Bal. Car'd. For'd.		

WRIGHT AVIATION COMPANY
110 NE Oddfellows Road
Bainbridge Island, WA 98110-5055

No. 354

Date ______ 20__ 4-126/4811

PAY TO THE ORDER OF ______ $ ______

For Classroom Use Only

______ Dollars

kitty hawk NATIONAL BANK
17801 Yester Way, Seattle, WA 98104-0010

⑆481101735⑆ 1364289⑈

No. 355 $ ______
Date ______
To ______
______
For ______

	Dollars	Cents
Bal. Bro't. For'd.		
Amt. Deposited		
Total		
Amt. This Check		
Bal. Car'd. For'd.		

WRIGHT AVIATION COMPANY
110 NE Oddfellows Road
Bainbridge Island, WA 98110-5055

No. 355

Date ______ 20__ 4-126/4811

PAY TO THE ORDER OF ______ $ ______

For Classroom Use Only

______ Dollars

kitty hawk NATIONAL BANK
17801 Yester Way, Seattle, WA 98104-0010

⑆481101735⑆ 1364289⑈

No. 356 $ ______
Date ______
To ______
______
For ______

	Dollars	Cents
Bal. Bro't. For'd.		
Amt. Deposited		
Total		
Amt. This Check		
Bal. Car'd. For'd.		

WRIGHT AVIATION COMPANY
110 NE Oddfellows Road
Bainbridge Island, WA 98110-5055

No. 356

Date ______ 20__ 4-126/4811

PAY TO THE ORDER OF ______ $ ______

For Classroom Use Only

______ Dollars

kitty hawk NATIONAL BANK
17801 Yester Way, Seattle, WA 98104-0010

⑆481101735⑆ 1364289⑈

Name ______________________

Mastery Problem, Concluded

No. 357 $ ________
Date ________
To ________
____
For ________

	Dollars	Cents
Bal. Bro't. For'd.		
Amt. Deposited		
Total		
Amt. This Check		
Bal. Car'd. For'd.		

WRIGHT AVIATION COMPANY
110 NE Oddfellows Road
Bainbridge Island, WA 98110-5055

No. **357**

Date ________ 20__ 4-126/4811

PAY TO THE ORDER OF ________ $ ________

For Classroom Use Only

________ Dollars

kitty hawk NATIONAL BANK
17801 Yester Way, Seattle, WA 98104-0010

⑆481101735⑆ 1364289⑈

No. **358** $ ________
Date ________
To ________
____
For ________

	Dollars	Cents
Bal. Bro't. For'd.		
Amt. Deposited		
Total		
Amt. This Check		
Bal. Car'd. For'd.		

Reviewing Your Business Vocabulary

Choose the words that match the statements. Write each word you choose next to the statement number it matches. All words will be used once.

Statements

1. Shows the purpose of a check and a description of the payment .... voucher
2. A fee for bank services .... service charge
3. Safe form of cash to use when taking a trip .... travel checks
4. A form used to indicate to the bank which signature to accept on signed checks .... signature card
5. A card that allows you to use an ATM .... ATM access card
6. A check with a special stub attached .... voucher check
7. A book of checks .... check book
8. A machine that allows 24-hour banking .... automated teller machine (ATM)
9. A number assigned to banks .... ABA number
10. A detailed record of a checking account sent by a bank .... bank statement
11. The money left in a checking account per the bank's records .... bank statement balance
12. Checks issued by the drawer but not yet paid by the bank .... outstanding checks
13. Money paid for the use of money .... Interest
14. The part of a check kept by the drawer .... check stub
15. Brought into agreement .... reconciled
16. A name signed falsely by someone else .... forged signature
17. A signature on the back of a check .... endorsement
18. Transferable to another party .... negotiable
19. An account used by only one person .... Individual checking account
20. A book for recording checks when stubs are not used .... check register
21. An endorsement by signature only .... bank endorsement
22. The left side of a check .... Trailing edge
23. The party who writes a check .... drawer
24. A central place where banks exchange checks .... clearing house
25. The money left in a checking account per the depositor's records .... checkbook balance
26. An endorsement which names the party to whom the check is transferred .... full endorsement
27. A check that is guaranteed by a bank .... certified check
28. A code number for access to an ATM .... pin
29. The bank that pays a check .... drawee
30. The right side of a check .... leading edge
31. A card that when used subtracts an amount directly from your bank account .... debit card
32. An account used by two or more people .... joint checking account
33. An endorsement which limits the use of a check .... restrictive endorsement
34. The party who receives a check and will be paid .... payee
35. A deposit that is part cash received and part deposit .... split deposit
36. Checks that have been paid by the bank .... canceled checks
37. Clear and easy to read .... legible
38. A statement that brings the checkbook and bank statement balances into agreement .... bank reconciliation statement

Name ______________________________

Reviewing Your Business Vocabulary, Concluded

Statements

39. Unusable . . . . void
40. A machine used to print the amount on checks . . . . check protector
41. When there is not enough money in an account to pay a check . . . . insufficient funds
42. To send out . . . . issue
43. A deposit slip on which the depositor's name and address are preprinted . . . . personalized deposit slip
44. The use of a computer to transfer money from one party to another . . . . electronic funds transfer
45. A form instructing a bank not to pay a check . . . . stop payment order
46. A deposit not shown on a bank statement . . . . outstanding deposit
47. A written order by the drawer to the drawee to pay the payee . . . . check

Words

- 9 ABA number
- 5 ATM access card
- 8 automated teller machine (ATM)
- 38 bank reconciliation statement
- 10 bank statement
- 11 bank statement balance
- 21 blank endorsement
- 36 canceled checks
- 27 certified check
- 47 check
- 40 check protector
- 20 check register
- 14 check stub
- 7 checkbook
- 25 checkbook balance
- 24 clearinghouse
- 31 debit card
- 29 drawee
- 23 drawer
- 44 electronic funds transfer
- 17 endorsement
- 16 forged signature
- 26 full endorsement
- 19 individual checking account
- 41 insufficient funds
- 13 interest
- 42 issue
- 32 joint checking account
- 30 leading edge
- 37 legible
- 18 negotiable
- 12 outstanding checks
- 46 outstanding deposit
- 34 payee
- 43 personalized deposit slip
- 28 PIN
- 15 reconciled
- 33 restrictive endorsement
- 2 service charge
- 4 signature card
- 35 split deposit
- 45 stop-payment order
- 22 trailing edge
- 3 travelers' checks
- 39 void
- 1 voucher
- 6 voucher check

(This page is without text copy.)

Name ______________________

Score __________

Sample Problem, page 251

PETTY CASH VOUCHER

No. ______

Date ______________ 20__

$	¢

Pay to ______________________________

For ______________________________

Approved by

____

Payment Received

____

Problem 31–1, page 253

a.

PETTY CASH VOUCHER

No. ______

Date ______________ 20__

$	¢

Pay to ______________________________

For ______________________________

Approved by

____

Payment Received

____

Problem 31–1, Concluded

PETTY CASH VOUCHER

No. ______

Date ______________ 20__

$	¢

Pay to ________________________________

For ________________________________

Approved by ________________

Payment Received ________________

PETTY CASH VOUCHER

No. ______

Date ______________ 20__

$	¢

Pay to ________________________________

For ________________________________

Approved by ________________

Payment Received ________________

PETTY CASH VOUCHER

No. ______

Date ______________ 20__

$	¢

Pay to ________________________________

For ________________________________

Approved by ________________

Payment Received ________________

b. 1. ________________________________

2. ________________________________

Name ______________________

Problem 31–2, page 253

a.

PETTY CASH VOUCHER

No. ______

Date ______________ 20__

$	¢

Pay to ______________________________

For ______________________________

Approved by ______________________ Payment Received ______________________

PETTY CASH VOUCHER

No. ______

Date ______________ 20__

$	¢

Pay to ______________________________

For ______________________________

Approved by ______________________ Payment Received ______________________

PETTY CASH VOUCHER

No. ______

Date ______________ 20__

$	¢

Pay to ______________________________

For ______________________________

Approved by ______________________ Payment Received ______________________

Problem 31–2, Concluded

PETTY CASH VOUCHER		
	No. ______	
	Date ____________ 20__	
Pay to ____________________		$ ¢
For ____________________		
Approved by	Payment Received	
____________	____________	

b. **1.** ____________________

2. ____________________

Problem 31-3

You work for Kord Kutchins, a ticket agent. He puts you in charge of the petty cash fund, which was started on October 1 with a balance of $175.00.

Directions

a. Fill out a petty cash voucher for each of the following payments made from the petty cash fund. Approve each voucher with your own initials, but do not fill in the signature. Start with Voucher No. 1.

Oct.	3	Paid $9.95 to Enid Wolfe, an office clerk, for copying charges.
	7	Paid $16.30 to Tom Parsons, a delivery person, for gasoline.
	12	Paid $9.05 to Will Bertini, a sales clerk, for printing charges.
	16	Paid $18.60 to Myra Gold, an office clerk, for stationery.
	19	Paid $25.00 to Corby Message Service for telegram delivery.
	24	Paid $41.90 to Downtown Deli for an office lunch.
	27	Paid $4.15 to Eloise Shuler, an office clerk, for message pads.
	31	Paid $8.37 to Clay Herman, an accounting clerk, for a rubber stamp.

b. Answer the following questions:

1. How much money have you spent in October?
2. How much should be left in the fund at the end of October?

Name ______________________________

Problem 31–3, Continued

a.

PETTY CASH VOUCHER

No. ______

Date ______________ 20__

Pay to ______________________________

For ______________________________

$	¢

Approved by ______________________

Payment Received ______________________

PETTY CASH VOUCHER

No. ______

Date ______________ 20__

Pay to ______________________________

For ______________________________

$	¢

Approved by ______________________

Payment Received ______________________

PETTY CASH VOUCHER

No. ______

Date ______________ 20__

Pay to ______________________________

For ______________________________

$	¢

Approved by ______________________

Payment Received ______________________

Problem 31–3, Continued

PETTY CASH VOUCHER

No. ______

Date ______________ 20__

	$	¢
Pay to ______________________		
For ______________________		

Approved by ______________________

Payment Received ______________________

PETTY CASH VOUCHER

No. ______

Date ______________ 20__

	$	¢
Pay to ______________________		
For ______________________		

Approved by ______________________

Payment Received ______________________

PETTY CASH VOUCHER

No. ______

Date ______________ 20__

	$	¢
Pay to ______________________		
For ______________________		

Approved by ______________________

Payment Received ______________________

Name ____________________

Problem 31–3, Concluded

PETTY CASH VOUCHER

No. ______

Date ______________ 20__

$	¢

Pay to ______________________________

For ______________________________

Approved by ______________ Payment Received ______________

PETTY CASH VOUCHER

No. ______

Date ______________ 20__

$	¢

Pay to ______________________________

For ______________________________

Approved by ______________ Payment Received ______________

b. 1. ______________________________

2. ______________________________

(This page is without text copy.)

Name ________________________________

Score ______________

Sample Problem, page 255

PETTY CASH RECORD									
PAID FOR	VO. NO.	TOTAL PAYMENTS		DISTRIBUTION OF PAYMENTS					
				OFFICE EXPENSE		DELIVERY EXPENSE		GENERAL EXPENSE	

Problem 32–1, page 257

PETTY CASH RECORD									
PAID FOR	VO. NO.	TOTAL PAYMENTS		DISTRIBUTION OF PAYMENTS					
				OFFICE EXPENSE		DELIVERY EXPENSE		GENERAL EXPENSE	

Problem 32–2, page 258

PETTY CASH RECORD									
PAID FOR	VO. NO.	TOTAL PAYMENTS		DISTRIBUTION OF PAYMENTS					
				OFFICE EXPENSE		DELIVERY EXPENSE		GENERAL EXPENSE	

Problem 32–3, page 258

PETTY CASH RECORD											
PAID FOR	VO. NO.	TOTAL PAYMENTS		DISTRIBUTION OF PAYMENTS							
				OFFICE EXPENSE		DELIVERY EXPENSE		SHIPPING EXPENSE		GENERAL EXPENSE	

Problem 32–4

You are in charge of the petty cash fund for the Wabash Lighting Company.

Directions

a. Prepare a petty cash record with Distribution of Payments columns for Office Expense, Delivery Expense, Shipping Expense, and General Expense. Enter the petty cash vouchers listed below in this record.

Voucher Number	Paid For	Amount
101	Printer ribbons	$19.62
102	Cab fare for deliveries	8.50
103	Truck lubrication	14.50
104	Cleaning supplies	11.63
105	Boxes for shipping	21.07
106	Paper towels	10.04
107	Gas for truck	10.40
108	Stamps for office	10.00
109	Duplicate keys	0.65
110	Shipping labels	14.26

b. Rule and foot the amount columns.

c. Check your totals by crossfooting.

d. If the totals agree, record the final totals and double rule the amount columns.

PETTY CASH RECORD

PAID FOR	VO. NO.	TOTAL PAYMENTS		DISTRIBUTION OF PAYMENTS							
				OFFICE EXPENSE		DELIVERY EXPENSE		SHIPPING EXPENSE		GENERAL EXPENSE	

(This page is without text copy.)

Name ______________________

Score ____________

Sample Problem, page 261

PETTY CASH BOOK															
Date		Explanation	Vo. No.	Receipts		Payments		Distribution of Payments							
								Office Expense		Delivery Expense		Other Items			
												Item	Amount		

Problem 33-1, page 264

PETTY CASH BOOK															
Date		Explanation	Vo. No.	Receipts		Payments		Distribution of Payments							
								Office Expense		Delivery Expense		Other Items			
												Item	Amount		

Problem 33–2, page 264

PETTY CASH BOOK								
					Distribution of Payments			
							Other Items	
Date	Explanation	Vo. No.	Receipts	Payments	Shipping Expense	Delivery Expense	Item	Amount

Name ________________________

Problem 33–3, page 265

PETTY CASH BOOK

DATE	EXPLANATION	VO. NO.	RECEIPTS	PAYMENTS	DISTRIBUTION OF PAYMENTS				
					TRAVEL EXPENSE	VAN EXPENSE	TELEPHONE EXPENSE	OTHER ITEMS	
								ITEM	AMOUNT

Problem 33–4

You are in charge of the petty cash fund for Kingsley's Diner. On September 1, your employer cashed Check No. 510 for $200.00 to start the petty cash fund. Each payment from the fund must be classified into one of these four categories:

Kitchen Expense—supplies used in the kitchen, such as sponges and steel wool; repairs to kitchen equipment
Maintenance Expense—expenses of keeping the diner clean; repairs to the diner
Office Expense—stationery and stamps
General Expense—any expense that does not fit in the other categories

Directions

a. Prepare a petty cash book with special column headings for Kitchen Expense, Maintenance Expense, and Office Expense.

b. Record the opening balance.

c. Record these vouchers issued in September:

Voucher Number	Date	Paid For	Amount
1	Sept. 2	Waxing floors	$30.00
2	5	Kitchen supplies	17.95
3	7	Replace diner windows	19.75
4	9	Laundry service	16.50
5	12	Taxi fare	8.50
6	15	Oven repair	30.50
7	17	Kitchen sponges	12.10
8	24	Stamps for office	10.00
9	29	Clean parking lot	15.50
10	30	Office stationery	17.60

d. Rule and foot the amount columns.

e. Check the totals by crossfooting.

f. Record the final totals and double rule the amount columns.

g. Find the new balance and enter it in the petty cash book as of October 1.

Name ____________________

Problem 33–4, Concluded

PETTY CASH BOOK

DATE	EXPLANATION	VO. NO.	RECEIPTS	PAYMENTS	DISTRIBUTION OF PAYMENTS				
					KITCHEN EXPENSE	MAINT. EXPENSE	OFFICE EXPENSE	OTHER ITEMS	
								ITEM	AMOUNT

(This page is without text copy.)

Name ______________________________

Score ____________

Sample Problem 1, page 267

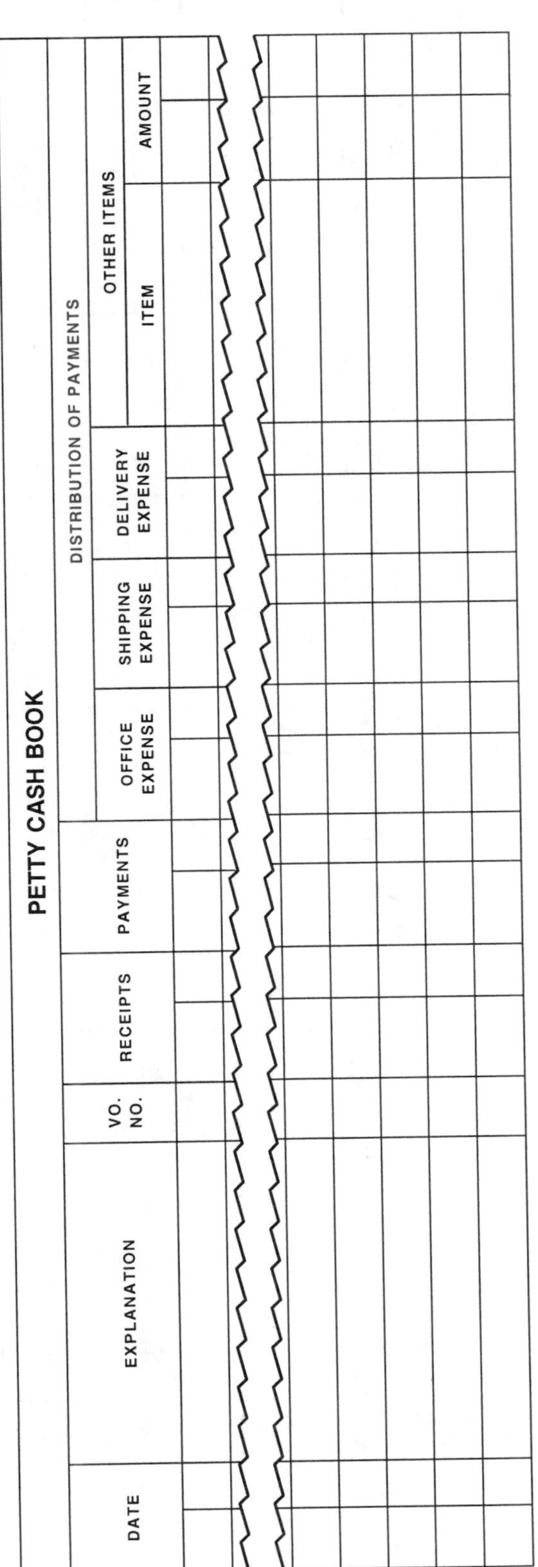

PETTY CASH BOOK

DATE	EXPLANATION	VO. NO.	RECEIPTS	PAYMENTS	DISTRIBUTION OF PAYMENTS				
					OFFICE EXPENSE	SHIPPING EXPENSE	DELIVERY EXPENSE	OTHER ITEMS	
								ITEM	AMOUNT

Sample Problem 2A (Cash Shortage), page 268

PETTY CASH BOOK

DATE	EXPLANATION	VO. NO.	RECEIPTS	PAYMENTS	DISTRIBUTION OF PAYMENTS				
					OFFICE EXPENSE	SHIPPING EXPENSE	DELIVERY EXPENSE	OTHER ITEMS	
								ITEM	AMOUNT

Sample Problem 2B (Cash Overage), page 269

PETTY CASH BOOK

DATE	EXPLANATION	VO. NO.	RECEIPTS	PAYMENTS	DISTRIBUTION OF PAYMENTS				
					OFFICE EXPENSE	SHIPPING EXPENSE	DELIVERY EXPENSE	OTHER ITEMS	
								ITEM	AMOUNT

Name ______________________________

Problem 34–1, page 272

	Original balance	Balance, petty cash book	Currency in box	(Shortage) Overage	Corrected balance	Amount to replenish
a.	$100.00	$ 5.00	$ 5.00	—0—	$ 5.00	$ 95.00
b.	$150.00	$ 7.00	$ 6.00	($1.00)	$ 6.00	$144.00
c.	$200.00	$19.00	$19.00	________	________	________
d.	$150.00	$17.50	$15.50	________	________	________
e.	$ 50.00	$ 9.50	$12.50	________	________	________
f.	$ 75.00	$15.75	$17.95	________	________	________
g.	$125.00	$42.60	$42.60	________	________	________
h.	$250.00	$37.25	$36.95	________	________	________
i.	$175.00	$41.18	$40.98	________	________	________
j.	$100.00	$56.19	$57.22	________	________	________

Problem 34–2, page 272

PETTY CASH BOOK

DATE	EXPLANATION	VO. NO.	RECEIPTS	PAYMENTS	DISTRIBUTION OF PAYMENTS				
					OFFICE EXPENSE	DELIVERY EXPENSE	SHIPPING EXPENSE	OTHER ITEMS	
								ITEM	AMOUNT

Name ______________________________

Problem 34–2, Concluded

PETTY CASH BOOK

DATE	EXPLANATION	VO. NO.	RECEIPTS	PAYMENTS	DISTRIBUTION OF PAYMENTS				
					OFFICE EXPENSE	DELIVERY EXPENSE	SHIPPING EXPENSE	OTHER ITEMS	
								ITEM	AMOUNT

Problem 34–3

You are the petty cash clerk for Nichols' Sports Shop. On June 1, your employer starts the petty cash fund by cashing Check No. 1104 for $175.00. Each payment from the fund is classified as office expense, delivery expense, telephone expense, or general expense.

Directions

a. Prepare a petty cash book with special column headings for Office Expense, Delivery Expense, and Telephone Expense.

b. Record the opening balance.

c. Record the following vouchers issued in June:

Voucher Number	Date	Paid For	Amount
1	June 3	Office supplies	$12.74
2	7	Gas for truck	18.50
3	10	Sales rep phone calls	11.96
4	12	Floor cleaning	15.00
5	14	Truck repairs	35.00
6	19	Repair broken window	20.00
7	25	Sales rep phone calls	19.03
8	30	Stamps	10.00

d. Rule and foot the amount columns.

e. Check the totals by crossfooting.

f. Record the final totals and double rule the amount columns.

g. Find the new balance and enter it as of July 1.

h. Begin a new page of the petty cash book for July and enter the new balance.

i. A count of currency in the box adds to $31.27. Calculate and record any cash shortage or overage and find, if necessary, the corrected balance.

j. Your employer cashes Check No. 1277 to replenish the fund. Calculate the amount of this check and record it in the petty cash book.

k. Record the following vouchers issued in July:

Voucher Number	Date	Paid For	Amount
9	July 3	Gas for truck	$21.10
10	7	Sales rep phone calls	12.87
11	12	Stationery	25.10
12	17	New tire	42.50
13	21	File folders	15.00
14	26	Cab fare for deliveries	6.50
15	29	Sales rep phone calls	13.09
16	31	Flowers	15.00

l. Rule and foot the amount columns.

m. Check your totals by crossfooting.

n. Record the final totals and double rule the amount columns.

o. Find the new balance and enter it as of August 1.

Name ______________________________

Problem 34–3, Continued

PETTY CASH BOOK

DATE		EXPLANATION	VO. NO.	RECEIPTS	PAYMENTS	DISTRIBUTION OF PAYMENTS				
						OFFICE EXPENSE	DELIVERY EXPENSE	TELEPHONE EXPENSE	OTHER ITEMS	
									ITEM	AMOUNT

Problem 34–3, Concluded

PETTY CASH BOOK

DATE	EXPLANATION	VO. NO.	RECEIPTS	PAYMENTS	DISTRIBUTION OF PAYMENTS				
					OFFICE EXPENSE	DELIVERY EXPENSE	TELEPHONE EXPENSE	OTHER ITEMS	
								ITEM	AMOUNT

i.

j.

Name ___________________________

Problem 34–4

You are the petty cash clerk for Inground Pool Company. On May 1, your employer starts the petty cash fund by cashing Check No. 610 for $150.00. Each payment from the fund is classified as pool expense, office expense, delivery expense, or general expense.

Directions

a. Prepare a petty cash book with special column headings for Pool Expense, Office Expense, and Delivery Expense.

b. Record the opening balance.

c. Record the following vouchers issued in May:

Voucher Number	Date	Paid For	Amount
1	May 2	Pool supplies	$14.75
2	8	Office stationery	12.90
3	12	Pool cleaning	35.00
4	15	Gas for van	12.65
5	17	Office cleaning	15.00
6	22	Pool filters	25.00
7	27	Stamps	5.00
8	31	Repairs to van	25.00

d. Rule and foot the amount columns.

e. Check your totals by crossfooting.

f. Record the final totals and double rule the amount columns.

g. Find the new balance and enter it as of June 1.

h. Begin a new page of the petty cash book for June and enter the new balance.

i. A count of currency in the box adds to $6.70. Calculate and record any cash shortage or overage and find, if necessary, the corrected balance.

j. Your employer issues Check No. 701 to replenish the fund. Calculate the amount of this check and record it in the petty cash book.

k. Record the following vouchers issued in June:

Voucher Number	Date	Paid For	Amount
9	June 4	Gas for van	$16.10
10	8	Pool supplies	17.95
11	10	Office file folders	8.75
12	14	Broken window in van	15.00
13	17	Coffee filters	5.50
14	21	Cab fare for deliveries	4.85
15	26	Sales rep phone calls	12.65
16	30	Pool cleaning	35.00

l. Rule and foot the amount columns.

m. Check your totals by crossfooting.

n. Record the final totals and double rule the amount columns.

o. Find the new balance and enter it as of July 1.

Problem 34–4, Continued

PETTY CASH BOOK

DATE	EXPLANATION	VO. NO.	RECEIPTS	PAYMENTS	DISTRIBUTION OF PAYMENTS				
					POOL EXPENSE	OFFICE EXPENSE	DELIVERY EXPENSE	OTHER ITEMS	
								ITEM	AMOUNT

Name ______________________________

Problem 34–4, Concluded

PETTY CASH BOOK

DATE		EXPLANATION	VO. NO.	RECEIPTS	PAYMENTS	DISTRIBUTION OF PAYMENTS				
						POOL EXPENSE	OFFICE EXPENSE	DELIVERY EXPENSE	OTHER ITEMS	
									ITEM	AMOUNT

i.

j.

(This page is without text copy.)

Name ______________________

Score __________

Reinforcement Activities

CHAPTER 6
Jobs 31–34

Check Your Reading, page 274

1. ______________________

2. ______________________

3. a. ______________________

3. b. ______________________

Discussion, page 274

____

Critical Thinking, page 274

Factors to consider before buying a car:

____

Five most important factors:

____

Communication in the Workplace, page 275

Focus on Careers, page 275

1.

2.

3.

Global Business: International Mail Activity, page 275

You have a 10-ounce document to mail to a foreign country. Select a country and contact your local post office or another delivery service to obtain the following information for your document:

1. What is the cost per ounce under each category of mail, including any special delivery services?

2. What is the usual delivery time under each category of mail?

Reviewing What You Have Learned, page 276

1.
2.
3.
4.
5.
6.
7.
8.
9.

Name ______________________________

Mastery Problem, page 276

PETTY CASH VOUCHER

No. ______
Date ______________ 20__

$	¢

Pay to ______________________________

For ______________________________

Approved by ______________________

Payment Received ______________________

PETTY CASH VOUCHER

No. ______
Date ______________ 20__

$	¢

Pay to ______________________________

For ______________________________

Approved by ______________________

Payment Received ______________________

PETTY CASH VOUCHER

No. ______
Date ______________ 20__

$	¢

Pay to ______________________________

For ______________________________

Approved by ______________________

Payment Received ______________________

Mastery Problem, Continued

PETTY CASH VOUCHER

No. ______

Date ______________ 20__

Pay to ______________________ | $ | ¢ |

For ______________________

Approved by ______________ Payment Received ______________

PETTY CASH VOUCHER

No. ______

Date ______________ 20__

Pay to ______________________ | $ | ¢ |

For ______________________

Approved by ______________ Payment Received ______________

PETTY CASH VOUCHER

No. ______

Date ______________ 20__

Pay to ______________________ | $ | ¢ |

For ______________________

Approved by ______________ Payment Received ______________

Name ______________________________

Mastery Problem, Continued

PETTY CASH VOUCHER

No. ______

Date ______________ 20__

$	¢

Pay to ______________________________

For ______________________________

Approved by ______________________

Payment Received ______________________

PETTY CASH VOUCHER

No. ______

Date ______________ 20__

$	¢

Pay to ______________________________

For ______________________________

Approved by ______________________

Payment Received ______________________

Mastery Problem, Continued

PETTY CASH BOOK

DATE	EXPLANATION	VO. NO.	RECEIPTS	PAYMENTS	DISTRIBUTION OF PAYMENTS				
					OFFICE EXPENSE	GENERAL EXPENSE	SHIPPING EXPENSE	OTHER ITEMS	
								ITEM	AMOUNT

Mastery Problem, Concluded

PETTY CASH BOOK

DATE	EXPLANATION	VO. NO.	RECEIPTS	PAYMENTS	DISTRIBUTION OF PAYMENTS				
					OFFICE EXPENSE	GENERAL EXPENSE	SHIPPING EXPENSE	OTHER ITEMS	
								ITEM	AMOUNT

j.

k.

Reviewing Your Business Vocabulary

Choose the words that match the statements. Write each word you choose next to the statement it matches. All words will be used.

Statements

1. Currency set aside for making small cash payments . . . . . ________
2. A column in a petty cash book for a specific expense . . . . ________
3. Small . . . . ________
4. A storage box for petty cash . . . . ________
5. Entered again in a second column . . . . ________
6. A person who keeps records of petty cash . . . . ________
7. When actual currency is less than the balance in the petty cash book . . . . ________
8. Add an amount to the petty cash fund to bring it back to its original balance . . . . ________
9. A record of payment from the petty cash fund . . . . ________
10. A form used to record and classify petty cash receipts and payments . . . . ________
11. When actual currency is more than the balance in the petty cash book . . . . ________
12. Bills and coins . . . . ________
13. Types of business expenses . . . . ________

Words

cash overage	extended	petty cash box	petty cash voucher
cash shortage	petty	petty cash clerk	replenish the fund
classifications	petty cash book	petty cash fund	special column
currency			

Name ______________________________

Score ____________

Comprehensive Project 2

CHAPTERS 4–6

You are a clerk for Midway Delivery Service. Your job is to collect cash from the delivery person on each route, deposit it in the bank, keep the checkbook, and maintain the petty cash records.

Phase 1: Collecting and Depositing Cash

During the week of March 1–5, 20--, you make the following collections from your delivery people:

	Route	**Delivery Person**	**Amount**
Monday, March 1	101	Louis Acre	$210.85
	103	Jeanne Molloy	147.30
	107	Roger Wilson	318.99
	109	Carl Holliday	504.12
Tuesday, March 2	102	Bea Lund	$601.19
	104	Carmen Ortiz	347.12
	105	Sean Walsh	508.16
	106	Millie Davis	195.08
	107	Roger Wilson	256.19
	108	Henry Dodge	155.17
	109	Carl Holliday	306.08
Wednesday, March 3	101	Louis Acre	$104.12
	102	Bea Lund	316.36
	103	Jeanne Molloy	127.00
	104	Carmen Ortiz	430.19
	106	Millie Davis	271.12
	107	Roger Wilson	649.21
	108	Henry Dodge	258.44
Thursday, March 4	101	Louis Acre	161.56
	102	Bea Lund	904.18
	103	Jeanne Molloy	872.67
	105	Sean Walsh	292.99
	106	Millie Davis	483.32
	107	Roger Wilson	208.11
	108	Henry Dodge	512.27
Friday, March 5	102	Bea Lund	$890.63
	103	Jeanne Molloy	109.44
	104	Carmen Ortiz	758.92
	105	Sean Walsh	614.41
	107	Roger Wilson	225.57
	108	Henry Dodge	436.63
	109	Carl Holliday	347.77

Directions

a. Write a receipt for each collection on March 1. Sign your name as cashier. Number your receipts beginning with 101.

b. Record the receipts from March 1 in the record of cashier's collections. Write in your name as cashier.

c. Record the receipts from March 2–5 in the record of cashier's collections. You do not have to write receipts for these dates.

d. Complete the record of cashier's collections by totaling and crossfooting.

Comprehensive Project 2, Continued

No. ____	**Midway Delivery Service**
Date: ____	No. ____
Received from: ____	Date: ____ 20__
____	Received from: ____ $ ____
Route: ____	____ Dollars
Amount: $ ____	Route: ____ For: ____
	____ Cashier

No. ____	**Midway Delivery Service**
Date: ____	No. ____
Received from: ____	Date: ____ 20__
____	Received from: ____ $ ____
Route: ____	____ Dollars
Amount: $ ____	Route: ____ For: ____
	____ Cashier

No. ____	**Midway Delivery Service**
Date: ____	No. ____
Received from: ____	Date: ____ 20__
____	Received from: ____ $ ____
Route: ____	____ Dollars
Amount: $ ____	Route: ____ For: ____
	____ Cashier

No. ____	**Midway Delivery Service**
Date: ____	No. ____
Received from: ____	Date: ____ 20__
____	Received from: ____ $ ____
Route: ____	____ Dollars
Amount: $ ____	Route: ____ For: ____
	____ Cashier

Comprehensive Project 2, Continued

MIDWAY DELIVERY SERVICE

Record of Cashier's Collections

Cashier ______________________________ Week of ______________ 20 __

Route	Employee	Monday		Tuesday		Wednesday		Thursday		Friday		Totals	

e. You count the following cash at the end of the week.

Quantity	Denomination
68	$50 bills
351	$20 bills
145	$10 bills
83	$ 5 bills
159	$ 1 bills
57	$0.50 coins
139	$0.25 coins
137	$0.10 coins
70	$0.05 coins
71	$0.01 coins

Prepare a tally sheet. Your total should match the grand total of the record of cashier's collections, if you have done your work correctly.

f. Prepare a deposit slip on March 5, 20--, for the bills and coins listed on the tally sheet. Your company uses two different banks. This deposit is made at the Home National Bank.

Comprehensive Project 2, Continued

No.	TALLY SHEET Date ______ 20--	
No.	**Bills**	
	Packages of $100 bills × $10,000.00	
	Loose $100 bills	
	Packages of $50 bills × $5,000.00	
	Loose $50 bills	
	Packages of $20 bills × $2,000.00	
	Loose $20 bills	
	Packages of $10 bills × $1,000.00	
	Loose $10 bills	
	Packages of $5 bills × $500.00	
	Loose $5 bills	
	Packages of $1 bills × $100.00	
	Loose $1 bills	
	Total bills to be deposited	
No.	**Coins**	
	Rolls of half-dollars × $10.00	
	Loose half-dollars	
	Rolls of quarters × $10.00	
	Loose quarters	
	Rolls of dimes × $5.00	
	Loose dimes	
	Rolls of nickels × $2.00	
	Loose nickels	
	Rolls of pennies × $0.50	
	Loose pennies	
	Total coins to be deposited	
	Total cash to be deposited	

For DEPOSIT to the Account of

MIDWAY DELIVERY SERVICE
29 RAMSEY STREET
BALTIMORE, MD 21230-5782

DATE ______________ 20____

HOME National Bank
Baltimore, Maryland

Subject to the Terms and Conditions of this Bank's Collection Agreement

⑆1477208161⑆ 353⑈1701⑈

5-19/1477

	Dollars	Cents
BILLS		
COINS		
Checks as Follows Properly Endorsed		
TOTAL DEPOSIT		

Comprehensive Project 2, Continued

Phase 2: Keeping the Checkbook

Directions

a. Enter a balance brought forward of $4,776.13 on Check Stub No. 416.

b. Record the March 5 deposit from step (f) of Phase 1 on Check Stub No. 416. Find the total.

c. Record the following checks and deposits during March on your check stubs. Write the checks. You are authorized to sign the checks.

March	9	Wrote Check No. 416 for $965.00 to Parsons Realty for office rent.
	15	Wrote Check No. 417 for $3,500.00 to Payroll for delivery salaries.
	16	Wrote Check No. 418 for $4,700.00 to Taylor Autos for down payment on a truck.
	19	Made a deposit of $11,146.18. (It is not necessary to write the deposit slip.)
	24	Wrote Check No. 419 for $215.99 to Eastern Power Company for electric bill.
	28	Wrote Check No. 420 for $147.95 to Carson Office Supply Company for office supplies.
	31	Deposited checks received of $975.00.
	31	Wrote Check No. 421 for $1,475.80 to Maxie's Uniforms for the drivers' uniforms. (Carry the balance forward to Check Stub No. 422.)

No. **416** $________
Date ________
To ________
____
For ________

	Dollars	Cents
Bal. Bro't. For'd.		
Amt. Deposited		
Total		
Amt. This Check		
Bal. Car'd. For'd.		

MIDWAY DELIVERY SERVICE
29 Ramsey Street
Baltimore, MD 21230-5782

No. **416**

Date ____________ 20___ 5-19/1477

PAY TO THE ORDER OF ____________ $________

For Classroom Use Only

____________ Dollars

HOME National Bank
47 Ramsey Street, Baltimore, MD 21230-5784 ____________

⑆147720816⑆ 35317016⑈

No. **417** $________
Date ________
To ________
____
For ________

	Dollars	Cents
Bal. Bro't. For'd.		
Amt. Deposited		
Total		
Amt. This Check		
Bal. Car'd. For'd.		

MIDWAY DELIVERY SERVICE
29 Ramsey Street
Baltimore, MD 21230-5782

No. **417**

Date ____________ 20___ 5-19/1477

PAY TO THE ORDER OF ____________ $________

For Classroom Use Only

____________ Dollars

HOME National Bank
47 Ramsey Street, Baltimore, MD 21230-5784 ____________

⑆147720816⑆ 35317016⑈

Comprehensive Project 2, Continued

No. **418** $ ____
Date ____
To ____
For ____

	Dollars	Cents
Bal. Bro't. For'd.		
Amt. Deposited		
Total		
Amt. This Check		
Bal. Car'd. For'd.		

MIDWAY DELIVERY SERVICE
29 Ramsey Street
Baltimore, MD 21230-5782

No. **418**

Date ____ 20__ 5-19/1477

PAY TO THE ORDER OF ____ $____

For Classroom Use Only

____ Dollars

HOME National Bank
47 Ramsey Street, Baltimore, MD 21230-5784

⑆147720816⑆ 3531701⑈

No. **419** $ ____
Date ____
To ____
For ____

	Dollars	Cents
Bal. Bro't. For'd.		
Amt. Deposited		
Total		
Amt. This Check		
Bal. Car'd. For'd.		

MIDWAY DELIVERY SERVICE
29 Ramsey Street
Baltimore, MD 21230-5782

No. **419**

Date ____ 20__ 5-19/1477

PAY TO THE ORDER OF ____ $____

For Classroom Use Only

____ Dollars

HOME National Bank
47 Ramsey Street, Baltimore, MD 21230-5784

⑆147720816⑆ 3531701⑈

No. **420** $ ____
Date ____
To ____
For ____

	Dollars	Cents
Bal. Bro't. For'd.		
Amt. Deposited		
Total		
Amt. This Check		
Bal. Car'd. For'd.		

MIDWAY DELIVERY SERVICE
29 Ramsey Street
Baltimore, MD 21230-5782

No. **420**

Date ____ 20__ 5-19/1477

PAY TO THE ORDER OF ____ $____

For Classroom Use Only

____ Dollars

HOME National Bank
47 Ramsey Street, Baltimore, MD 21230-5784

⑆147720816⑆ 3531701⑈

Comprehensive Project 2, Continued

No. 421	$
Date	
To	
For	

	Dollars	Cents
Bal. Bro't. For'd.		
Amt. Deposited		
Total		
Amt. This Check		
Bal. Car'd. For'd.		

MIDWAY DELIVERY SERVICE
29 Ramsey Street
Baltimore, MD 21230-5782

No. **421**

Date ______________ 20___ 5-19/1477

PAY TO THE ORDER OF ______________________ $________

For Classroom Use Only

______________________________________ Dollars

HOME National Bank
47 Ramsey Street, Baltimore, MD 21230-5784

⑆1477208161⑆ 3531701⑈

d. You receive the following bank statement as of March 31 from the Home National Bank. Prepare a bank reconciliation statement as of March 31. You must find the outstanding checks and the outstanding deposit by comparing your checkbook records with the bank statement. Be sure to include the interest earned and the service charge on your bank reconciliation statement.

HOME National Bank
47 Ramsey Street, Baltimore, MD 21230-5784

Account of:

Midway Delivery Service
29 Ramsey Street
Baltimore, MD 21230-5782

Account no.: ˙353-1701

Statement Date:	03/31/--
Beginning Balance:	4,776.13
Total Deposits/Credits:	23,745.84
Total Checks/Debits:	9,327.95
Ending Balance:	19,194.02

Date	Checks/Debits	Deposits/Credits	Balance
03/01/--			4,776.13
03/05/--		12,525.16	17,301.29
03/12/--	965.00		16,336.29
03/15/--	3,500.00		12,836.29
03/19/--		11,146.18	23,982.47
03/19/--	4,700.00		19,282.47
03/31/--	147.95		19,134.52
03/31/--	15.00 SERVICE CHARGE		19,119.52
03/31/--		74.50 INTEREST	19,194.02

Comprehensive Project 2, Continued

e. Adjust Check Stub No. 422 for the interest and the service charge.

No. **422** $ ______

Date ______

To ______

For ______

	Dollars	Cents
Bal. Bro't. For'd.		
Amt. Deposited		
Total		
Amt. This Check		
Bal. Car'd. For'd.		

Phase 3: Petty Cash Duties

It is now June 1. Your employer directs you to write Check No. 456 for $200 payable to Petty Cash to establish a petty cash fund. Each payment from the fund must be classified into either delivery expense, office expense, or general expense.

Directions

a. Prepare a petty cash voucher for each of the following payments from the fund. Approve each voucher with your own initials, but do not fill in the signature. Start with Voucher No. 1.

June 3 Paid $27.45 to Jeanne Molloy for delivery expenses.
6 Paid $19.50 to Carson Office Supply Company for office supplies.
12 Paid $4.85 to Carl Holliday for delivery expenses.
17 Paid $31.63 to Master Locks for a new office lock.
24 Paid $13.06 to Millie Davis for delivery expenses.
30 Paid $15.60 to Carson Office Supply Company for stationery.

Comprehensive Project 2, Continued

b. Record the opening balance in the petty cash book.

c. Record the vouchers issued in the petty cash book.

d. Rule and foot the amount columns of the petty cash book.

e. Check your totals by crossfooting.

f. Record the final totals and double rule the amount columns.

g. Find the new balance as of July 1 and enter it in the petty cash book.

h. Begin a new page in the petty cash book and enter the balance as of July 1.

i. A count of currency in the petty cash box shows $85.71. Calculate and enter any cash shortage or overage, and find, if necessary, the corrected balance.

j. Your employer directs you to cash Check No. 471 to replenish the fund. Calculate the amount of this check and record it in the petty cash book.

a.

PETTY CASH VOUCHER

No. ______

Date ______________ 20__

Pay to ______________________ | $ | ¢ |

For ______________________

Approved by ______________ Payment Received ______________

PETTY CASH VOUCHER

No. ______

Date ______________ 20__

Pay to ______________________ | $ | ¢ |

For ______________________

Approved by ______________ Payment Received ______________

Comprehensive Project 2, Continued

PETTY CASH VOUCHER

No. _______

Date _______________ 20__

Pay to _______________________________ | $ | ¢ |

For _______________________________

Approved by _______________

Payment Received _______________

PETTY CASH VOUCHER

No. _______

Date _______________ 20__

Pay to _______________________________ | $ | ¢ |

For _______________________________

Approved by _______________

Payment Received _______________

PETTY CASH VOUCHER

No. _______

Date _______________ 20__

Pay to _______________________________ | $ | ¢ |

For _______________________________

Approved by _______________

Payment Received _______________

Name ______________________

Comprehensive Project 2, Continued

PETTY CASH VOUCHER

No. ______

Date ______________ 20__

$	¢

Pay to ______________________

For ______________________

Approved by ______________________

Payment Received ______________________

b.–g.

PETTY CASH BOOK															
Date		Explanation	Vo. No.	Receipts		Payments		Distribution of Payments							
								Delivery Expense		Office Expense		Other Items			
												Item	Amount		

Comprehensive Project 2, Concluded

h.

PETTY CASH BOOK																
Date		Explanation	Vo. No.	Receipts		Payments		Distribution of Payments							
								Delivery Expense		Office Expense		Other Items		
												Item	Amount	

i.

j.

Name ____________________

Score __________

Sample Problem, page 282

BAYVIEW OFFICE MART
411 East Broadway Avenue
Tampa, FL 33605-5451
555-2245

NO. 6271

SOLD TO: ____________________ __________ 20__

STREET: ____________________

CITY, STATE, ZIP: ____________________

SOLD BY	CASH	CHARGE	COD	DELIVER BY

QUANTITY	DESCRIPTION	UNIT PRICE		AMOUNT	

This slip must accompany all returns

____
Customer signature for charge sales

Problem 35–1, page 286

Sales Slip #1

BAYVIEW OFFICE MART
411 East Broadway Avenue
Tampa, FL 33605-5451
555-2245

NO. 6283

SOLD TO: ______________________ ____________ 20__
STREET: ______________________
CITY, STATE, ZIP: ______________________

SOLD BY	CASH	CHARGE	COD	DELIVER BY

QUANTITY	DESCRIPTION	UNIT PRICE	AMOUNT

This slip must accompany all returns

____
Customer signature for charge sales

Sales Slip #2

BAYVIEW OFFICE MART
411 East Broadway Avenue
Tampa, FL 33605-5451
555-2245

NO. 6284

SOLD TO: ______________________ ____________ 20__
STREET: ______________________
CITY, STATE, ZIP: ______________________

SOLD BY	CASH	CHARGE	COD	DELIVER BY

QUANTITY	DESCRIPTION	UNIT PRICE	AMOUNT

This slip must accompany all returns

____
Customer signature for charge sales

Sales Slip #3

BAYVIEW OFFICE MART
411 East Broadway Avenue
Tampa, FL 33605-5451
555-2245

NO. 6285

SOLD TO: ______________________ ____________ 20__
STREET: ______________________
CITY, STATE, ZIP: ______________________

SOLD BY	CASH	CHARGE	COD	DELIVER BY

QUANTITY	DESCRIPTION	UNIT PRICE	AMOUNT

This slip must accompany all returns

____
Customer signature for charge sales

Sales Slip #4

BAYVIEW OFFICE MART
411 East Broadway Avenue
Tampa, FL 33605-5451
555-2245

NO. 6286

SOLD TO: ______________________ ____________ 20__
STREET: ______________________
CITY, STATE, ZIP: ______________________

SOLD BY	CASH	CHARGE	COD	DELIVER BY

QUANTITY	DESCRIPTION	UNIT PRICE	AMOUNT

This slip must accompany all returns

____
Customer signature for charge sales

Problem 35–1, Concluded

Sales Slip #5

BAYVIEW OFFICE MART
411 East Broadway Avenue
Tampa, FL 33605-5451
555-2245

NO. 6287

SOLD TO: ______________________ ____________ 20__

STREET: ______________________

CITY, STATE, ZIP: ______________________

SOLD BY	CASH	CHARGE	COD	DELIVER BY	
QUANTITY	DESCRIPTION	UNIT PRICE		AMOUNT	

This slip must accompany all returns

____
Customer signature for charge sales

Sales Slip #6

BAYVIEW OFFICE MART
411 East Broadway Avenue
Tampa, FL 33605-5451
555-2245

NO. 6288

SOLD TO: ______________________ ____________ 20__

STREET: ______________________

CITY, STATE, ZIP: ______________________

SOLD BY	CASH	CHARGE	COD	DELIVER BY	
QUANTITY	DESCRIPTION	UNIT PRICE		AMOUNT	

This slip must accompany all returns

____
Customer signature for charge sales

Sales Slip #7

BAYVIEW OFFICE MART
411 East Broadway Avenue
Tampa, FL 33605-5451
555-2245

NO. 6289

SOLD TO: ______________________ ____________ 20__

STREET: ______________________

CITY, STATE, ZIP: ______________________

SOLD BY	CASH	CHARGE	COD	DELIVER BY	
QUANTITY	DESCRIPTION	UNIT PRICE		AMOUNT	

This slip must accompany all returns

____
Customer signature for charge sales

Sales Slip #8

BAYVIEW OFFICE MART
411 East Broadway Avenue
Tampa, FL 33605-5451
555-2245

NO. 6290

SOLD TO: ______________________ ____________ 20__

STREET: ______________________

CITY, STATE, ZIP: ______________________

SOLD BY	CASH	CHARGE	COD	DELIVER BY	
QUANTITY	DESCRIPTION	UNIT PRICE		AMOUNT	

This slip must accompany all returns

____
Customer signature for charge sales

(This page is without text copy.)

Name ______________________

Score __________

Sample Problem, page 289

No. 786

13089 Franklin Road
Boise, ID 83709-5162
555-3939

SOLD TO: Brach Engineering April 12, 20--

STREET: 211B 1st Street, Apt. 24

CITY, STATE, ZIP: Boise, ID 83705-1928

SOLD BY 04	CASH ✓	CHECK	CHARGE	DELIVER BY

QUANTITY	DESCRIPTION	UNIT PRICE		AMOUNT	
3 ea.	Surge protectors	3	29	9	87
1 ea.	Two-button wheel mouse	24	88	24	88
	Amount of sale			34	75
	5% sales tax				
	Total				

Customer signature for charge sales ______________________

THIS SLIP MUST ACCOMPANY ALL RETURNS

Problem 36–1, page 292

No.	Amount of Sale		Amount of Sales Tax		Total	
1		40				
2		09				
3		42				
4		91				
5	3	64				
6	10	12				
7	4	53				
8	19	82				
9	20	30				
10	135	48				

Problem 36–2, page 292

No.	Amount of Sale		Amount of Sales Tax		Total	
1		75				
2		90				
3		07				
4	6	30				
5	5	27				
6	28	66				
7	47	99				
8	321	37				
9	405	44				
10	612	53				

Name ______________________

Problem 36–3, page 292

San Juan Bookstore — Cash and Carry Only
66 N. Pine Street
Spartanburg, SC 29302-7145 DATE Feb. 3, 20--

SOLD TO: Stacey Moynihan
STREET: 6892 North Street
CITY, STATE, ZIP: Spartanburg, SC 29301-8861

SOLD BY 06 | CASH ✓ | CHECK | DELIVER BY

QUANTITY	DESCRIPTION	AMOUNT
3	Book covers @ $0.79	
2	Dictionaries @ $20.49	
	Amount of sale	
	7% sales tax	
	Total	

No. 8041

San Juan Bookstore — Cash and Carry Only
66 N. Pine Street
Spartanburg, SC 29302-7145 DATE Feb. 3, 20--

SOLD TO: Tommy Prak
STREET: 2809 Oak Street
CITY, STATE, ZIP: Spartanburg, SC 29316-7201

SOLD BY 06 | CASH | CHECK ✓ | DELIVER BY

QUANTITY	DESCRIPTION	AMOUNT
1	Nonfiction @ $17.36	
3	Mystery paperbacks	
	@ $4.88	
	Amount of sale	
	7% sales tax	
	Total	

No. 8042

San Juan Bookstore — Cash and Carry Only
66 N. Pine Street
Spartanburg, SC 29302-7145 DATE Feb. 3, 20--

SOLD TO: Tamara Preston
STREET: 7280 Peachtree Road
CITY, STATE, ZIP: Spartanburg, SC 29302-0060

SOLD BY 06 | CASH ✓ | CHECK | DELIVER BY

QUANTITY	DESCRIPTION	AMOUNT
4	Book holders @ $6.99	
5	Leather bookmarks @ $3.08	
	Amount of sale	
	7% sales tax	
	Total	

No. 8043

San Juan Bookstore — Cash and Carry Only
66 N. Pine Street
Spartanburg, SC 29302-7145 DATE Feb. 3, 20--

SOLD TO: REI Industries
STREET: 919 Ranch Road
CITY, STATE, ZIP: Spartanburg, SC 29316-7848

SOLD BY 06 | CASH ✓ | CHECK | DELIVER BY

QUANTITY	DESCRIPTION	AMOUNT
2	Teen paperbacks @ $4.98	
1	Video cassette @ $10.99	
	Amount of sale	
	7% sales tax	
	Total	

No. 8044

Problem 36–4

You are a salesclerk for Bentley Enterprises, Inc.

Directions

Complete the following four sales slips. Find the sales tax by multiplying the amount of the sale by the sales tax rate of 6.5%.

Bentley Enterprises, Inc. — Cash and Carry Only
7740 Toll House Road
DATE June 21, 20--
SOLD TO: Mandy Williams
STREET: 8310 Estates Lane
CITY, STATE, ZIP: Granite City, IL 62040-8362

SOLD BY 3	CASH ✓	CHECK	DELIVER BY

QUANTITY	DESCRIPTION	AMOUNT
4	Dual cables @ $5.68	
6	Wire sets @ $3.78	
	Amount of sale	
	6.5% sales tax	
	Total	

No. 880

Bentley Enterprises, Inc. — Cash and Carry Only
7740 Toll House Road
DATE June 21, 20--
SOLD TO: Barry Vashon
STREET: 24 duBraul St.
CITY, STATE, ZIP: Granite City, IL 62040-2440

SOLD BY 3	CASH	CHECK ✓	DELIVER BY

QUANTITY	DESCRIPTION	AMOUNT
8	Cable taps @ $1.98	
15	Terminators @ $1.09	
	Amount of sale	
	6.5% sales tax	
	Total	

No. 881

Bentley Enterprises, Inc. — Cash and Carry Only
7740 Toll House Road
DATE June 21, 20--
SOLD TO: Coleen McCarty
STREET: 1007 Branching Avenue
CITY, STATE, ZIP: Granite City, IL 62040-1023

SOLD BY 3	CASH ✓	CHECK	DELIVER BY

QUANTITY	DESCRIPTION	AMOUNT
4	R15 connectors @ $2.28	
8	R30 connectors @ $3.16	
	Amount of sale	
	6.5% sales tax	
	Total	

No. 882

Bentley Enterprises, Inc. — Cash and Carry Only
7740 Toll House Road
DATE June 21, 20--
SOLD TO: Anna White
STREET: 14 Elders Lane
CITY, STATE, ZIP: Granite City, IL 62040-1459

SOLD BY 3	CASH ✓	CHECK	DELIVER BY

QUANTITY	DESCRIPTION	AMOUNT
16	V22 receptacles @ $0.23	
50	Plastic caps @ $0.89	
	Amount of sale	
	6.5% sales tax	
	Total	

No. 883

Name ______________________

Score __________

Sample Problem 1, page 294

Sterling VCR and Camcorder Repair
2023 Forbus Street
Poughkeepsie, NY 12603-4041

NO. **6247**

NAME: Kim Thorpe
ADDRESS: 428 Ferris Lane
Poughkeepsie, NY 12603-0052

MAKE	MODEL	SERIAL NO.	DATE
RCA	XR-96	2649118	4/18/--

DESCRIPTION	PARTS		LABOR	
Repair damaged video head	26	45	54	00
Replace switch	2	95	10	00
TOTALS	29	40	64	00
PARTS FORWARD →			29	40
SUBTOTAL			93	40
SALES TAX — 7%				
TOTAL BILL				

Sample Problem 2, page 295

Lexington Automotive — 20630 Franklin Street, Santa Clara, CA 95052-6021 — NO. **681**

NAME: Peter Johansen

ADDRESS: 3648 Sunlite Drive
Santa Clara, CA 95050-1011

YEAR	MAKE	LICENSE NO.	MILEAGE	DATE
2000	Toyota	3NJR 556	6,328	6/12/--

DESCRIPTION	PARTS		LABOR	
Replace thermostat	14	89	24	80
Rotate tires			15	90
Change oil	10	00	19	95
TOTALS	24	89	60	65
PARTS FORWARD →			24	89
SUBTOTAL			85	54
SALES TAX — 8.25% (ON PARTS ONLY)				
TOTAL BILL				

Problem 37–1, page 296

Bill No.	Labor		Parts		Total Labor and Parts (Subtotal)		Sales Tax		Final Total	
Example	20	00	6	20	26	20	1	57	27	77
1	6	30	32	10						
2	58	79	6	89						
3	103	42	46	70						
4	212	36	83	45						
5	421	71	108	38						

Name ______________________________

Problem 37–2, page 297

Bill #1

Gibraltar Auto Repair
1701 Main Street
Poughkeepsie, NY 12601-7280

NO. 00201

NAME: Yoshihiro Ihara
ADDRESS: 470 Innis Avenue
Poughkeepsie, NY 12603-1560

YEAR	MAKE	LICENSE NO.	MILEAGE	DATE
1999	Dodge Viper	OSR-736	20,752	10/21/--

DESCRIPTION	PARTS		LABOR	
20,000 mile checkup			70	00
Replace front brake pads	40	95	90	75
TOTALS				
PARTS FORWARD ⟶				
SUBTOTAL				
SALES TAX — 7%				
TOTAL BILL				

Bill #2

Gibraltar Auto Repair
1701 Main Street
Poughkeepsie, NY 12601-7280

NO. 00202

NAME: Christine Campoy
ADDRESS: 27086 Gifford Avenue
Poughkeepsie, NY 12601-2243

YEAR	MAKE	LICENSE NO.	MILEAGE	DATE
1998	Chevrolet	MNX-824	41,260	10/21/--

DESCRIPTION	PARTS		LABOR	
Replace radiator hose	19	99	31	50
Repair air conditioner	62	39	76	00
TOTALS				
PARTS FORWARD ⟶				
SUBTOTAL				
SALES TAX — 7%				
TOTAL BILL				

Problem 37–2, Concluded

Bill #3

Gibraltar Auto Repair
1701 Main Street
Poughkeepsie, NY 12601-7280

NO. 00203

NAME: Kevin McGuire
ADDRESS: 36805 Poplar Street
Poughkeepsie, NY 12601-2032

YEAR	MAKE	LICENSE NO.	MILEAGE	DATE
2000	Saturn	NXL-829	12,311	10/21/--

DESCRIPTION	PARTS		LABOR	
Change oil and oil filter	16	90	19	00
Replace defective water pump	61	49	65	00
TOTALS				
PARTS FORWARD →				
SUBTOTAL				
SALES TAX — 7%				
TOTAL BILL				

Bill #4

Gibraltar Auto Repair
1701 Main Street
Poughkeepsie, NY 12601-7280

NO. 00204

NAME: Erin Foglia
ADDRESS: 9847 Montgomery Street
Poughkeepsie, NY 12601-3161

YEAR	MAKE	LICENSE NO.	MILEAGE	DATE
1968	Ford Mustang	AYE-741	147,211	10/21/--

DESCRIPTION	PARTS		LABOR	
Replace belts	41	66	52	50
Service transmission	29	00	46	00
TOTALS				
PARTS FORWARD →				
SUBTOTAL				
SALES TAX — 7%				
TOTAL BILL				

Name ______________________________

Problem 37–3, page 298

Bill #1

Cheswick Small Engine and Appliance Repair
3982 South Naper Blvd.
Naperville, IL 60565

NO. 7542

NAME Karen Hoffman
ADDRESS 2136 N. Loomis St.
Naperville, IL 60563-5101

APPLIANCE Floor waxer/polisher
DATE April 12, 20--

DESCRIPTION	PARTS		LABOR	
Repair floor waxer/polisher			19	25
Replace wax container	10	50	5	50
TOTALS				
PARTS FORWARD ⟶				
SUBTOTAL				
SALES TAX — 6.5%—on parts only				
TOTAL BILL				

Bill #2

Cheswick Small Engine and Appliance Repair
3982 South Naper Blvd.
Naperville, IL 60565

NO. 7543

NAME William Proteau
ADDRESS 4370 N. Mill Street
Naperville, IL 60563-2148

APPLIANCE Snow blower
DATE April 12, 20--

DESCRIPTION	PARTS		LABOR	
Replace rotor	16	29	20	55
Replace chain	18	98	7	00
TOTALS				
PARTS FORWARD ⟶				
SUBTOTAL				
SALES TAX — 6.5%—on parts only				
TOTAL BILL				

Problem 37–3, Concluded

Bill #3

Cheswick Small Engine and Appliance Repair
3982 South Naper Blvd.
Naperville, IL 60565

NO. 7544

NAME Selby McDade
ADDRESS 5081 Olympus Drive
Naperville, IL 60565-3001

APPLIANCE Log splitter
DATE April 12, 20--

DESCRIPTION	PARTS		LABOR	
Tune up	21	66	28	60
Replace wheel	8	79	6	95
TOTALS				
PARTS FORWARD →				
SUBTOTAL				
SALES TAX — 6.5%—on parts only				
TOTAL BILL				

Bill #4

Cheswick Small Engine and Appliance Repair
3982 South Naper Blvd.
Naperville, IL 60565

NO. 7545

NAME Eric Hicklin
ADDRESS 3791 Ogden Avenue
Naperville, IL 60540-6843

APPLIANCE Chain saw
DATE April 12, 20--

DESCRIPTION	PARTS		LABOR	
Replace blade	9	49	7	25
Clean fuel system	10	60	9	60
TOTALS				
PARTS FORWARD →				
SUBTOTAL				
SALES TAX — 6.5%—on parts only				
TOTAL BILL				

Name ____________________

Score __________

Sample Problem 1, page 300

Shop Fair Department Store
89 West Street
Reno, NV 89501-7311

0019634

Date: __________
20 __

A-724-6118

SOLD TO: JESSICA VARGAS

STREET: ____________________

CITY, STATE, ZIP: ____________________

SOLD BY	CASH	CHECK	CHARGE

QUANTITY	DESCRIPTION	AMOUNT	

THIS SLIP MUST ACCOMPANY ALL RETURNS

____

Sample Problem 2, page 301

ACCOUNT NUMBER
7417 4611 8263 8809

6/99 6/03

NICK BARRETT

0897125
DALEY FURNITURE MART
1733 N. FLINTWOOD ROAD
PARKER, CO 80134-7201

SALE AMOUNT

INVOICE NUMBER
760021

DATE	AUTHORIZATION NO.	SALES CLERK	DEPT.

QUAN.	DESCRIPTION	PRICE	AMOUNT	
SIGN HERE X		SUBTOTAL		
		SALES TAX		
SALES SLIP		TOTAL		

VISA OR MasterCard

MERCHANT COPY

MERCHANT: RETAIN THIS COPY FOR YOUR RECORDS

Problem 38–1, page 304

a.

Sale #1

BECK'S AUTOMOTIVE
99 Statler Street
Tacoma, WA 98409-2298

NO. 11260

132 9783

ELLEN FRATZKE
Sold To ____________ ________ 20__

Street ____________

City, State, ZIP ____________

Sold By	Cash	Charge	
Quantity	Description	Amount	

This slip must accompany all returns

____
Customer's Signature for charge sales

Sale #2

BECK'S AUTOMOTIVE
99 Statler Street
Tacoma, WA 98409-2298

NO. 11261

189 0192

BRAD VOGLE
Sold To ____________ ________ 20__

Street ____________

City, State, ZIP ____________

Sold By	Cash	Charge	
Quantity	Description	Amount	

This slip must accompany all returns

____
Customer's Signature for charge sales

Sale #3

BECK'S AUTOMOTIVE
99 Statler Street
Tacoma, WA 98409-2298

NO. 11262

101 9703

JULIE TIERNEY
Sold To ____________ ________ 20__

Street ____________

City, State, ZIP ____________

Sold By	Cash	Charge	
Quantity	Description	Amount	

This slip must accompany all returns

____
Customer's Signature for charge sales

Sale #4

BECK'S AUTOMOTIVE
99 Statler Street
Tacoma, WA 98409-2298

NO. 11263

074 2276

BRIAN ZANELLA
Sold To ____________ ________ 20__

Street ____________

City, State, ZIP ____________

Sold By	Cash	Charge	
Quantity	Description	Amount	

This slip must accompany all returns

____
Customer's Signature for charge sales

b. ____

Name ______________________________

Problem 38–2, page 304

Sale #1

ACCOUNT NUMBER
4044 1978 6022 1967

7/99 7/03

NAVID VAHIDI

1778439
GOLFPRO STORE
88 LAKEVIEW DR.
MORGAN HILL, CA 95037-6131

SALE AMOUNT

INVOICE NUMBER
8647

DATE	AUTHORIZATION NO.	SALES CLERK	DEPT.

QUAN.	DESCRIPTION	PRICE	AMOUNT	
SIGN HERE X		SUBTOTAL		
		SALES TAX		
SALES SLIP		TOTAL		

VISA OR MasterCard

MERCHANT: RETAIN THIS COPY FOR YOUR RECORDS

MERCHANT COPY

Sale #2

ACCOUNT NUMBER
4048 6141 2544 9718

8/00 8/04

KAREN HYLAND

1778439
GOLFPRO STORE
88 LAKEVIEW DR.
MORGAN HILL, CA 95037-6131

SALE AMOUNT

INVOICE NUMBER
8648

DATE	AUTHORIZATION NO.	SALES CLERK	DEPT.

QUAN.	DESCRIPTION	PRICE	AMOUNT	
SIGN HERE X		SUBTOTAL		
		SALES TAX		
SALES SLIP		TOTAL		

VISA OR MasterCard

MERCHANT: RETAIN THIS COPY FOR YOUR RECORDS

MERCHANT COPY

Problem 38–2, Concluded

Sale #3

ACCOUNT NUMBER
8029 6622 6511 9899

SALE AMOUNT

INVOICE NUMBER
8649

7/99 7/03

DEAN FOREMAN

1778439
GOLFPRO STORE
88 LAKEVIEW DR.
MORGAN HILL, CA 95037-6131

DATE	AUTHORIZATION NO.	SALES CLERK	DEPT.

QUAN.	DESCRIPTION	PRICE	AMOUNT	
SIGN HERE X		SUBTOTAL		
		SALES TAX		
SALES SLIP		TOTAL		

MERCHANT COPY

MERCHANT: RETAIN THIS COPY FOR YOUR RECORDS

VISA OR MasterCard

Sale #4

ACCOUNT NUMBER
2170 3620 6541 1577

SALE AMOUNT

INVOICE NUMBER
8650

5/00 5/03

JAMIE CONWAY

1778439
GOLFPRO STORE
88 LAKEVIEW DR.
MORGAN HILL, CA 95037-6131

DATE	AUTHORIZATION NO.	SALES CLERK	DEPT.

QUAN.	DESCRIPTION	PRICE	AMOUNT	
SIGN HERE X		SUBTOTAL		
		SALES TAX		
SALES SLIP		TOTAL		

MERCHANT COPY

MERCHANT: RETAIN THIS COPY FOR YOUR RECORDS

VISA OR MasterCard

Name ____________________

Score __________

Sample Problem, page 307

ACCOUNT NUMBER
7768 4272 8616 0003

12/00 12/04

LEAH GOETZE

0798876
THE GREAT OUTDOORS
2507 YAKLE BLVD.
RUTLAND, VT 05701-1985

MERCHANT'S SIGNATURE X ____________________

CREDIT SLIP

CREDIT SLIP NUMBER
264371

DATE		CLERK	REG/DEPT

QUAN.	DESCRIPTION	UNIT PRICE	AMOUNT	
CUSTOMER'S SIGNATURE X		SUBTOTAL		
		SALES TAX		
SALES SLIP		TOTAL		

VISA OR MasterCard

MERCHANT: RETAIN THIS COPY FOR YOUR RECORDS

VISA — GREAT EASTERN BANK — MasterCard

Transaction Date	Reference	Transaction Description		New Loans, Fees, & Purchases	Payments & Credits
11/02/--	07139827	Summit Ski Lodge	Rutland, VT	35.89	
11/03/--	82647362	Boulevard Motors	Rutland, VT	138.95	
11/04/--	15243416	Payment -- Thank You			103.44
11/06/--	60798986	The Great Outdoors	Rutland, VT		47.61
11/11/--	10183928	Fifth Street Station	Rutland, VT	18.86	
11/17/--	38563847	Clermont TV	Rutland, VT	19.76	

Problem 39–1, page 309

Return #1

ACCOUNT NUMBER
4313 7261 8798 2983

3/99 3/04

AMANDA PRETROK

7184366
EDISON ELECTRIC, INC.
272A ALTAMONT RD.
EDISON, NJ 08817-2690

MERCHANT'S SIGNATURE X ____________________

CREDIT SLIP

CREDIT SLIP NUMBER
067217

DATE		CLERK	REG/DEPT

QUAN.	DESCRIPTION	UNIT PRICE	AMOUNT	
CUSTOMER'S SIGNATURE X		SUBTOTAL		
		SALES TAX		
SALES SLIP		TOTAL		

VISA OR MasterCard

MERCHANT: RETAIN THIS COPY FOR YOUR RECORDS

Return #2

ACCOUNT NUMBER
0071 7125 1837 3674

8/00 8/04

TIEN TUONG

7184366
EDISON ELECTRIC, INC.
272A ALTAMONT RD.
EDISON, NJ 08817-2690

MERCHANT'S SIGNATURE X ____________________

CREDIT SLIP

CREDIT SLIP NUMBER
067218

DATE		CLERK	REG/DEPT

QUAN.	DESCRIPTION	UNIT PRICE	AMOUNT	
CUSTOMER'S SIGNATURE X		SUBTOTAL		
		SALES TAX		
SALES SLIP		TOTAL		

VISA OR MasterCard

MERCHANT: RETAIN THIS COPY FOR YOUR RECORDS

Name ______________________________

Problem 39–1, Concluded

Return #3

ACCOUNT NUMBER
6299 2846 9785 6531

7/00 7/05

ROBERT WHELAN

7184366
EDISON ELECTRIC, INC.
272A ALTAMONT RD.
EDISON, NJ 08817-2690

MERCHANT'S SIGNATURE X ______________________

CREDIT SLIP

CREDIT SLIP NUMBER
067219

DATE		CLERK	REG/DEPT

QUAN.	DESCRIPTION	UNIT PRICE	AMOUNT	
CUSTOMER'S SIGNATURE X		SUBTOTAL		
		SALES TAX		
SALES SLIP		**TOTAL**		

VISA OR MasterCard

MERCHANT: RETAIN THIS COPY FOR YOUR RECORDS

Return #4

ACCOUNT NUMBER
7302 4040 4698 4274

2/99 2/03

MOSADDAR TURABI

7184366
EDISON ELECTRIC, INC.
272A ALTAMONT RD.
EDISON, NJ 08817-2690

MERCHANT'S SIGNATURE X ______________________

CREDIT SLIP

CREDIT SLIP NUMBER
067220

DATE		CLERK	REG/DEPT

QUAN.	DESCRIPTION	UNIT PRICE	AMOUNT	
CUSTOMER'S SIGNATURE X		SUBTOTAL		
		SALES TAX		
SALES SLIP		**TOTAL**		

VISA OR MasterCard

MERCHANT: RETAIN THIS COPY FOR YOUR RECORDS

Problem 39–2, page 309

Return #1

ACCOUNT NUMBER
1773 2981 1816 0899

8/99 8/04

CLARE O'BRIEN

4189226
BAYSIDE GIFT SHOP
12400 TURN POINT ROAD
FRIDAY HARBOR, WA 98250-0600

CREDIT SLIP

CREDIT SLIP NUMBER
867153

DATE		CLERK	REG/DEPT

QUAN.	DESCRIPTION	UNIT PRICE	AMOUNT	
CUSTOMER'S SIGNATURE X		SUBTOTAL		
		SALES TAX		
SALES SLIP		**TOTAL**		

MERCHANT'S SIGNATURE **X** ____________________

MERCHANT: RETAIN THIS COPY FOR YOUR RECORDS

VISA OR MasterCard

Return #2

ACCOUNT NUMBER
3711 4980 7163 1432

5/00 5/05

ROBERT LAFRANCE

4189226
BAYSIDE GIFT SHOP
12400 TURN POINT ROAD
FRIDAY HARBOR, WA 98250-0600

CREDIT SLIP

CREDIT SLIP NUMBER
867154

DATE		CLERK	REG/DEPT

QUAN.	DESCRIPTION	UNIT PRICE	AMOUNT	
CUSTOMER'S SIGNATURE X		SUBTOTAL		
		SALES TAX		
SALES SLIP		**TOTAL**		

MERCHANT'S SIGNATURE **X** ____________________

MERCHANT: RETAIN THIS COPY FOR YOUR RECORDS

VISA OR MasterCard

Name ______________________________

Problem 39–2, Concluded

Return #3

ACCOUNT NUMBER
6230 5340 1655 9184

3/00 3/04

JOHN MCHUGH

4189226
BAYSIDE GIFT SHOP
12400 TURN POINT ROAD
FRIDAY HARBOR, WA 98250-0600

MERCHANT'S SIGNATURE X ______________

CREDIT SLIP

CREDIT SLIP NUMBER
867155

DATE		CLERK	REG/DEPT

QUAN.	DESCRIPTION	UNIT PRICE	AMOUNT	
CUSTOMER'S SIGNATURE X		SUBTOTAL		
		SALES TAX		
SALES SLIP		**TOTAL**		

VISA OR MasterCard

MERCHANT: RETAIN THIS COPY FOR YOUR RECORDS

Return #4

ACCOUNT NUMBER
9979 8648 6523 0019

10/99 10/03

MAGDY HUSSAR

4189226
BAYSIDE GIFT SHOP
12400 TURN POINT ROAD
FRIDAY HARBOR, WA 98250-0600

MERCHANT'S SIGNATURE X ______________

CREDIT SLIP

CREDIT SLIP NUMBER
867156

DATE		CLERK	REG/DEPT

QUAN.	DESCRIPTION	UNIT PRICE	AMOUNT	
CUSTOMER'S SIGNATURE X		SUBTOTAL		
		SALES TAX		
SALES SLIP		**TOTAL**		

VISA OR MasterCard

MERCHANT: RETAIN THIS COPY FOR YOUR RECORDS

(This page is without text copy.)

Name ______________________

Score __________

Reinforcement Activities

CHAPTER 7
Jobs 35–39

Check Your Reading, page 310

1. ______________________

2. ______________________

3. ______________________

4. ______________________

Discussion, page 310

1. ______________________

2. ______________________

3. a. ______________________

3. b. ______________________

3. c. ______________________

4. a. ______________________

4. b. ______________________

Critical Thinking, page 310

1. ______________________________

2. ______________________________

3. ______________________________

Communication in the Workplace, page 311

____

Focus on Careers, page 311

	Business or Place	Job Description
1.		
2.		
3.		
4.		
5.		

Reviewing What You Have Learned, page 312

1. ____________
2. ____________
3. ____________
4. ____________
5. ____________
6. ____________
7. ____________

Name ______________________________

Mastery Problem, page 312

Sale #1

HARTE'S ARTS AND CRAFTS STORE **NO. 12089**
1678 Vandalia Boulevard
Charleston, WV 25311-7918

__________ **20**

Sold To

Street

City, State, ZIP

Sold By	**Cash**	**Charge**	**C.O.D.**	**Deliver By**

Quantity	Description	Unit Price		Amount	

This slip must accompany all returns

Customer signature for charge sales

Sale #2

ACCOUNT NUMBER
4478 9924 0129 3627

8/99 8/03

SANDY CUMMINS

1089885
HARTE'S ARTS AND CRAFTS STORE
1678 VANDALIA BLVD.
CHARLESTON, WV 25311-7918

SALE AMOUNT

INVOICE NUMBER
445672

DATE	AUTHORIZATION NO.	SALES CLERK	REG/DEPT

QUAN.	DESCRIPTION	PRICE	AMOUNT	
SIGN HERE **X**		SUBTOTAL		
		SALES TAX		
SALES SLIP		**TOTAL**		

MERCHANT COPY

VISA OR MasterCard

MERCHANT: RETAIN THIS COPY FOR YOUR RECORDS

Mastery Problem, Concluded

Return #1

ACCOUNT NUMBER
2293 7612 6879 1029

9/99 9/02

GRAHAM DOUTHERD

1089885
HARTE'S ARTS AND CRAFTS STORE
1678 VANDALIA BLVD.
CHARLESTON, WV 25311-7918

MERCHANT'S SIGNATURE X ____________

CREDIT SLIP

CREDIT SLIP NUMBER
162576

DATE		CLERK	REG/DEPT

QUAN.	DESCRIPTION	UNIT PRICE	AMOUNT	
CUSTOMER'S SIGNATURE X		SUBTOTAL		
		SALES TAX		
SALES SLIP		**TOTAL**		

MERCHANT: RETAIN THIS COPY FOR YOUR RECORDS

VISA OR MasterCard

Name ______________________________

Reviewing Your Business Vocabulary

Choose the words that match the statements. Write each word you choose next to the statement number it matches. Be careful; some of the words listed should not be used.

Statements

1. A list of lost or stolen card numbers . . . . ______
2. About 500 sheets of paper . . . . ______
3. Sales made on credit . . . . ______
4. Twelve dozen . . . . ______
5. The price of each item . . . . ______
6. A sales slip used with bank credit cards . . . . ______
7. Three copies . . . . ______
8. A form used to return goods bought with a bank credit card . . . . ______
9. Questions or commands on a display screen . . . . ______
10. A scanner that reads bar codes on tags . . . . ______
11. A device that automatically checks credit cards . . . . ______
12. One hundred . . . . ______
13. One thousand . . . . ______
14. The last day on which a credit card can be used . . . . ______
15. Quantity times unit price . . . . ______
16. Store owners who sell directly to consumers . . . . ______
17. A mechanical device used to record sales . . . . ______
18. Percent of selling price collected by retailers for governments . . . . ______
19. A computer used to record sales . . . . ______

Words

authorization number	credit slip	POS terminal	sales tax
C	expiration date	prompts	triplicate
charge sales	extension	ream	unit price
credit card sales slip	gross	retailers	wand
credit card verification terminal	M	sales slip register	warning bulletin

(This page is without text copy.)

Name ______________________________

Score ______________

Sample Problem, page 317

NAME ______________________________ ACCOUNT NO. __________

ADDRESS ______________________________

DATE		ITEM	DEBIT	CREDIT	BALANCE

Problem 40–1, page 320

Account #1

NAME ______________________________ ACCOUNT NO. __________

ADDRESS ______________________________

DATE		ITEM	DEBIT	CREDIT	BALANCE

Problem 40–1, Continued

Account #2

NAME ACCOUNT NO.

ADDRESS

DATE		ITEM	DEBIT	CREDIT	BALANCE

Account #3

NAME ACCOUNT NO.

ADDRESS

DATE		ITEM	DEBIT	CREDIT	BALANCE

Account #4

NAME ACCOUNT NO.

ADDRESS

DATE		ITEM	DEBIT	CREDIT	BALANCE

Name ______________________________

Problem 40–1, Continued

Account #5

NAME ______________________________ ACCOUNT NO. ________

ADDRESS ______________________________

DATE		ITEM	DEBIT	CREDIT	BALANCE

Account #6

NAME ______________________________ ACCOUNT NO. ________

ADDRESS ______________________________

DATE		ITEM	DEBIT	CREDIT	BALANCE

Account #7

NAME ______________________________ ACCOUNT NO. ________

ADDRESS ______________________________

DATE		ITEM	DEBIT	CREDIT	BALANCE

Problem 40–1, Concluded

Account #8

NAME ACCOUNT NO.

ADDRESS

DATE		ITEM	DEBIT	CREDIT	BALANCE

Problem 40–2

You are an accounts receivable clerk for Grovers, a department store. Your job is to keep accounts for charge customers.

Directions

a. Open a three-column account for each charge customer.

b. Record in each customer account the charge sales made and the payments received.

c. Find the new balance after each debit or credit is recorded.

d. At the end of the month, foot the Debit and Credit columns of each account. Prove the balance of each account by subtracting the total credits from the total debits. Write your proofs in the Item column of the accounts.

Account #1

Customer's name: Sylvia Ruben
Address: 135 Cliffton Street, Oklahoma City, OK 73132-5511
Account number: 311

Sept.	2	Sold merchandise on credit to Sylvia Ruben for $162.00; invoice #216.
	6	Sold merchandise on credit to Sylvia Ruben for $276.30; invoice #248.
	18	Received a check from Sylvia Ruben for $350.00 in payment on account.
	24	Sold merchandise on credit to Sylvia Ruben for $185.80; invoice #428.
	30	Received a check from Sylvia Ruben for $274.10 in full payment of the account.

Name ______________________________

Problem 40–2, Continued

Account #2

Customer's name: Ivan Korolsky
Address: 37 Bryant Street, N., Oklahoma City, OK 73117-5511
Account number: 312

Sept.	5	Sold merchandise on credit to Ivan Korolsky for $165.00; invoice #242.
	8	Sold merchandise on credit to Ivan Korolsky for $438.25; invoice #263.
	12	Sold merchandise on credit to Ivan Korolsky for $263.75; invoice #325.
	25	Received a check from Ivan Korolsky for $603.25 in payment on account.
	30	Received a check from Ivan Korolsky for $263.75 in full payment of the account.

Account #3

Customer's name: Clara May
Address: 184 Cosby Drive, Oklahoma City, OK 73135-5511
Account number: 313

Sept.	2	Sold merchandise on credit to Clara May for $99.75; invoice #221.
	5	Sold merchandise on credit to Clara May for $125.00; invoice #239.
	12	Sold merchandise on credit to Clara May for $75.40; invoice #327.
	19	Sold merchandise on credit to Clara May for $95.75; invoice #395.
	27	Received a check from Clara May for $300.15 in payment on account.

Account #4

Customer's name: Vance Rieken
Address: 3135 Dorchester Drive, Oklahoma City, OK 73120-5511
Account number: 314

Sept.	1	Sold merchandise on credit to Vance Rieken for $176.85; invoice #201.
	6	Sold merchandise on credit to Vance Rieken for $98.90; invoice #251.
	8	Sold merchandise on credit to Vance Rieken for $68.30; invoice #271.
	19	Sold merchandise on credit to Vance Rieken for $74.00; invoice #397.
	28	Received a check from Vance Rieken for $350.00 in payment on account.

Account #5

Customer's name: Rita Vasquez
Address: 135 Carson Street, Oklahoma City, OK 73111-8561
Account number: 315

Sept.	4	Sold merchandise on credit to Rita Vasquez for $145.00; invoice #230.
	8	Sold merchandise on credit to Rita Vasquez for $156.30; invoice #272.
	14	Received a check from Rita Vasquez for $145.00 in payment on account.
	24	Sold merchandise on credit to Rita Vasquez for $258.10; invoice #431.
	30	Received a check from Rita Vasquez for $275.00 in payment on account.

Problem 40–2, Continued

Account #6

Customer's name: Herbert Ivany
Address: 275 Mardi Gras Street, Oklahoma City, OK 73112-9810
Account number: 316

Sept.	2	Sold merchandise on credit to Herbert Ivany for $250.00; invoice #218.
	6	Sold merchandise on credit to Herbert Ivany for $482.80; invoice #250.
	15	Sold merchandise on credit to Herbert Ivany for $174.95; invoice #357.
	22	Received a check from Herbert Ivany for $735.80 in payment on account.
	30	Received a check from Herbert Ivany for $150.00 in payment on account.

Account #7

Customer's name: Laura Times
Address: 214 Golf Drive, Oklahoma City, OK 73170-3511
Account number: 317

Sept.	8	Sold merchandise on credit to Laura Times for $295.55; invoice #284.
	14	Sold merchandise on credit to Laura Times for $92.00; invoice #346.
	19	Sold merchandise on credit to Laura Times for $125.40; invoice #396.
	25	Sold merchandise on credit to Laura Times for $245.85; invoice #462.
	29	Received a check from Laura Times for $758.80 in full payment of the account.

Account #8

Customer's name: Andrew Rey
Address: 407 Mueller Avenue, Oklahoma City, OK 73142-7483
Account number: 318

Sept.	8	Sold merchandise on credit to Andrew Rey for $146.85; invoice #292.
	10	Sold merchandise on credit to Andrew Rey for $57.80; invoice #311.
	18	Sold merchandise on credit to Andrew Rey for $62.30; invoice #389.
	27	Sold merchandise on credit to Andrew Rey for $85.70; invoice #783.
	30	Received a check from Andrew Rey for $265.00 in payment on account.

Name ______________________

Problem 40–2, Continued

Account #1

NAME ______________________ ACCOUNT NO. ________

ADDRESS ______________________

DATE		ITEM	DEBIT	CREDIT	BALANCE

Account #2

NAME ______________________ ACCOUNT NO. ________

ADDRESS ______________________

DATE		ITEM	DEBIT	CREDIT	BALANCE

Account #3

NAME ______________________ ACCOUNT NO. ________

ADDRESS ______________________

DATE		ITEM	DEBIT	CREDIT	BALANCE

Problem 40–2, Continued

Account #4

NAME ACCOUNT NO.

ADDRESS

DATE		ITEM	DEBIT	CREDIT	BALANCE

Account #5

NAME ACCOUNT NO.

ADDRESS

DATE		ITEM	DEBIT	CREDIT	BALANCE

Account #6

NAME ACCOUNT NO.

ADDRESS

DATE		ITEM	DEBIT	CREDIT	BALANCE

Name ______________________________

Problem 40–2, Concluded

Account #7

NAME ______________________________ ACCOUNT NO. __________

ADDRESS ______________________________

DATE		ITEM	DEBIT	CREDIT	BALANCE

Account #8

NAME ______________________________ ACCOUNT NO. __________

ADDRESS ______________________________

DATE		ITEM	DEBIT	CREDIT	BALANCE

(This page is without text copy.)

Name ______________________

Score ____________

Sample Problem, page 325

NAME ______________________ ACCOUNT NO. ______

ADDRESS ______________________

DATE		ITEM	DEBIT	CREDIT	BALANCE

Problem 41–1, page 327

Account #1

NAME ______________________ ACCOUNT NO. ______

ADDRESS ______________________

DATE		ITEM	DEBIT	CREDIT	BALANCE

Problem 41–1, Continued

Account #2

NAME ACCOUNT NO.

ADDRESS

DATE		ITEM	DEBIT	CREDIT	BALANCE

Account #3

NAME ACCOUNT NO.

ADDRESS

DATE		ITEM	DEBIT	CREDIT	BALANCE

Name ____________________

Problem 41–1, Continued

Account #4

NAME ____________________ ACCOUNT NO. ________

ADDRESS ____________________

DATE		ITEM	DEBIT	CREDIT	BALANCE

Account #5

NAME ____________________ ACCOUNT NO. ________

ADDRESS ____________________

DATE		ITEM	DEBIT	CREDIT	BALANCE

Problem 41–1, Continued

Account #6

NAME ACCOUNT NO.

ADDRESS

DATE		ITEM	DEBIT	CREDIT	BALANCE

Account #7

NAME ACCOUNT NO.

ADDRESS

DATE		ITEM	DEBIT	CREDIT	BALANCE

Name ______________________________

Problem 41–1, Concluded

Account #8

NAME ______________________________ ACCOUNT NO. ________

ADDRESS ______________________________

DATE		ITEM	DEBIT	CREDIT	BALANCE

Problem 41–2

You are an accounts receivable clerk for Beard's Department Store. Your job is to keep the accounts for charge customers.

Directions

a. Open a three-column account for each customer.

b. Record in each customer's account the charge sales made, the merchandise returned, and the payments received.

c. Find the new balance after each debit or credit is recorded.

d. At the end of the month, foot the Debit and Credit columns of each account. Prove the balance of each account by subtracting the total credits from the total debits. Write your proofs in the Item column of the accounts.

Account #1

Customer's name: Anton Marias
Address: 6129 Thomas Street, Memphis, TN 38127-2322
Account number: 3751

Jan.	3	Sold merchandise on credit to Anton Marias for $154.70; Inv. #782.
	17	Sold merchandise on credit to Anton Marias for $264.50; Inv. #1037.
	20	Issued Credit Memo #201 to Anton Marias for $36.75.
	21	Sold merchandise on credit to Anton Marias for $127.25; Inv. #1059.
	31	Received a check from Anton Marias for $509.70 in full payment of the account.

Problem 41–2, Continued

Account #2

Customer's name: Valerie Beck
Address: 1262 Princeton Avenue, Memphis, TN 38117-2276
Account number: 3752

Jan. 2 Sold merchandise on credit to Valerie Beck for $161.80; Inv. #771.

6 Sold merchandise on credit to Valerie Beck for $295.35; Inv. #921.

11 Received a check from Valerie Beck for $161.80 in payment on account.

14 Sold merchandise on credit to Valerie Beck for $136.70; Inv. #1021.

20 Received a check from Valerie Beck for $295.35 in payment on account.

25 Sold merchandise on credit to Valerie Beck for $154.10; Inv. #1063.

Account #3

Customer's name: Courtney Emerson
Address: 3124 Quince Road, Memphis, TN 38117-3297
Account number: 3753

Jan. 5 Sold merchandise on credit to Courtney Emerson for $462.50; Inv. #873.

7 Sold merchandise on credit to Courtney Emerson for $376.45; Inv. #940.

24 Issued Credit Memo #203 to Courtney Emerson for $66.50.

27 Sold merchandise on credit to Courtney Emerson for $311.20; Inv. #1071.

29 Received a check from Courtney Emerson for $900.00 in payment on account.

31 Sold merchandise on credit to Courtney Emerson for $182.85; Inv. #2005.

Account #4

Customer's name: Dora Haney
Address: 614 Rayner Street, Memphis, TN 38114-8765
Account number: 3754

Jan. 9 Sold merchandise on credit to Dora Haney for $113.65; Inv. #1006.

11 Sold merchandise on credit to Dora Haney for $271.70; Inv. #1016.

13 Issued Credit Memo #191 to Dora Haney for $27.75.

18 Received a check from Dora Haney for $300.00 in payment on account.

21 Sold merchandise on credit to Dora Haney for $188.35; Inv. #1052.

24 Received a check from Dora Haney for $245.95 in full payment of the account.

Name ______________________________

Problem 41–2, Continued

Account #5

Customer's name: Saul Klein
Address: 1287 Summer Avenue, Memphis, TN 38112-7413
Account number: 3755

Jan.	3	Sold merchandise on credit to Saul Klein for $228.30; Inv. #779.
	17	Issued Credit Memo #197 to Saul Klein for $24.80.
	18	Sold merchandise on credit to Saul Klein for $467.75; Inv. #1041.
	24	Received a check from Saul Klein for $500.00 in payment on account.
	28	Sold merchandise on credit to Saul Klein for $636.75; Inv. #1083.
	31	Received a check from Saul Klein for $600.00 in payment on account.

Account #6

Customer's name: Enid Halleck
Address: 831 Riverdale Road, Memphis, TN 38138-7067
Account number: 3756

Jan.	2	Sold merchandise on credit to Enid Halleck for $181.70; Inv. #770.
	6	Sold merchandise on credit to Enid Halleck for $195.85; Inv. #937.
	11	Received a check from Enid Halleck for $300.00 in payment on account.
	14	Sold merchandise on credit to Enid Halleck for $203.40; Inv. #1025.
	20	Received a check from Enid Halleck for $200.00 in payment on account.
	25	Sold merchandise on credit to Enid Halleck for $313.10; Inv. #1064.

Account #7

Customer's name: Flora Meade
Address: 1399 Tillman Street, Memphis, TN 38112-6173
Account number: 3757

Jan.	5	Sold merchandise on credit to Flora Meade for $172.80; Inv. #868.
	7	Sold merchandise on credit to Flora Meade for $276.65; Inv. #943.
	14	Issued Credit Memo #195 to Flora Meade for $66.50.
	17	Sold merchandise on credit to Flora Meade for $101.20; Inv. #1038.
	19	Received a check from Flora Meade for $400.00 in payment on account.
	27	Sold merchandise on credit to Flora Meade for $262.85; Inv. #1072.

Problem 41–2, Continued

Account #8

Customer's name: Alan Landow
Address: 2737 Rozelle Street, Memphis, TN 38114-2387
Account number: 3758

Jan.	9	Sold merchandise on credit to Alan Landow for $107.65; Inv. #1007.
	12	Sold merchandise on credit to Alan Landow for $39.20; Inv. #1017.
	13	Issued Credit Memo #192 to Alan Landow for $17.75.
	18	Received a check from Alan Landow for $100.00 in payment on account.
	21	Sold merchandise on credit to Alan Landow for $158.35; Inv. #1047.
	24	Received a check from Alan Landow for $187.45 in full payment of the account.

Account #1

NAME ACCOUNT NO.

ADDRESS

DATE		ITEM	DEBIT	CREDIT	BALANCE

Account #2

NAME ACCOUNT NO.

ADDRESS

DATE		ITEM	DEBIT	CREDIT	BALANCE

Name ______________________________

Problem 41–2, Continued

Account #3

NAME ______________________________ ACCOUNT NO. __________

ADDRESS ______________________________

DATE		ITEM	DEBIT	CREDIT	BALANCE

Account #4

NAME ______________________________ ACCOUNT NO. __________

ADDRESS ______________________________

DATE		ITEM	DEBIT	CREDIT	BALANCE

Problem 41–2, Continued

Account #5

NAME ACCOUNT NO.

ADDRESS

DATE		ITEM	DEBIT	CREDIT	BALANCE

Account #6

NAME ACCOUNT NO.

ADDRESS

DATE		ITEM	DEBIT	CREDIT	BALANCE

Name ____________________

Problem 41–2, Concluded

Account #7

NAME ACCOUNT NO.

ADDRESS

DATE		ITEM	DEBIT	CREDIT	BALANCE

Account #8

NAME ACCOUNT NO.

ADDRESS

DATE		ITEM	DEBIT	CREDIT	BALANCE

(This page is without text copy.)

Name ______________________

Score __________

Sample Problem, page 331

CUSTOMER STATEMENT

MORENO DEPARTMENT STORE
5 Cade Street
Miami, FL 33160-7823

TO: ______________________

____

____

______________________ 20 __

ACCOUNT NO. ______

DATE		ITEM	DEBIT		CREDIT		BALANCE	
		Previous balance →						

LAST AMOUNT IN THIS COLUMN IS THE BALANCE DUE ↑

Problem 42–1, page 333

Account #1

CUSTOMER STATEMENT

DEVOE'S DEPARTMENT STORE
7981 Marshall Road
Dayton, OH 45459-6172

TO: ______________________

______________________ ______________________ 20 __

______________________ ACCOUNT NO. ______

DATE		ITEM	DEBIT		CREDIT		BALANCE	
		Previous balance ⟶						

LAST AMOUNT IN THIS COLUMN IS THE BALANCE DUE ↑

Account #2

CUSTOMER STATEMENT

DEVOE'S DEPARTMENT STORE
7981 Marshall Road
Dayton, OH 45459-6172

TO: ______________________

______________________ ______________________ 20 __

______________________ ACCOUNT NO. ______

DATE		ITEM	DEBIT		CREDIT		BALANCE	
		Previous balance ⟶						

LAST AMOUNT IN THIS COLUMN IS THE BALANCE DUE ↑

Name ______________________________

Problem 42–1, Continued

Account #3

CUSTOMER STATEMENT

DEVOE'S DEPARTMENT STORE

7981 Marshall Road
Dayton, OH 45459-6172

TO: ______________________________

______________________________ 20 __

______________________________ ACCOUNT NO. ______

DATE		ITEM	DEBIT		CREDIT		BALANCE	
		Previous balance →						

LAST AMOUNT IN THIS COLUMN IS THE BALANCE DUE ↑

Account #4

CUSTOMER STATEMENT

DEVOE'S DEPARTMENT STORE

7981 Marshall Road
Dayton, OH 45459-6172

TO: ______________________________

______________________________ 20 __

______________________________ ACCOUNT NO. ______

DATE		ITEM	DEBIT		CREDIT		BALANCE	
		Previous balance →						

LAST AMOUNT IN THIS COLUMN IS THE BALANCE DUE ↑

Problem 42–1, Continued

Account #5

CUSTOMER STATEMENT

DEVOE'S DEPARTMENT STORE
7981 Marshall Road
Dayton, OH 45459-6172

TO: ______________________

______________________ ______________________ 20 __

______________________ ACCOUNT NO. ______

DATE		ITEM	DEBIT		CREDIT		BALANCE	
		Previous balance →						

LAST AMOUNT IN THIS COLUMN IS THE BALANCE DUE ↑

Account #6

CUSTOMER STATEMENT

DEVOE'S DEPARTMENT STORE
7981 Marshall Road
Dayton, OH 45459-6172

TO: ______________________

______________________ ______________________ 20 __

______________________ ACCOUNT NO. ______

DATE		ITEM	DEBIT		CREDIT		BALANCE	
		Previous balance →						

LAST AMOUNT IN THIS COLUMN IS THE BALANCE DUE ↑

Name ______________________

Problem 42–1, Concluded

Account #7

CUSTOMER STATEMENT

DEVOE'S DEPARTMENT STORE

7981 Marshall Road
Dayton, OH 45459-6172

TO: ______________________

______________________ 20 __

ACCOUNT NO. ______

DATE		ITEM	DEBIT		CREDIT		BALANCE	
		Previous balance →						

LAST AMOUNT IN THIS COLUMN IS THE BALANCE DUE ↑

Account #8

CUSTOMER STATEMENT

DEVOE'S DEPARTMENT STORE

7981 Marshall Road
Dayton, OH 45459-6172

TO: ______________________

______________________ 20 __

ACCOUNT NO. ______

DATE		ITEM	DEBIT		CREDIT		BALANCE	
		Previous balance →						

LAST AMOUNT IN THIS COLUMN IS THE BALANCE DUE ↑

(This page is without text copy.)

Name ____________________

Score __________

Reinforcement Activities

CHAPTER 8
Jobs 40–42

Check Your Reading, page 336

1. ____________________

2. a. ____________________

2. b. ____________________

2. c. ____________________

2. d. ____________________

3. ____________________

Discussion, page 336

____

Ethics in the Workplace, page 336

____

Communication in the Workplace, page 337

1.

2.

CUSTOMER STATEMENT

ZUGGIE'S, INC.
16 Wetzler Street
San Antonio, TX 78237-8823

TO: ______________________

______________________ ______________________ 20 __

______________________ ACCOUNT NO. ______

DATE		ITEM	DEBIT		CREDIT		BALANCE	
		Previous balance →						

LAST AMOUNT IN THIS COLUMN IS THE BALANCE DUE ↑

3.

Name ____________________

Focus on Careers, page 338

1. ____________________

2. ____________________

3. ____________________

4. ____________________

Reviewing What You Have Learned, page 338

1. ____________________
2. ____________________
3. ____________________
4. ____________________
5. ____________________
6. ____________________
7. ____________________
8. ____________________
9. ____________________
10. ____________________

Mastery Problem, page 339

a.–b.

NAME Joshua Reynolds ACCOUNT NO. 109

ADDRESS 7612 Raitt Street, Chattanooga, TN 37411-8879

DATE		ITEM	DEBIT	CREDIT	BALANCE
20-- May	6	Inv. #811	251 89		251 89
	15	Inv. #945	36 19		288 08

Mastery Problem, Continued

NAME Janice O'Clair ACCOUNT NO. 183

ADDRESS 6133 Toro Street, Chattanooga, TN 37404-2617

DATE		ITEM	DEBIT	CREDIT	BALANCE
20-- May	3	Inv. #536	207 82		207 82
	12	Inv. #794	321 64		529 46

c.

CUSTOMER STATEMENT

BAILEY'S, INC.
5 Hardel Street
Ogden, UT 84401-4879

TO: ____________________

____________________ ____________________ 20 __

____________________ ACCOUNT NO. _______

DATE		ITEM	DEBIT	CREDIT	BALANCE
		Previous balance →			

LAST AMOUNT IN THIS COLUMN IS THE BALANCE DUE ↑

Name ______________________

Mastery Problem, Concluded

CUSTOMER STATEMENT

BAILEY'S, INC.
5 Hardel Street
Ogden, UT 84401-4879

TO: ______________________

______________________ 20 __

______________________ ACCOUNT NO. ______

DATE		ITEM	DEBIT		CREDIT		BALANCE	
		Previous balance →						

LAST AMOUNT IN THIS COLUMN IS THE BALANCE DUE ↑

Reviewing Your Business Vocabulary

Choose the words that match the statements. Write each word you choose next to the statement number it matches. Be careful; some of the words listed should not be used. Some words may be used more than once.

Statements

1. A customer account . . . . ______
2. Total debits minus total credits . . . . ______
3. An increase in a customer account . . . . ______
4. A decrease in a customer account . . . . ______
5. Part payments of the amount due . . . . ______
6. Has debit, credit, and balance columns . . . . ______
7. The balance found after each entry is made . . . . ______
8. The column used to record a charge sale in a customer account . . . . ______
9. The column used to record a payment or a return in customer account . . . . ______
10. A form that shows that a charge customer has returned merchandise and owes less money . . . . ______
11. The balance of the account at the end of last month . . . . . ______
12. A monthly report listing all transactions in a customer account during the month . . . . ______
13. Billing groups of customers at different times during the month . . . . ______
14. An employee who keeps records for charge customers . . . ______

Words

account balance	credit memo	payments on account	subtotal
accounts receivable account	customer statement	previous balance	three-column account
accounts receivable clerk	cycle billing	running balance	transaction
credit	debit		

Sample Problem, page 343

SALES INVOICE

NORTHWESTERN ATHLETIC SHOE WHOLESALER

1600 Dallas Parkway, Dallas, TX 75240-0810

555-3285

SOLD TO ______________________ INVOICE NO. ____________

DATE ____________ 20__

OUR ORDER NO. ____________

CUSTOMER ORDER NO. ____________

TERMS ______________________ SHIPPED VIA ____________

QUANTITY	STOCK NO.	DESCRIPTION	UNIT PRICE		AMOUNT	

2/17/05

Problem 43–1, page 346

	Date of Invoice		Terms of Invoice	Due Date
a.	Feb. 4	14	10 days	Feb 14
b.	Sept. 7	23	20 days	Sept 27
c.	Mar. 21	10	30 days	April 20
d.	Apr. 3	27	30 days	May 3
e.	Nov. 17	13	30 days	Dec 17
f.	July 19	12	60 days	Sept 17
g.	Dec. 12	19	60 days	Feb 10
h.	Mar. 22	8	90 days	June 20

	Date of Invoice		Terms of Invoice	Due Date
i.	Mar. 8	23	15 days	March 23
j.	Jan. 17	14	20 days	Feb 6
k.	July 27	4	30 days	Aug 26
l.	Nov. 23	7	30 days	Dec 23
m.	Jan. 16	15	30 days	Feb 15
n.	Mar. 3	28	75 days	May 17
o.	May 19	12	90 days	Aug 17
p.	Sept. 11	19	90 days	Dec 10

Problem 43–2, page 346

2/17/05

Sale #1

SALES INVOICE

PHONECOM, INC.

5640 Church Street, Lancaster, PA 17603-1250
555-3928

SOLD TO Phone Store, Inc
78 River Road
Bismark, ND 58504-6131

INVOICE NO. 17053
DATE Jan 8 20__
OUR ORDER NO. 1710
CUSTOMER ORDER NO. 66B
SHIPPED VIA truck

TERMS 30 days

QUANTITY	STOCK NO.	DESCRIPTION	UNIT PRICE		AMOUNT	
10 ea.	43-781	Big Button phone	12	99	129	90
5 ea	43-629	32 Memory Speaker Phone	41	99	209	95
		Total invoice			339	85

Name ______________________________

Problem 43–2, Continued

2/17/05

Sale #2

SALES INVOICE

PHONECOM, INC.
5640 Church Street, Lancaster, PA 17603-1250
555-3928

SOLD TO Phone Electronics
6759 White Oak Drive
Gadsden, Al 35907-6244

TERMS 30 days

INVOICE NO. 17054
DATE Jan 8 20__
OUR ORDER NO. 1711
CUSTOMER ORDER NO. 6-483
SHIPPED VIA Truck

QUANTITY	STOCK NO.	DESCRIPTION	UNIT PRICE		AMOUNT	
10 ea.	#279-11	Surface Mount Dual Jack	3	99	39	90
10 ea.	279-12	Modular Jack with Wiring Block Ivory	2	99	29	90
10 ea	279-15	Quick Connect Jack, White	1	99	19	90
		total invoice			89.	70

Problem 43–2, Continued

2/17/05

Sale #3

SALES INVOICE
PHONECOM, INC.
5640 Church Street, Lancaster, PA 17603-1250
555-3928

SOLD TO Phone Hut
91 Washington Square
Wilmington, DE 19802-2584

INVOICE NO. 17055
DATE Jan 8 20
OUR ORDER NO. 1712
CUSTOMER ORDER NO. 11-803
SHIPPED VIA truck

TERMS 30 days

QUANTITY	STOCK NO.	DESCRIPTION	UNIT PRICE		AMOUNT	
5 ea	43-109	900MHZ Cordless Phone	59	99	299	95
5 ea	43-5811	All-Digital Answer Machine	39	99	199	95
		Total invoice			499	80

Name ________________________

Problem 43–2, Continued

2/17/05

Sale #4

SALES INVOICE

PHONECOM, INC.

5640 Church Street, Lancaster, PA 17603-1250
555-3928

SOLD TO TeleMart Inc
1100 Webster Street
Yakima, WA 98902-1217

INVOICE NO. 17056
DATE Jan 8 20 5
OUR ORDER NO. 1713
CUSTOMER ORDER NO. 729
SHIPPED VIA truck

TERMS 30 days

QUANTITY	STOCK NO.	DESCRIPTION	UNIT PRICE		AMOUNT	
2 ea	43-972	90-Memory Caller ID	11	95	23	90
5 ea	17-8116	Dual-Band PCS Phone	69	90	349	50
		Total invoice			363	40

Problem 43–2, Continued

2/17/05

Sale #5

SALES INVOICE

PHONECOM, INC.

5640 Church Street, Lancaster, PA 17603-1250
555-3928

SOLD TO Fone Mart
8870 E. Clay Street
Richmond, VA 23223-5510

INVOICE NO. 17057
DATE Jan 8 20—
OUR ORDER NO. 1714
CUSTOMER ORDER NO. A-66
SHIPPED VIA truck

TERMS 30 days

QUANTITY	STOCK NO.	DESCRIPTION	UNIT PRICE		AMOUNT	
6 ea.	M30-1712	Maxion 30-Number Pager	15	80	94	80
5 ea	LH-600	Lightweight Headset Phone	39	50	197	50
2 dz.	279-600	25 ft. phone Cord, White	18	79	450	96
		Total invoice			743	26

Name ______________________

Problem 43–2, Concluded

2/17/05

Sale #6

SALES INVOICE
PHONECOM, INC.
5640 Church Street, Lancaster, PA 17603-1250
555-3928

SOLD TO Cellular Six
52946 Glenside Avenue
Baton Rouge, LA 70808-5626

INVOICE NO. 17058
DATE Jan 8 20__
OUR ORDER NO. 1715
CUSTOMER ORDER NO. 17312
SHIPPED VIA truck

TERMS ______________________

QUANTITY	STOCK NO.	DESCRIPTION	UNIT PRICE		AMOUNT	
1 dz.	17-435	leather phone case	19	50	234	00
1 dz.	273-1217	Car DC Adapters	21	00	252	00
10 ea	23-1019	Extended Service Battery	29	98	299	80
		total invoice			785	80

(This page is without text copy.)

Name ______________________

Score ____________

Sample Problem, page 349

NAME PDM Industrial — ACCOUNT NO. 120

ADDRESS 1200 Paragon Road, Dayton, OH 45459-6004 — TERMS 20 days

DATE		ITEM	DEBIT	CREDIT	BALANCE

NAME Quement Promotions, Inc. — ACCOUNT NO. 125

ADDRESS 960 Quail Lane, Dayton, OH 45434-2501 — TERMS 20 days

DATE		ITEM	DEBIT	CREDIT	BALANCE

NAME Tafoya Distributors, Inc. — ACCOUNT NO. 130

ADDRESS 4692 Poplar Street, Dayton, OH 45415-5025 — TERMS 20 days

DATE		ITEM	DEBIT	CREDIT	BALANCE

Sample Problem, Concluded

Problem 44–1, page 359

NAME ACCOUNT NO.

ADDRESS TERMS

DATE		ITEM	DEBIT	CREDIT	BALANCE

NAME ACCOUNT NO.

ADDRESS TERMS

DATE		ITEM	DEBIT	CREDIT	BALANCE

Name

Problem 44–1, Concluded

NAME ACCOUNT NO.

ADDRESS TERMS

DATE		ITEM	DEBIT	CREDIT	BALANCE

Problem 44–2, page 353

NAME ACCOUNT NO.

ADDRESS TERMS

DATE		ITEM	DEBIT	CREDIT	BALANCE

Problem 44–2, Concluded

NAME ACCOUNT NO.

ADDRESS TERMS

DATE		ITEM	DEBIT	CREDIT	BALANCE

NAME ACCOUNT NO.

ADDRESS TERMS

DATE		ITEM	DEBIT	CREDIT	BALANCE

Name ______________________________

Problem 44–3

You are employed by the Madison Wholesale Company to keep the records of charge customers.

Directions

a. Open an account for each of the following customers. The terms for all customers are 20 days.
Bix & Aronson, 1521 Court Street, Detroit, MI 48209-7318, Acct. #110
Lambert & Associates, 20234 Southwest Road, Detroit, MI 48225-3251, Acct. #120
Wallace & Daughters, Inc., 19 Apple Road, Detroit, MI 48219-1721, Acct. #130

b. Record the following transactions in the order in which they occurred:

List of Duplicate Sales Invoices

Date	Invoice Number	Customer	Amount
Nov. 2	325	Lambert & Associates	$285.60
3	326	Bix & Aronson	321.45
4	327	Wallace & Daughters, Inc.	162.50
9	328	Bix & Aronson	23.90
11	329	Lambert & Associates	403.20
15	330	Wallace & Daughters, Inc.	509.00
18	331	Bix & Aronson	143.35

List of Duplicate Credit Memos

Date	Credit Memo No.	Customer	Amount
Nov. 16	187	Bix & Aronson	$82.75
21	188	Lambert & Associates	56.00

List of Cash Received

Date	Customer	Amount
Nov. 20	Lambert & Associates	$285.60
21	Bix & Aronson	238.70
23	Wallace & Daughters, Inc.	162.50
25	Bix & Aronson	23.90
30	Lambert & Associates	347.20

c. To check the final balance of each account, foot the Debit and Credit columns at the end of the month. Subtract the total credits from the total debits. Show your math in the Item columns.

d. Prepare a schedule of accounts receivable on November 30.

Problem 44–3, Continued

NAME ACCOUNT NO.

ADDRESS TERMS

DATE		ITEM	DEBIT	CREDIT	BALANCE

NAME ACCOUNT NO.

ADDRESS TERMS

DATE		ITEM	DEBIT	CREDIT	BALANCE

NAME ACCOUNT NO.

ADDRESS TERMS

DATE		ITEM	DEBIT	CREDIT	BALANCE

Name ______________________

Problem 44–3, Concluded

(This page is without text copy.)

Name ______________________

Score ____________

Using a Sales Journal

CHAPTER 9 Job 45

Sample Problem, page 356

SALES JOURNAL PAGE 1

	DATE		CUSTOMER'S NAME	INV. NO.	POST. REF.	AMOUNT	
1							1
2							2
3							3
4							4
5							5
6							6
7							7

NAME Electronic Solutions ACCOUNT NO. 120

ADDRESS 88 Catawba Road, Sevierville, TN 37876-0008 TERMS 30 days

DATE		ITEM	POST. REF.	DEBIT	CREDIT	BALANCE

NAME Phi-Alpha Electronics ACCOUNT NO. 140

ADDRESS 150 Burridge Drive, Sevierville, TN 37862-2404 TERMS 30 days

DATE		ITEM	POST. REF.	DEBIT	CREDIT	BALANCE

NAME TechMart Corporation ACCOUNT NO. 160

ADDRESS 22701 Beach Front Drive, Sevierville, TN 37876-1150 TERMS 30 days

DATE		ITEM	POST. REF.	DEBIT	CREDIT	BALANCE

 2/17/05

Problem 45–1, page 358

SALES JOURNAL PAGE 1

	DATE		CUSTOMER'S NAME	INV. NO.	POST. REF.	AMOUNT	
1	20-- Aug	5	Byington Corporation	1082	115	540 00	1
2		9	Escobar & Evans Inc	1084	120	472 00	2
3		21	American Communication Inc	1086	110	987 00	3
4		24	Escobar & Evans Inc	1085	120	653 00	4
5		27	Byington Corporation	1083	115	1,229 00	5
6		29	American Communication Inc	1087	110	810	6
7						4,691 00 / 4,691 00	7

NAME Byington Corporation ACCOUNT NO. 115 (2)

ADDRESS TERMS 30 days

DATE		ITEM	POST. REF.	DEBIT	CREDIT	BALANCE
✓ Aug	5	invoice #1082	S1	540 00		540 00
✓	27	invoice #1083	S1	1,229 00		1,769 00
				1,769 00		

NAME Escobar & Evans Inc ACCOUNT NO. 120 (3)

ADDRESS TERMS 30 days

DATE		ITEM	POST. REF.	DEBIT	CREDIT	BALANCE
✓ Aug	9	invoice #1084	S1	472 00		472 00
✓	24	Invoice #1085	S1	653 00		1,125 00
				1,125 00		

NAME American Communications Inc ACCOUNT NO. 110 (1)

ADDRESS TERMS 30 days

DATE		ITEM	POST. REF.	DEBIT	CREDIT	BALANCE
✓ Aug	21	Invoice #1086	S1	987 00		987 00
	29	Invoice #1087	S1	810 00		1,797 00
				1,797 00		

Name ______________________

Problem 45–2, page 359

SALES JOURNAL

PAGE

	DATE		CUSTOMER'S NAME	INV. NO.	POST. REF.	AMOUNT	
1							1
2							2
3							3
4							4
5							5
6							6
7							7

NAME ACCOUNT NO.

ADDRESS TERMS

DATE		ITEM	POST. REF.	DEBIT	CREDIT	BALANCE

NAME ACCOUNT NO.

ADDRESS TERMS

DATE		ITEM	POST. REF.	DEBIT	CREDIT	BALANCE

NAME ACCOUNT NO.

ADDRESS TERMS

DATE		ITEM	POST. REF.	DEBIT	CREDIT	BALANCE

Problem 45–3

You work in the accounting department of Sterling Enterprises, Inc.

Directions

a. Open an account for each customer. The terms for all customers are 30 days.
Archer Industries, 121 Lackland Ave., El Paso, TX 79915-2701, Acct. #110
Rojas, Inc., 808 Sorocco Drive, El Paso, TX 79936-3556, Acct. #140
T. Springer Company, 52718 Anise Road, El Paso, TX 79924-1429, Acct. #170

b. Record the following sales in a sales journal. Number the journal page 9.

Nov.	2	Sold merchandise to Archer Industries for $874.85. (Start with Invoice #831.)
	5	Sold merchandise to T. Springer Company for $1,548.50.
	9	Sold merchandise to Rojas, Inc., for $543.95.
	19	Sold merchandise to T. Springer Company for $733.70.
	23	Sold merchandise to Archer Industries for $569.45.
	29	Sold merchandise to Rojas, Inc., for $1,132.60.

c. Post daily from the sales journal to the customer accounts. Do not forget to enter an account number in the sales journal and the posting reference S9 in the account as you post.

d. Foot, total, and rule the sales journal for the month.

e. Check the balance in each customer account by footing the Debit column.

SALES JOURNAL PAGE

	DATE		CUSTOMER'S NAME	INV. NO.	POST. REF.	AMOUNT	
1							1
2							2
3							3
4							4
5							5
6							6
7							7

NAME ACCOUNT NO.

ADDRESS TERMS

DATE		ITEM	POST. REF.	DEBIT	CREDIT	BALANCE

Name ______________________________

Problem 45–3, Concluded

NAME ______________________________ ACCOUNT NO. __________

ADDRESS ______________________________ TERMS __________

DATE		ITEM	POST. REF.	DEBIT	CREDIT	BALANCE

NAME ______________________________ ACCOUNT NO. __________

ADDRESS ______________________________ TERMS __________

DATE		ITEM	POST. REF.	DEBIT	CREDIT	BALANCE

Problem 45–4

You are employed by Sugihara & Sons as an accounts receivable clerk.

Directions

a. Open an account for each customer. The terms for all customers are 30 days.
Amber Corporation, 7318 Mountain Ave., Tucson, AZ 85741-3617, Acct. #101
Dougherty's, 10788 Pomona Road, Tucson, AZ 85747-9038, Acct. #110
Tyler & Sons, Inc., 9579 Water Street, Tucson, AZ 85730-1113, Acct. #120

b. Record the following sales in a sales journal. Number the journal page 1.

June 3 Sold merchandise to Amber Corporation for $348.65. (Start with Invoice #761.)
9 Sold merchandise to Dougherty's for $511.24.
15 Sold merchandise to Tyler & Sons, Inc., for $628.50.
20 Sold merchandise to Dougherty's for $219.00.
22 Sold merchandise to Tyler & Sons, Inc., for $726.85.
27 Sold merchandise to Amber Corporation for $473.55.

c. Post daily from the sales journal to the customer accounts.

d. Foot, total, and rule the sales journal for the month.

e. Check the balance in each customer account by footing the Debit column.

f. Prepare a schedule of accounts receivable for June.

Problem 45–4, Continued

SALES JOURNAL PAGE

	DATE		CUSTOMER'S NAME	INV. NO.	POST. REF.	AMOUNT	
1							1
2							2
3							3
4							4
5							5
6							6
7							7

NAME ACCOUNT NO.

ADDRESS TERMS

DATE		ITEM	POST. REF.	DEBIT	CREDIT	BALANCE

NAME ACCOUNT NO.

ADDRESS TERMS

DATE		ITEM	POST. REF.	DEBIT	CREDIT	BALANCE

NAME ACCOUNT NO.

ADDRESS TERMS

DATE		ITEM	POST. REF.	DEBIT	CREDIT	BALANCE

Name ______________________________

Problem 45–4, Concluded

Problem 45–5

You are employed by Paramount Distributors as an accounts receivable clerk.

Directions

a. Open an account for each customer. The terms for all customers are 30 days.
Castle Stores, 146 Second St., Savannah, GA 31419-5228, Acct. #110
Johns Company, 14389 Wasington Road, Savannah, GA 31411-3906, Acct. #130
Reed & Pierce, 19 Cohen St., Savannah, GA 31407-1583, Acct. #150

b. Record the following sales in a sales journal. Number the journal page 3.

Feb.	1	Sold merchandise to Castle Stores for $283.15. (Start with Invoice #921.)
	4	Sold merchandise to Johns Company for $872.78.
	9	Sold merchandise to Reed & Pierce for $495.30.
	16	Sold merchandise to Castle Stores for $607.40.
	23	Sold merchandise to Reed & Pierce for $143.58.
	27	Sold merchandise to Johns Company for $319.75.

c. Post daily from the sales journal to the customer accounts.

d. Foot, total, and rule the sales journal for the month.

e. Check the balance in each customer account by footing the Debit column.

f. Prepare a schedule of accounts receivable for February.

Problem 45–5, Continued

SALES JOURNAL PAGE

	DATE		CUSTOMER'S NAME	INV. NO.	POST. REF.	AMOUNT	
1							1
2							2
3							3
4							4
5							5
6							6
7							7

NAME ACCOUNT NO.

ADDRESS TERMS

DATE		ITEM	POST. REF.	DEBIT	CREDIT	BALANCE

NAME ACCOUNT NO.

ADDRESS TERMS

DATE		ITEM	POST. REF.	DEBIT	CREDIT	BALANCE

NAME ACCOUNT NO.

ADDRESS TERMS

DATE		ITEM	POST. REF.	DEBIT	CREDIT	BALANCE

Name ______________________

Problem 45–5, Concluded

(This page is without text copy.)

Name ______________________

Score ____________

Using a Cash Receipts Journal

CHAPTER 9
Job 46

Sample Problem, page 361

CASH RECEIPTS JOURNAL — PAGE 1

	DATE		RECEIVED FROM	FOR	POST. REF.	AMOUNT	
1							1
2							2
3							3
4							4
5							5
6							6
7							7

NAME Discount Tire — ACCOUNT NO. 110

ADDRESS 2640 Signal Hill Road, Manassas, VA 20111-7252 — TERMS 45 days

DATE		ITEM	POST. REF.	DEBIT	CREDIT	BALANCE
20-- May	4	Invoice #561	S1	1 204 60		1 204 60
	24	Invoice #565	S1	624 50		1 829 10

NAME Morris Tire & Wheel Outlet — ACCOUNT NO. 120

ADDRESS 4890 Sudley Road, Manassas, VA 20109-1310 — TERMS 45 days

DATE		ITEM	POST. REF.	DEBIT	CREDIT	BALANCE
20-- May	7	Invoice #562	S1	278 45		278 45
	16	Invoice #564	S1	623 10		901 55
	25	Invoice #566	S1	846 53		1 748 08

Sample Problem, Concluded

NAME Tire Warehouse **ACCOUNT NO.** 130

ADDRESS 93 River Road, Manassas, VA 20111-6347 **TERMS** 45 days

DATE		ITEM	POST. REF.	DEBIT	CREDIT	BALANCE
20-- May	9	Invoice #563	S1	630 15		630 15

Problem 46–1, page 364

2/24/05

CASH RECEIPTS JOURNAL PAGE 5

	DATE		RECEIVED FROM	FOR	POST. REF.	AMOUNT	
1	20 Mar	5	Brady Heating & Cooling	invoice, 2/6	115	1008 00	1
2		8	Dali Brothers Furnace & Heating	invoice 2/10	125	190 00	2
3		12	Allied Heating, Inc	invoice 2/13	105	980 00	3
4		20	Dali Brothers Furnace & Heating	invoice 2/21	125	666 00	4
5		22	Brady Heating & Cooling	invoice 2/23	115	421 00	5
6			Total			3265 00 3265 00	6
7							7

NAME Allied Heating, Inc. **ACCOUNT NO.** 105

ADDRESS 63 Ash Street, Scranton, PA 18509-3721 **TERMS** 30 days

DATE		ITEM	POST. REF.	DEBIT	CREDIT	BALANCE
20-- Feb.	13	Invoice #182	S2	980 00		980 00
20 Mar	12	Cash	CR5		980 00	—

Name ______________________________

Problem 46–1, Concluded

NAME Brady Heating & Cooling ACCOUNT NO. 115

ADDRESS 274 Delaware Street, Scranton, PA 18512-2402 TERMS 30 days

DATE		ITEM	POST. REF.	DEBIT	CREDIT	BALANCE
20-- Feb.	6	Invoice #180	S2	1 008 00		1 008 00
	23	Invoice #184	S2	421 00		1 429 00
20 Mar.	5	Cash	CR5		1008 00	421 00
	22	Cash	CR5		421 00	—

NAME Dali Brothers' Furnace & Heating ACCOUNT NO. 125

ADDRESS 16 Erie Street, Scranton, PA 18510-7658 TERMS 30 days

DATE		ITEM	POST. REF.	DEBIT	CREDIT	BALANCE
20-- Feb.	10	Invoice #181	S2	190 00		190 00
	21	Invoice #183	S2	666 00		856 00
20 Mar.	8	Cash	CR5		190 00	666 00
	20	Cash	CR5		666 00	—

Problem 46–2, page 365

CASH RECEIPTS JOURNAL PAGE

	DATE		RECEIVED FROM	FOR	POST. REF.	AMOUNT	
1							1
2							2
3							3
4							4
5							5
6							6
7							7
8							8

Problem 46–2, Concluded

NAME Eli Johnson Formalwear — ACCOUNT NO. 160

ADDRESS 171 Memorial Drive, Waycross, GA 31501-9322 — TERMS 45 days

DATE		ITEM	POST. REF.	DEBIT	CREDIT	BALANCE
20-- Apr.	5	Invoice #262	S1	620 00		620 00

NAME Milo's Tuxedos — ACCOUNT NO. 170

ADDRESS 99 State Street, Waycross, GA 31501-6253 — TERMS 45 days

DATE		ITEM	POST. REF.	DEBIT	CREDIT	BALANCE
20-- Apr.	2	Invoice #260	S1	390 00		390 00
	20	Invoice #264	S1	1142 00		1532 00

NAME South City Tux Shoppe — ACCOUNT NO. 180

ADDRESS 231 Mary Street, Waycross, GA 31501-7082 — TERMS 45 days

DATE		ITEM	POST. REF.	DEBIT	CREDIT	BALANCE
20-- Apr.	3	Invoice #261	S1	481 00		481 00
	13	Invoice #263	S1	506 00		987 00
	24	Invoice #265	S1	774 00		1761 00

Name ______________________________

Problem 46–3

You are an accounts receivable clerk for Mandarith Wholesale Company.

Directions

a. The customer accounts that follow show the sales recorded in October.

b. Record the following cash receipts in a cash receipts journal. Number the journal page 6.

Nov. 3 Received a check for $519.45 from A. Vaughn & Sons for the invoice of October 5.

7 Received a check for $817.60 from Latham Company for the invoice of October 8.

13 Received a check for $541.15 from Hyten Gift Shops, Inc., for the invoice of October 14.

18 Received a check for $312.00 from A. Vaughn & Sons for the invoice of October 21.

24 Received a check for $831.50 from Hyten Gift Shops, Inc., for the invoice of October 25.

c. Post daily from the cash receipts journal to the Credit column of the customer accounts.

d. Foot, total, and rule the Amount column of the cash receipts journal.

e. Check the balance in each customer account by footing the Debit and Credit columns. Subtract the total credits from the total debits. The answer should agree with the final balance shown in the account.

CASH RECEIPTS JOURNAL PAGE

	DATE		RECEIVED FROM	FOR	POST. REF.	AMOUNT	
1							1
2							2
3							3
4							4
5							5
6							6
7							7

Problem 46–3, Concluded

NAME Hyten Gift Shops, Inc. ACCOUNT NO. 109

ADDRESS 12 D Street, Anchorage, AK 99506-1785 TERMS 30 days

DATE		ITEM	POST. REF.	DEBIT	CREDIT	BALANCE
20-- Oct.	14	Invoice #753	S6	541 15		541 15
	25	Invoice #755	S6	831 50		1,372 65

NAME Latham Company ACCOUNT NO. 110

ADDRESS 582 King Street, Anchorage, AK 99515-4305 TERMS 30 days

DATE		ITEM	POST. REF.	DEBIT	CREDIT	BALANCE
20-- Oct.	8	Invoice #752	S6	817 60		817 60

NAME A. Vaughn & Sons ACCOUNT NO. 111

ADDRESS 66 Short Street, Anchorage, AK 99516-6116 TERMS 30 days

DATE		ITEM	POST. REF.	DEBIT	CREDIT	BALANCE
20-- Oct.	5	Invoice #751	S6	519 45		519 45
	21	Invoice #754	S6	312 00		831 45

Name ______________________________

Problem 46–4

You are an accounts receivable clerk for Dynamic Packaging Products.

Directions

a. The customer accounts that follow show the sales recorded in September.

b. Record the following cash receipts in the cash receipts journal. Number the journal page 3.

Oct.	17	Received a check for $527.84 from Morgan & Smith for the invoice of September 2.
	19	Received a check for $719.30 from Tyler Shipping for the invoice of September 5.
	23	Received a check for $912.15 from Donnelly Corporation for the invoice of September 8.
	30	Received a check for $301.15 from Donnelly Corporation for the invoice of September 14.
	31	Received a check for $265.50 from Tyler Shipping for the invoice of September 16.

c. Post daily from the cash receipts journal to the Credit column of the customer accounts.

d. Foot, total, and rule the Amount column of the cash receipts journal.

e. Check the balance in each customer account by footing the Debit and Credit columns. Subtract the total credits from the total debits. The answer should agree with the final balance shown in the account.

CASH RECEIPTS JOURNAL

PAGE

	DATE		RECEIVED FROM	FOR	POST. REF.	AMOUNT	
1							1
2							2
3							3
4							4
5							5
6							6
7							7

NAME Donnelly Corporation ACCOUNT NO. 106

ADDRESS 9624 Carlson Road, Topeka, KS 66611-3616 TERMS 45 days

DATE		ITEM	POST. REF.	DEBIT	CREDIT	BALANCE
20-- Sept.	8	Invoice #443	S3	912 15		912 15
	14	Invoice #444	S3	301 15		1213 30
	29	Invoice #447	S3	275 12		1488 42

Problem 46–4, Concluded

NAME Morgan & Smith **ACCOUNT NO.** 110

ADDRESS 8 Croco Road, Topeka, KS 66608-7013 **TERMS** 45 days

DATE		ITEM	POST. REF.	DEBIT	CREDIT	BALANCE
20-- Sept.	2	Invoice #441	S3	527 84		527 84
	30	Invoice #448	S3	178 80		706 64

NAME Tyler Shipping **ACCOUNT NO.** 120

ADDRESS 842 First Street, Topeka, KS 66606-1953 **TERMS** 45 days

DATE		ITEM	POST. REF.	DEBIT	CREDIT	BALANCE
20-- Sept.	5	Invoice #442	S3	719 30		719 30
	16	Invoice #445	S3	265 50		984 80
	26	Invoice #446	S3	436 22		1421 02

Name ______________________

Score ____________

Sample Problem, page 368

SALES JOURNAL PAGE 1

	DATE		CUSTOMER'S NAME	INV. NO.	POST. REF.	AMOUNT	
1							1
2							2
3							3
4							4
5							5
6							6

CASH RECEIPTS JOURNAL PAGE 1

	DATE		RECEIVED FROM	FOR	POST. REF.	AMOUNT	
1							1
2							2
3							3
4							4
5							5
6							6

NAME Village Floral ACCOUNT NO. 180

ADDRESS 5362 Avalon Lane, Oklahoma City, OK 73118-2170 TERMS 10 days

DATE		ITEM	POST. REF.	DEBIT	CREDIT	BALANCE

Problem 47–1, page 370

SALES JOURNAL

PAGE

	DATE		CUSTOMER'S NAME	INV. NO.	POST. REF.	AMOUNT	
1							1
2							2
3							3
4							4
5							5
6							6
7							7
8							8

CASH RECEIPTS JOURNAL

PAGE

	DATE		RECEIVED FROM	FOR	POST. REF.	AMOUNT	
1							1
2							2
3							3
4							4
5							5

NAME ACCOUNT NO.

ADDRESS TERMS

DATE		ITEM	POST. REF.	DEBIT	CREDIT	BALANCE

Name

Problem 47–1, Concluded

NAME ACCOUNT NO.

ADDRESS TERMS

DATE		ITEM	POST. REF.	DEBIT	CREDIT	BALANCE

NAME ACCOUNT NO.

ADDRESS TERMS

DATE		ITEM	POST. REF.	DEBIT	CREDIT	BALANCE

Problem 47–2, page 371

SALES JOURNAL

PAGE

	DATE		CUSTOMER'S NAME	INV. NO.	POST. REF.	AMOUNT	
1							1
2							2
3							3
4							4
5							5
6							6
7							7
8							8

CASH RECEIPTS JOURNAL

PAGE

	DATE		RECEIVED FROM	FOR	POST. REF.	AMOUNT	
1							1
2							2
3							3
4							4
5							5

NAME

ACCOUNT NO.

ADDRESS

TERMS

DATE		ITEM	POST. REF.	DEBIT	CREDIT	BALANCE

Name

Problem 47–2, Concluded

NAME ACCOUNT NO.

ADDRESS TERMS

DATE		ITEM	POST. REF.	DEBIT	CREDIT	BALANCE

NAME ACCOUNT NO.

ADDRESS TERMS

DATE		ITEM	POST. REF.	DEBIT	CREDIT	BALANCE

Problem 47–3

You are employed as an assistant bookkeeper by Reynolds Interstate Wholesalers, Inc.

Directions

a. Open an account for each of the following customers. The terms for all customers are 10 days.
Baker Company, 731 Howard Street, Louisville, KY 40223-5826, Acct. #105
Green Market, 37 Pershing Ave., Stockton, CA 95209-2007, Acct. #110
Taliano's, 53 Dodd Road, St. Paul, MN 55110-7374, Acct. #120

b. Record the following transactions using a sales journal and a cash receipts journal. Use page 2 for both journals. Post to the customer accounts as soon as you have recorded each transaction.

Feb.	2	Sold merchandise to Baker Company for $543.35. (Start with Invoice #801.)
	6	Sold merchandise to Green Market for $248.80.
	9	Sold merchandise to Baker Company for $806.70.
	12	Received a check for $543.35 from Baker Company for the invoice of February 2.
	14	Sold merchandise to Taliano's for $1,113.20.
	16	Sold merchandise to Green Market for $729.95.
	16	Received a check for $248.80 from Green Market for the invoice of February 6.
	19	Received a check for $806.70 from Baker Company for the invoice of February 9.
	21	Sold merchandise to Taliano's for $527.50.
	23	Sold merchandise to Green Market for $763.75.
	24	Received a check for $1,113.20 from Taliano's for the invoice of February 14.
	26	Received a check for $729.95 from Green Market for the invoice of February 16.

c. Foot, total, and rule the sales and cash receipts journals.

d. Check the balance at the end of the month in each account. Show all footings.

e. Prepare a schedule of accounts receivable on February 28. (Did you get a total of $1,291.25?)

SALES JOURNAL

PAGE

	DATE		CUSTOMER'S NAME	INV. NO.	POST. REF.	AMOUNT	
1							1
2							2
3							3
4							4
5							5
6							6
7							7
8							8

Name

Problem 47–3, Continued

CASH RECEIPTS JOURNAL PAGE

	DATE		RECEIVED FROM	FOR	POST. REF.	AMOUNT	
1							1
2							2
3							3
4							4
5							5
6							6

NAME ACCOUNT NO.

ADDRESS TERMS

DATE		ITEM	POST. REF.	DEBIT	CREDIT	BALANCE

NAME ACCOUNT NO.

ADDRESS TERMS

DATE		ITEM	POST. REF.	DEBIT	CREDIT	BALANCE

Problem 47–3, Concluded

NAME ACCOUNT NO.

ADDRESS TERMS

DATE		ITEM	POST. REF.	DEBIT	CREDIT	BALANCE

Name ____________________

Score ____________

Using a Sales Returns and Allowances Journal

CHAPTER 9
Job 48

Sample Problem, page 373

SALES RETURNS AND ALLOWANCES JOURNAL PAGE

	DATE		CUSTOMER'S NAME	CREDIT MEMO NO.	POST. REF.	AMOUNT	
1							1
2							2
3							3
4							4
5							5
6							6

NAME San Juan Jewelers ACCOUNT NO. 160

ADDRESS 1700 Northland Drive, Rockville, RI 02873-1511 TERMS 30 days

DATE		ITEM	POST. REF.	DEBIT	CREDIT	BALANCE
20-- Mar.	5	Invoice #1172	S1	1 700 00		1 700 00
	13	Invoice #1174	S1	980 00		2 680 00

NAME Taylor's Jewelry & Design ACCOUNT NO. 180

ADDRESS 1229 Avery Avenue, Buffalo, NY 14216-1780 TERMS 30 days

DATE		ITEM	POST. REF.	DEBIT	CREDIT	BALANCE
20-- Mar.	2	Invoice #1171	S1	1 260 00		1 260 00
	12	Invoice #1173	S1	810 00		2 070 00

Problem 48–1, page 377

SALES RETURNS AND ALLOWANCES JOURNAL PAGE 1

	DATE		CUSTOMER'S NAME	CREDIT MEMO NO.	POST. REF.	AMOUNT	
1	20-- Oct	15	Cypress Landscape, Inc	85	120	40 00	1
2		17	Gish Landscape Design & Installation	86	140	22 00	2
3		20	Valley Pride Landscaping	87	160	175 00	3
4		23	Gish Landscape Design & Installation	88	140	36 00	4
5		26	Valley Pride Landscaping	89	160	80 00	5
6		31	Total			353 00 353 00	6

NAME Cypress Landscape, Inc. **ACCOUNT NO.** 120

ADDRESS 2650 Brighton Drive, Valencia, CA 91355-0606 **TERMS** 30 days

DATE		ITEM	POST. REF.	DEBIT	CREDIT	BALANCE
20-- Oct.	6	Invoice #1202	S1	430 00		430 00
	13	Invoice #1205	S1	163 00		593 00
	15	Credit memo #85	SR1		40	553 00

NAME Gish Landscape Design & Installation **ACCOUNT NO.** 140

ADDRESS 1742 Calvert Drive, Valencia, CA 91354-2242 **TERMS** 30 days

DATE		ITEM	POST. REF.	DEBIT	CREDIT	BALANCE
20-- Oct.	10	Invoice #1204	S1	362 00		362 00
	14	Invoice #1206	S1	403 00		765 00
	17	Credit memo #86	SR1		22 00	743 00
	23	Credit memo #88	SR1		36 00	707 00

Name ______________________

Problem 48–1, Concluded

NAME Valley Pride Landscaping ACCOUNT NO. 160

ADDRESS 360 Decoro Drive, Valencia, CA 91354-6242 TERMS 30 days

DATE		ITEM	POST. REF.	DEBIT	CREDIT	BALANCE
20-- Oct.	8	Invoice #1203	S1	5 1 1 00		5 1 1 00
	18	Invoice #1207	S1	3 2 2 00		8 3 3 00
	20	Credit memo # 87	SR1		1 7 5 00	6 5 8 00
	26	Credit memo # 89	SR1		8 0 00	5 7 8 00

Problem 48–2, page 378

SALES RETURNS AND ALLOWANCES JOURNAL PAGE

	DATE		CUSTOMER'S NAME	CREDIT MEMO NO.	POST. REF.	AMOUNT	
1							1
2							2
3							3
4							4
5							5
6							6

NAME Aqua Clear Pool Service ACCOUNT NO. 105

ADDRESS 63421 Berrent Street, Houston, TX 77003-8045 TERMS 30 days

DATE		ITEM	POST. REF.	DEBIT	CREDIT	BALANCE
20-- July	6	Invoice #639	S7	9 2 0 00		9 2 0 00
	18	Invoice #643	S7	4 7 2 00		1 3 9 2 00

Problem 48–2, Concluded

NAME Diablo Pool & Spa Service — ACCOUNT NO. 125

ADDRESS 2715 Rancho Verde Drive, Houston, TX 77078-6004 — TERMS 30 days

DATE		ITEM	POST. REF.	DEBIT	CREDIT	BALANCE
20-- July	10	Invoice #641	S7	891 00		891 00
	21	Invoice #644	S7	646 00		1 537 00

NAME Saratoga Pool Treatment — ACCOUNT NO. 145

ADDRESS 10 Market Square, Houston, TX 77078-4368 — TERMS 30 days

DATE		ITEM	POST. REF.	DEBIT	CREDIT	BALANCE
20-- July	9	Invoice #640	S7	602 00		602 00
	15	Invoice #642	S7	230 00		832 00

Problem 48–3, page 378

SALES RETURNS AND ALLOWANCES JOURNAL — PAGE

	DATE		CUSTOMER'S NAME	CREDIT MEMO NO.	POST. REF.	AMOUNT	
1							1
2							2
3							3
4							4
5							5
6							6

Name ______________________________

Problem 48–3, Concluded

NAME Allied Business Solutions **ACCOUNT NO.** 110

ADDRESS 99 Moorefield Bridge Road, Danville, VA 24540-6021 **TERMS** 30 days

DATE		ITEM	POST. REF.	DEBIT	CREDIT	BALANCE
20-- Jan.	11	Invoice #1235	S11	762 40		762 40
	19	Invoice #1237	S11	881 33		1643 73

NAME Golden State Office Systems **ACCOUNT NO.** 115

ADDRESS 9640 Koch Lane, San Jose, CA 95125-5010 **TERMS** 30 days

DATE		ITEM	POST. REF.	DEBIT	CREDIT	BALANCE
20-- Jan.	5	Invoice #1233	S11	390 12		390 12
	22	Invoice #1238	S11	683 63		1073 75

NAME Premier Copier Sales & Services **ACCOUNT NO.** 120

ADDRESS 38902 Blue Heron Road, Corvallis, OR 97330-1822 **TERMS** 30 days

DATE		ITEM	POST. REF.	DEBIT	CREDIT	BALANCE
20-- Jan.	8	Invoice #1234	S11	98 99		98 99
	15	Invoice #1236	S11	641 60		740 59

Problem 48–4

You are the accounts receivable clerk for LaserWorks Distributors.

Directions

a. Use the sales returns and allowances journal to record the following data taken from the credit memos issued during the month. Number the journal page 28.

Date	Customer's Name	Credit Memo No.	Amount
July 15	Enron Associates	624	$42.25
18	Sigma Technologies, Inc.	625	22.40
22	Enron Associates	626	18.20
25	Sigma Technologies, Inc.	627	68.80
28	Thornton & Company	628	33.00

b. Post from the sales returns and allowances journal to the customer accounts.

c. Foot, total, and rule the sales returns and allowances journal.

d. Check the balance at the end of the month in each account. Show all footings in each account.

SALES RETURNS AND ALLOWANCES JOURNAL

PAGE

	DATE		CUSTOMER'S NAME	CREDIT MEMO NO.	POST. REF.	AMOUNT	
1							1
2							2
3							3
4							4
5							5
6							6

NAME Enron Associates ACCOUNT NO. 121

ADDRESS 587 Sarah Street, Fresno, CA 93725-7218 TERMS 30 days

DATE		ITEM	POST. REF.	DEBIT	CREDIT	BALANCE
20-- July	5	Invoice #302	S28	511 40		511 40
	13	Invoice #304	S28	771 25		1282 65

Name ______________________________

Problem 48–4, Concluded

NAME Sigma Technologies ACCOUNT NO. 122

ADDRESS 1056 Clarissa Avenue, Fresno, CA 93710-2123 TERMS 30 days

DATE		ITEM	POST. REF.	DEBIT	CREDIT	BALANCE
20-- July	8	Invoice #303	S28	307 50		307 50
	15	Invoice #305	S28	717 25		1 024 75

NAME Thornton & Company ACCOUNT NO. 123

ADDRESS 2401 16th Street, Fresno, CA 93727-1433 TERMS 30 days

DATE		ITEM	POST. REF.	DEBIT	CREDIT	BALANCE
20-- July	2	Invoice #301	S28	198 95		198 95
	21	Invoice #306	S28	262 20		461 15

Problem 48–5

You are an employee in the accounting department of Gulf Coast Wholesalers, Inc.

Directions

a. Post to the customer accounts from each journal that follows. Follow the order of dates.

b. Foot, total, and rule the journals.

c. Check the balance in each account at the end of the month.

d. Prepare a schedule of accounts receivable on November 30. (Did you get a total of $836.60?)

Problem 48–5, Continued

SALES JOURNAL

PAGE 6

DATE		CUSTOMER'S NAME	INV. NO.	POST. REF.	AMOUNT
20-- Nov.	3	Diversion Dynamics	513		708 00
	5	FDX Racing, Inc.	514		245 20
	6	Elgin Engineering	515		448 35
	8	FDX Racing, Inc.	516		961 60
	15	Diversion Dynamics	517		306 45

CASH RECEIPTS JOURNAL

PAGE 6

DATE		RECEIVED FROM	FOR	POST. REF.	AMOUNT
20-- Nov.	24	Diversion Dynamics	Invoice, 11/3		708 00
	26	FDX Racing, Inc.	On account		100 00
	27	Elgin Engineering	Bal. Inv., 11/6		430 10
	29	FDX Racing, Inc.	On account		430 00

SALES RETURNS AND ALLOWANCES JOURNAL

PAGE 6

DATE		CUSTOMER'S NAME	CREDIT MEMO NO.	POST. REF.	AMOUNT
20-- Nov.	11	Elgin Engineering	412		18 25
	16	FDX Racing, Inc.	413		110 50
	23	Diversion Dynamics	414		36 15

Problem 48–5, Continued

NAME Diversion Dynamics **ACCOUNT NO.** 101

ADDRESS 4822 Beech Street, Beaumont, TX 77708-4212 **TERMS** 30 days

DATE		ITEM	POST. REF.	DEBIT	CREDIT	BALANCE

NAME Elgin Engineering **ACCOUNT NO.** 102

ADDRESS 1512 43rd Street, Beaumont, TX 77705-5006 **TERMS** 30 days

DATE		ITEM	POST. REF.	DEBIT	CREDIT	BALANCE

NAME FDX Racing, Inc. **ACCOUNT NO.** 103

ADDRESS 23 Laurel Street, Beaumont, TX 77707-8137 **TERMS** 30 days

DATE		ITEM	POST. REF.	DEBIT	CREDIT	BALANCE

Problem 48–5, Concluded

Problem 48–6

You are an accounts receivable clerk for Digital Distributors, Inc.

Directions

a. Post to the customer accounts from each journal that follows. Follow the order of dates.

b. Foot, total, and rule the journals.

c. Check the balance in each account at the end of the month.

d. Prepare a schedule of accounts receivable on March 31. (Did you get a total of $1,500.95?)

SALES JOURNAL PAGE 11

	DATE		CUSTOMER'S NAME	INV. NO.	POST. REF.	AMOUNT	
1	20-- Mar.	3	Garino Company	419		611 25	1
2		6	Chen's	420		865 40	2
3		6	Pulaski & Company	421		593 15	3
4		7	Chen's	422		904 75	4
5		9	Pulaski & Company	423		731 65	5
6							6

Problem 48–6, Continued

CASH RECEIPTS JOURNAL

PAGE 11

	DATE		RECEIVED FROM	FOR	POST. REF.	AMOUNT	
1	20-- Mar.	23	Garino Company	Bal. Inv., 3/3		574 85	1
2		25	Chen's	On account		450 00	2
3		29	Pulaski & Company	Invoice, 3/6		593 15	3
4		30	Chen's	On account		450 00	4
5							5

SALES RETURNS AND ALLOWANCES JOURNAL

PAGE 11

	DATE		CUSTOMER'S NAME	CREDIT MEMO NO.	POST. REF.	AMOUNT	
1	20-- Mar.	13	Garino Company	61		36 40	1
2		17	Pulaski & Company	62		44 35	2
3		19	Chen's	63		56 50	3
4							4

NAME Chen's ACCOUNT NO. 101

ADDRESS 6849 Wakefield Road, Roanoke, VA 24012-7712 TERMS 30 days

DATE		ITEM	POST. REF.	DEBIT	CREDIT	BALANCE

Problem 48–6, Concluded

NAME Garino Company **ACCOUNT NO.** 110

ADDRESS 12649 Hollins Road, Roanoke, VA 24014-1011 **TERMS** 30 days

DATE		ITEM	POST. REF.	DEBIT	CREDIT	BALANCE

NAME Pulaski & Company **ACCOUNT NO.** 120

ADDRESS 120 52nd Street, Roanoke, VA 24018-8361 **TERMS** 30 days

DATE		ITEM	POST. REF.	DEBIT	CREDIT	BALANCE

Name ______________________

Score __________

Reinforcement Activities

CHAPTER 9
Jobs 43–48

Check Your Reading, page 380

1. ______________________

2. ______________________

3. a. ______________________

3. b. ______________________

4. ______________________

5.

Discussion, page 380

1. By Hours:

   Advantage: ______

   Disadvantage: ______

2. By Number of Orders Completed:

   Advantage: ______

   Disadvantage: ______

3. By Effort:

   Advantage: ______

   Disadvantage: ______

Critical Thinking, page 380

1. ______
2. ______
3. ______

Communication in the Workplace, page 381

1. ______
2. ______
3. ______

Focus on Careers, page 381

1. ______________________

____

____

____

2. ______________________

____

____

____

Global Business—Foreign Currency Activity, page 381

You are a new clerk being trained by Kimika Embree. She gives you the following checks written in foreign currencies and asks you to convert them into U.S. dollars. Use the following table and round to the nearest cent.

Country	Currency	U.S. Dollar Equivalent
Belgium	franc	0.02660
Canada	dollar	0.66578
	Euro	1.07078
Italy	lira	0.00055
Greece	drachma	0.00328
Japan	yen	0.00821
South Korea	won	0.00089

Amount in Foreign Currency	Amount in U.S. Dollars
1,500 Belgian francs	______________
500 Canadian dollars	______________
100 Euros	______________
20,000 Italian lira	______________
5,000 Greek drachmas	______________
4,000 Japanese yen	______________
30,000 South Korean won	______________

Reviewing What You Have Learned, page 382

1. ______________________
2. ______________________
3. ______________________
4. ______________________
5. ______________________
6. ______________________
7. ______________________
8. ______________________
9. ______________________

Mastery Problem, page 383

Sale #1

SALES INVOICE

Quasar Electronics
7822 Ganredy Avenue, Mobile, AL 36606-8774
555-1289

SOLD TO ______________________
____
____

SHIP VIA ______________________

INVOICE NO. 58922
DATE ______________ 20__
OUR ORDER NO. ______________
CUSTOMER ORDER NO. ______________
TERMS ______________

QUANTITY	STOCK NO.	DESCRIPTION	UNIT PRICE		AMOUNT	

Sale #2

SALES INVOICE

Quasar Electronics
7822 Ganredy Avenue, Mobile, AL 36606-8774
555-1289

SOLD TO ______________________
____
____

SHIP VIA ______________________

INVOICE NO. 58923
DATE ______________ 20__
OUR ORDER NO. ______________
CUSTOMER ORDER NO. ______________
TERMS ______________

QUANTITY	STOCK NO.	DESCRIPTION	UNIT PRICE		AMOUNT	

Name ______________________

Mastery Problem, Continued

Sale #3

SALES INVOICE

Quasar Electronics
7822 Ganredy Avenue, Mobile, AL 36606-8774
555-1289

SOLD TO ______________________

INVOICE NO. 58924

DATE ______________ 20__

OUR ORDER NO. ______________

CUSTOMER ORDER NO. ______________

TERMS ______________

SHIP VIA ______________

QUANTITY	STOCK NO.	DESCRIPTION	UNIT PRICE		AMOUNT	

Sale #4

SALES INVOICE

Quasar Electronics
7822 Ganredy Avenue, Mobile, AL 36606-8774
555-1289

SOLD TO ______________________

INVOICE NO. 58925

DATE ______________ 20__

OUR ORDER NO. ______________

CUSTOMER ORDER NO. ______________

TERMS ______________

SHIP VIA ______________

QUANTITY	STOCK NO.	DESCRIPTION	UNIT PRICE		AMOUNT	

Mastery Problem, Concluded

SALES JOURNAL PAGE 1

	DATE		CUSTOMER'S NAME	INV. NO.	POST. REF.	AMOUNT	
1							1
2							2
3							3
4							4
5							5
6							6
7							7

Name ______________________________

Reviewing Your Business Vocabulary

Choose the words that match the statements. Write each word you choose next to the statement number it matches. Be careful; some of the words listed should not be used.

Statements

1. The date by which an invoice should be paid . . . . ____________
2. A record of all cash received . . . . ____________
3. A business that sells directly to the customer . . . . ____________
4. A form on which a customer's request for merchandise is first recorded . . . . ____________
5. The column in which increases in a customer account are recorded . . . . ____________
6. The column in which decreases in a customer account are recorded . . . . ____________
7. A list of customers who owe money . . . . ____________
8. The length of time the customer has to pay a bill, such as 10 days . . . . ____________
9. To record in a journal . . . . ____________
10. A business that sells in large quantities to retailers . . . . . . ____________
11. A bill . . . . ____________
12. To transfer data from one record to another . . . . ____________
13. A record of all charge sales . . . . ____________
14. Abbreviations, such as S1, which show where entries were posted from . . . . ____________
15. A journal in which you record credit memos . . . . ____________
16. A form that shows that the balance of an account has been reduced because of a return or allowance . . . . ____________
17. A reduction in price given for damaged merchandise or to correct an overcharge . . . . ____________
18. A group of customer accounts . . . . ____________
19. When the price on a sales invoice is more than it should be . . . . ____________

Words

accounts receivable ledger
allowance
cash receipts journal
computer terminal
credit
credit memo
debit
due date
extension
journalize
overcharge
post
posting references
retailer
sales invoice
sales journal
sales order
sales returns and allowances journal
schedule of accounts receivable
terms
wholesaler

(This page is without text copy.)

Name ______________________

Score ____________

Comprehensive Project 3 | **CHAPTERS 7–9**

You are an accounting clerk for KPM Wholesale Trading Co. Your job is to record all transactions with credit customers in the journals and in the ledger accounts.

Phase 1

Directions

a. Record the transactions below using a sales journal, cash receipts journal, and sales returns and allowances journal. Number all journal pages 7.

b. Post to the customer accounts as soon as you have recorded each transaction in the proper journal.

Aug.	2	Sold merchandise to The Depot, Inc., for $780.00. (Start with Invoice #545.)
	4	Sold merchandise to C & C Stores, Inc., for $893.00.
	7	Received a check for $399.00 from The Depot, Inc., for the balance due on the invoice of July 27.
	8	Received a check for $519.00 from Duvaney's, Inc., for the balance due on the invoice of July 28.
	10	Sold merchandise to The Depot, Inc., for $702.00.
	11	Issued Credit Memo #98 for $83.00 to C & C Stores, Inc., for merchandise returned.
	12	Received a check for $780.00 from The Depot, Inc., for the invoice of August 2.
	13	Sold merchandise to Duvaney's, Inc., for $375.00.
	13	Sold merchandise to C & C Stores, Inc., for $955.00.
	14	Received a check for $810.00 from C & C Stores, Inc., for the balance due on the invoice of August 4.
	17	Issued Credit Memo #99 for $56.00 to Duvaney's, Inc., for merchandise returned.
	20	Received a check for $702.00 from The Depot, Inc., for the invoice of August 10.
	22	Sold merchandise to Duvaney's, Inc., for $649.00.
	23	Received a check for $319.00 from Duvaney's, Inc., for the balance due on the invoice of August 13.
	29	Issued Credit Memo #100 for $31.00 to C & C Stores, Inc., as an allowance for an overcharge.

SALES JOURNAL PAGE

	DATE		CUSTOMER'S NAME	INV. NO.	POST. REF.	AMOUNT	
1							1
2							2
3							3
4							4
5							5
6							6
7							7
8							8

Comprehensive Project 3, Continued

CASH RECEIPTS JOURNAL

PAGE

	DATE		RECEIVED FROM	FOR	POST. REF.	AMOUNT	
1							1
2							2
3							3
4							4
5							5
6							6
7							7
8							8

SALES RETURNS AND ALLOWANCES JOURNAL

PAGE

	DATE		CUSTOMER'S NAME	CREDIT MEMO NO.	POST. REF.	AMOUNT	
1							1
2							2
3							3
4							4
5							5
6							6

NAME C & C Stores, Inc. ACCOUNT NO. 110

ADDRESS 5123 Howe Road, Flint, MI 48519-4476 TERMS 10 days

DATE		ITEM	POST. REF.	DEBIT	CREDIT	BALANCE
20-- July	17	Invoice #542	S6	732 00		732 00
	27	Cash	CR6		732 00	—

Comprehensive Project 3, Continued

NAME The Depot, Inc. ACCOUNT NO. 120

ADDRESS 6522 Cook Avenue, Billings, MT 59102-4615 TERMS 10 days

DATE		ITEM	POST. REF.	DEBIT	CREDIT	BALANCE
20-- July	27	Invoice #543	S6	446 00		446 00
	30	Credit Memo #97	SR6		47 00	399 00

NAME Duvaney's, Inc. ACCOUNT NO. 130

ADDRESS 9754 Lieber Road, Indianapolis, IN 46260-8809 TERMS 10 days

DATE		ITEM	POST. REF.	DEBIT	CREDIT	BALANCE
20-- July	28	Invoice #544	S6	578 00		578 00
	29	Credit Memo #96	SR6		59 00	519 00

c. Foot, total, and rule the sales journal, cash receipts journal, and sales returns and allowances journal.

d. Check the balance at the end of the month in each account. Show all footings.

e. Prepare a schedule of accounts receivable on August 31. (Did you get a total of $1,573.00?)

Comprehensive Project 3, Continued

Phase 2

Your employer, KPM Wholesale Trading Co., sends statements of account to all its credit customers at the end of each month. Statements of account were sent out at the end of July. It is part of your job to prepare the statements at the end of August.

Directions

Prepare statements of account using the three customer accounts you completed in Phase 1 of this Comprehensive Project. Date all statements August 31. Remember to start each statement with the previous balance. If necessary, refer back to Illustration 42A (page 331) in the text as a guide.

CUSTOMER STATEMENT

KPM WHOLESALE TRADING CO.
9212 Lehigh Avenue
Chicago, IL 60648-2283

TO: ____________________

____________________ ____________________ 20 __

____________________ ACCOUNT NO. ______

DATE		ITEM	DEBIT		CREDIT		BALANCE	
		Previous balance ——————→						

LAST AMOUNT IN THIS COLUMN IS THE BALANCE DUE ↑

Comprehensive Project 3, Concluded

CUSTOMER STATEMENT

KPM WHOLESALE TRADING CO.

9212 Lehigh Avenue
Chicago, IL 60648-2283

TO: ______________________

______________________ ______________________ 20 __

______________________ ACCOUNT NO. ______

DATE		ITEM	DEBIT		CREDIT		BALANCE	
		Previous balance ——————→						

LAST AMOUNT IN THIS COLUMN IS THE BALANCE DUE ↑

CUSTOMER STATEMENT

KPM WHOLESALE TRADING CO.

9212 Lehigh Avenue
Chicago, IL 60648-2283

TO: ______________________

______________________ ______________________ 20 __

______________________ ACCOUNT NO. ______

DATE		ITEM	DEBIT		CREDIT		BALANCE	
		Previous balance ——————→						

LAST AMOUNT IN THIS COLUMN IS THE BALANCE DUE ↑

(This page is without text copy.)